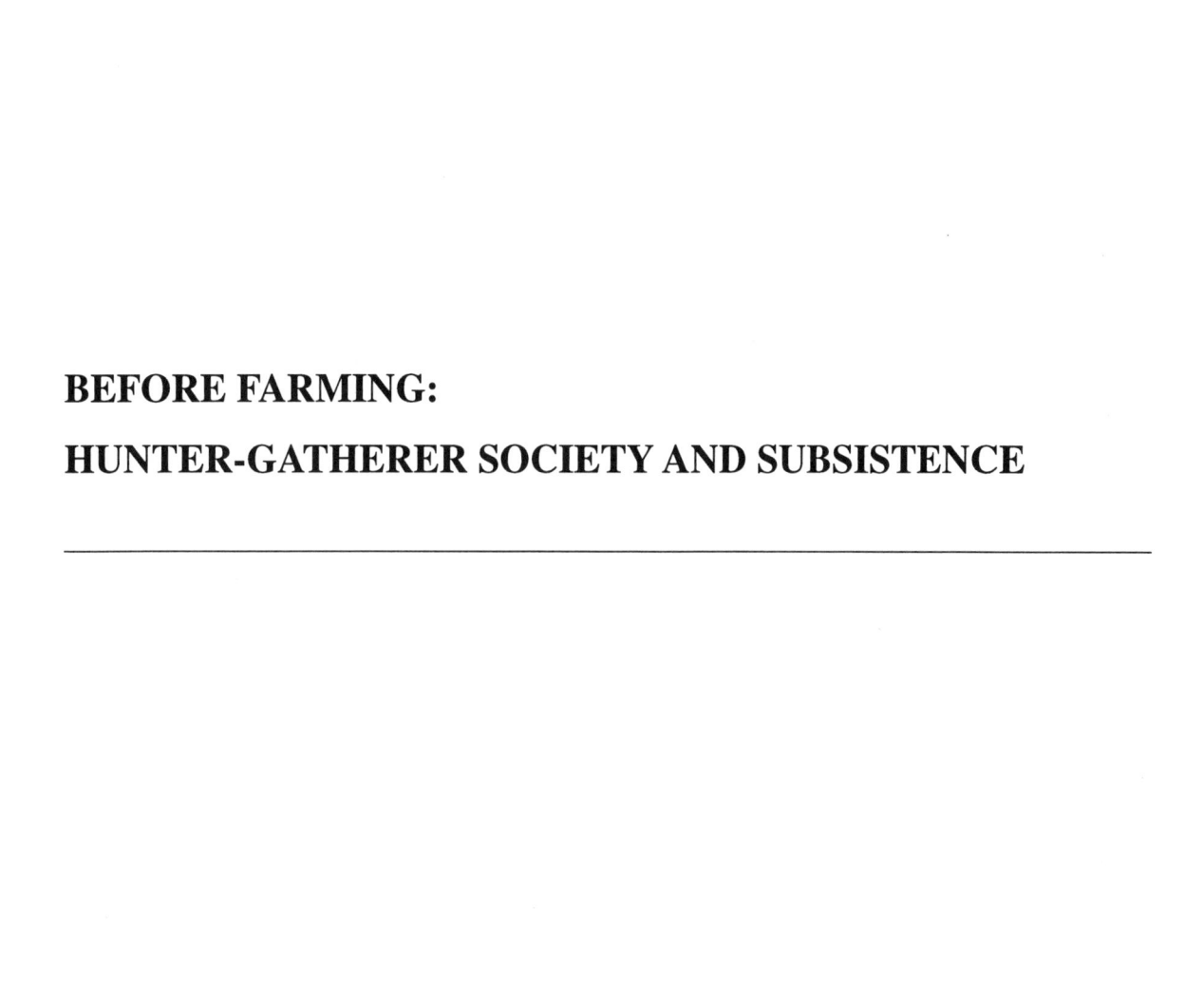

BEFORE FARMING:
HUNTER-GATHERER SOCIETY AND SUBSISTENCE

MASCA Research Papers in Science and Archaeology

Series Editor,
Kathleen Ryan

MASCA Research Papers in Science and Archaeology

Supplement to Volume 12, 1995

BEFORE FARMING:

HUNTER-GATHERER SOCIETY AND SUBSISTENCE

edited by

Douglas V. Campana

MASCA, University of Pennsylvania Museum of Archaeology and Anthropology
Philadelphia, Pennsylvania
1995

Published by
Museum Applied Science Center for Archaeology (MASCA)
University of Pennsylvania Museum of Archaeology and Anthropology
33rd and Spruce Streets, Philadelphia, PA 19104-6324

Copyright 1995 MASCA

ISSN 1048-5325

Printed by
Cushing-Malloy, Inc.
Ann Arbor, Michigan

Cover:
Engraved horse from the cave of Le Gabillou
(Dordogne), France. After drawing by Jean Gaussen, *La
Grotte Ornée de Gabillou (prés Mussidan, Dordogne)*
(Imprimeries Delmas, Bordeaux, 1964).

CONTENTS

Introduction   1
Douglas V. Campana

Examining Seasonality in Upper Paleolithic Art: Methodology and Research Applications   3
Sally Casey

Social Hunting and Multiple Predation   23
Jonathan C. Driver

Environmental and Socioeconomic Background to Domestication in the Southern Levant   39
Eitan Tchernov

Hunting, Gathering, or Husbandry? Management of Food Resources by the Late Mesolithic Communities of Temperate Europe   79
Marek Zvelebil

Prelude to Agriculture in North-Central Europe   105
Peter Bogucki

INTRODUCTION

Douglas V. Campana

*Valley Forge Division of Archaeology and Historic Architecture, National Park Service,
Valley Forge NHP, Valley Forge, PA 19482-0953*

The papers that make up this volume are quite disparate in subject and approach, but they are united by a common theme.

It has been commonplace, at least since Vere Gordon Childe introduced his concept of an agricultural revolution, to see the domestication of plants and animals as the turning point from which much of the complexity of later society arose. Certainly the cities and states of the Old and New Worlds, and the complex societies in which they were imbedded, were dependent upon an agricultural base. Still, the early agricultural societies did not appear full-blown in a cultural vacuum. Over millions of years humans had developed an increasingly varied set of relationships with the plants and animals in their environment upon which they depended for survival. Certainly the means and methods devised by early societies to exploit wild plants and animals exerted a strong influence upon the structure of those societies. It is clear today that by the period of the European Mesolithic and the Near Eastern Epi-paleolithic the efficient exploitation of wild food resources had produced a strong, well-structured social and economic base that was ripe for the introduction of domesticates.

It is not the intent of this volume to treat once again the topic of animal and plant domestication, a subject that has filled a multitude of books and papers. Instead, these essays focus on the relationships of people to the plants and animals in their environment before the introduction of agriculture. Any attempt to penetrate the structure of a preliterate society is a daunting task. Social structure is not directly preserved in the archaeological record. Fortunately, animal bones frequently endure, and plant remains are sometimes found as well. Over the years zooarchaeologists have devised (often controversial) criteria by which they can judge how early societies scavenged, hunted, or exploited animals. Such studies can provide at least some insight into the economic functioning of these societies. The art of early hunter-gatherers allows us to perceive another aspect of the relationship of early peoples with the animals and plants that they saw as sufficiently meaningful to portray. The interpretation of such art, however, is notoriously difficult. Most likely the meaning of paleolithic cave art will always remain largely a mystery. New examples of ancient art continue to be found, though, and there is much scope for the formulation and testing of hypotheses about its import.

In her essay Sally Casey considers an aspect of European Upper Paleolithic parietal art that is very seldom touched upon. These artists possessed an intimate familiarity with the animals with which they interacted. As successful hunters, Upper Paleolithic peoples must have known in detail the behavior of the game animals upon which they depended and how these animals must have appeared throughout the year. For some species seasonal changes in antler form and pelage were striking. Casey demonstrates that the Upper Paleolithic artists at Lascaux and Le Gabillou captured these seasonal differences in their paintings on the cave walls.

Jonathan C. Driver summarizes the evidence for social hunting in pre-agricultural societies, concentrating upon the Middle and Upper Paleolithic periods of the Old World. Driver describes the ecological, technological, and social conditions under which social hunting may have been economically important. According to Driver's model, social hunting is most likely in highly seasonal environments with little resource diversity and where hunters are dependent upon migratory large game. Social hunters must also possess adequate weapons and storage methods and the organization needed to conduct such a hunt. Driver also discusses the criteria for identifying social hunting in the archaeological record. These include the detection of facilities (either constructed or natural) for the driving or concentration of animals, and certain features of the faunal assemblages, such as distinctive age and sex ratios or a characteristic proportional representation of specific skeletal parts.

Eitan Tchernov provides us with a detailed account of the environmental, archaeological, and archeozoological evidence for the social and economic adaptations prevalent in the Levant just prior to the introduction of domesticated plants and animals. In concert with most scholars, Tchernov sees the beginnings of agriculture in the Levant as an outgrowth of a long period of increased sedentism that began with the late Epi-paleolithic Natufian people. Starting with a review of the evidence for Natufian sedentism, the issue then devolves to the root causes of that sedentism and the changes in social structure following the Kebaran period. Tchernov proposes a "thermodynamic" model (that some may see as controversial) to account for these changes. In Tchernov's view, once sedentism was established it had profound effects upon the Natufian subsistence economy. Depletion of resources in the vicinity of settlements forced the Natufian foragers to utilize a much broader base of animal and plant resources. At the same time they came to specialize in the hunting of a single large species—gazelle. Although the root causes are quite different, this two-sided economic adaptation shows a striking resemblance to that of the European Late Mesolithic societies, as discussed by Zvelebil and Bogucki. Tchernov summarizes the evidence for the Natufian subsistence economy, which included the gathering of wild grain and the hunting of gazelle. He continues with a discussion of the economic adaptations of the succeeding PPNA and PPNB periods—the earliest Neolithic during which domesticated cereals and animals became prevalent. Finally, Tchernov examines the range of hypotheses and opinions that have been put forward to account for these developments.

Marek Zvelebil takes us to the Late Mesolithic of Europe. Until recent years European Mesolithic societies have been seen as relatively simple and mobile, qualitatively different from the sedentary Neolithic communities that succeeded them. Zvelebil stresses the variability in Mesolithic subsistence economies and emphasizes the duality of their response to post-glacial European conditions. These societies on the one hand *diversified* their use of plants and animals (the use of a "broad spectrum" of resources) and on the other hand *specialized*, through the interception of seasonally aggregated species such as seal, waterfowl, and anadromous fish. He further suggests that some Mesolithic societies may have been on the road from species specialization to animal husbandry. Substantial evidence suggests that widespread burning was practiced during the Mesolithic, resulting in the spread of hazel in many areas. Hazel produces a large quantity of food; hazelnuts are very common in Mesolithic sites. Wild pigs could feed on such food, and in the third millennium B.C., when climatic conditions would have been adverse for pigs, Mesolithic dependence on pigs actually increases. Zvelebil presents the evidence for possible wild pig husbandry in the European Late Mesolithic.

Peter Bogucki concludes this volume by taking us to the brink of the introduction of agriculture into North-Central Europe. In a sense Bogucki takes up where Zvelebil leaves off. Bogucki reviews the subsistence practices of the Late Mesolithic societies of the North European Plain. Mesolithic groups near the coast enjoyed a diversity of aquatic resources as well as a variety of terrestrial animal species that congregated in the many available forest openings. Such openings were not available inland, but Mesolithic groups could, through forest burnings, create their own artificial glades that would have been attractive to game animals, and thereby provide a more reliable resource base. At the very end of the Mesolithic period these people were living in very close proximity with Neolithic herders, who brought with them domesticated livestock. Bogucki suggests that feral domesticated cattle found their way into these glades, where they could be readily captured by Mesolithic peoples. Such animals would be the initial stage leading to the adoption of domestic animals by these groups.

EXAMINING SEASONALITY IN UPPER PALEOLITHIC ART: METHODOLOGY AND RESEARCH APPLICATIONS

Sally Casey

Department of Anthropology, New York University, 25 Waverly Place, New York, NY 10003

In recent years seasonality studies have moved to the forefront of archaeological research. This growing interest is the result of an increased awareness on the part of archaeologists that a complex relationship exists between hunter-gatherers and the resources they exploit. Although many factors influence the relationship between humans and natural resources, one of the most significant variables is seasonality. Analyses of archaeological fauna from many European Upper Paleolithic sites (Spiess 1979; Pike-Tay 1989; Gordon 1988, for example) have shown a seasonal bias in site occupation and/or exploitation of resources, suggesting a seasonal influence on Upper Paleolithic subsistence and settlement. Seasonality, however, did not affect only the subsistence and settlement systems of Upper Paleolithic hunter-gatherers. Many of the graphic images which have been recovered from Upper Paleolithic excavations and discovered on cave walls exhibit aspects of animal behavior and appearance that are seasonally affected (Guthrie 1984; Schmid 1984; Marshack 1972, 1989; Mithen 1988, 1990). Seasonality, therefore, may have acted not only in an economic context of resource scheduling and procurement but also in a social or symbolic context through its incorporation into visual imagery.

This paper is an abbreviated version of a master's thesis submitted to the Department of Anthropology at New York University (Casey 1993). The role of seasonality in archaeological studies is discussed, as are the results of a systematic examination of seasonality represented in the visual images from two caves in the Périgord region of southwest France, Lascaux (Dordogne) and Le Gabillou (Dordogne). Information on the ethology and appearance of various extant animal species was used as a guide for understanding and interpreting seasonality represented in the parietal art at these two caves, and a brief description of these criteria is provided here for each species. I present here the results of my analysis of the seasonality represented in the visual images at Lascaux and Le Gabillou because although they cannot indicate seasonal occupation of the sites, they provide a forum for discussing the problems and prospects involved in the identification of seasonality in Upper Paleolithic art.

Positioning seasonality in archaeological research

It has long been known to anthropologists (Mauss 1904; Quimby 1962) that seasons affect the subsistence, movement, and resource scheduling of people dependent upon hunting, gathering, and/or fishing. Only within the last several years, however, have seasonality studies become integrated into archaeological research (Monks 1981). Seasonality in general is considered to be the time of year at which a particular event is most likely to occur (Monks 1981:79). This definition is inadequate, however, for addressing anthropological questions and must be expanded to include *human* action. Pike-Tay (1989:6) has re-defined seasonality as "the coincidence of human activity with naturally occurring seasonal events." It is this definition of seasonality which is adopted here.

Definitions of "season" may vary (Monks 1981), thus it is necessary to define its use in any particular study. Jochim (1976) has proposed the use of the term "economic season" in mapping resource utilization of hunting and gathering societies. Availability, as well as the timing of mating and reproductive events, varies among animal resources and these variations do not often conform to "standard" (winter, spring, summer, fall) seasonal distinctions. "Economic season" allows for variation (both temporal and preferential) among resources and defines season according to the different configuration of resource utilization (scheduling), and the various demographic responses by the population (Jochim 1976:44–45).

Differential resource utilization that is seasonally influenced can be recognized in the archaeological record. Several direct methods of determining seasonality from archaeofauna are available (Monks 1981), but the presence of migratory species may also indicate scheduling of resource procurement. The Upper Paleolithic of southwestern France has been considered a specialized reindeer economy due to the large number of reindeer bones which have been recovered from archaeological sites. Reindeer are migratory animals and, therefore, may have been available to Upper Paleolithic people only on a seasonal basis. The extent of reindeer migrations during the Upper Paleolithic has been debated (Bahn 1977; Sturdy 1975; White 1989), but even if available year-round, hunter-gatherers may have chosen only to exploit them on a seasonal basis (Burch 1972, 1991; Spiess 1979). Seasonal exploitation of large migratory herds such as reindeer may have also been tied to group aggregations (White 1985), during which information, potential mates, and exotic raw materials could be exchanged.

The effect of seasonality on the presence or absence of certain plant and animal species may be clear, but even when resources are available, such as reindeer, they may have been differentially exploited according to sex and season. It has been argued that seasonal fluctuations in the fat content of animals may be an important consideration in the selection of prey (Speth 1983; Spiess 1979). However, the desire for raw material such as antler may be equally influential. The Upper Paleolithic in Europe shows an increase in the use of antler as a raw material (Mellars 1973; White 1982, 1985). Reindeer (*Rangifer tarandus*) antler is only present seasonally, and it is possible that when present it was influential in the selection of prey (i.e., males with large antlers may be chosen over females with smaller, or no antlers). It is likely that hides of animals such as reindeer were also seasonally selected for, as they have certain "prime" times when they are more suitable for use as clothing or bedding (Spiess 1979:29–30; Sturdy 1975:362).

The same type of pattern of exploitation would apply to the gathering of plant food, as certain plants are only seasonally present in certain areas, and therefore could only be procured on a seasonal basis. Storage must be considered, however, as it is possible that resources (both plant and animal) were gathered at one time of the year and then used continually, or at some other point during the year (Winters 1969:117; Binford 1983).

The increased awareness by archaeologists that seasonality plays a crucial role in the economic and social patterning of hunting and gathering groups has been recognized by some to be also manifest archaeologically in the realm of visual imagery. Both Mithen (1988, 1990) and Marshack (1972) have noted the representation of seasons in the visual imagery of the Upper Paleolithic. Despite the importance of such a line of inquiry, only limited research has been done in this area. Marshack (1972) has most fully addressed this issue, but he fails to regard the images in their whole context. Rather than interpreting seasonality in selected images from different sites, analyses of the representation of seasons in prehistoric visual imagery must focus on how the seasonality is depicted in all of the images from a site. Just as one would not interpret a faunal assemblage by studying only select bones, one cannot reliably interpret seasonality in visual imagery by looking only at a selection of images.

The aim of this study is to employ an "objective" seasonal analysis of the parietal "art" at two caves, and to consider how information about the seasons represented may reflect the complex social and behavioral context of Upper Paleolithic groups. An understanding of the seasonality in hunting and gathering groups is requisite to our understanding of their subsistence and settlement systems. It has been shown that many of the images created by Upper Paleolithic hunter-gatherers have exhibited seasonal characteristics (Guthrie 1984; Schmid 1984; Marshack 1972, 1989; Mithen 1988, 1990), which may indicate some relationship between symbolic expression and larger social systems (such as subsistence and settlement). It is not being suggested here that visual representations be taken as evidence of seasonal occupation of a site, or seasonal exploitation of a particular resource (cf. Bahn 1977; Sieveking 1976), but rather that it may allow us to observe the relationship between these.

White (1985) has noted that over 80% of the portable images recovered from late Upper Paleolithic (Magdalenian) sites come from four large sites in the Périgord region of France: Limeuil, Laugerie-Basse, La Madeleine, and Rochereil. These sites are all located at river fords and may have been chosen in order to exploit migrating herds of reindeer during seasonal group aggregations (White 1982, 1985:148). White (1985:157) suggests that the presence of decorated artifacts at these sites indicates "a greater intensity of social interaction and ceremonial activity than when such art is lacking at a site." The presence of such sites may evidence the fact that visual representations are perhaps tied to aspects of hunter-gatherer subsistence and settlement (i.e., aggregation and dispersion of mobile hunting-gathering groups), but that there is more to this pattern than "subsistence ecology" alone (Conkey 1980:609).

Through analyzing the seasonality represented in the images at the caves of Lascaux and Le Gabillou, it is hoped that the influence of seasonality on the production of visual imagery may be seen. Seasonality, as I have already discussed, plays an important role in hunter-gatherer subsistence systems. This influence can be seen in the differential exploitation of resources (Spiess 1979; Speth 1983; Winters 1969) as well as in settlement patterns which may reflect seasonal movements and/or aggregation (Conkey 1980; White 1985). However, seasonality is also expressed in a social and symbolic context through its presence in visual imagery. The questions, therefore, which must be asked by archaeologists are: To what degree is there a relationship between seasonality and visual representation in the Upper Paleolithic, and how does this relationship reflect the social, economic, and symbolic contexts of visual imagery? This study is an attempt to develop a methodology capable of addressing these questions.

Seasonality in the visual record of the Upper Paleolithic: Looking at the images from Le Gabillou and Lascaux

The interpretations of seasonality given here were based on observed similarities to known seasonal characteristics of extant species (with the exception of aurochs, see Heck 1951) which are conspecific, or closely related to those represented in the visual imagery at Lascaux and Le Gabillou. Because variations exist in the behaviors of geographically isolated populations of extant animals which are considered conspecific (e.g., reindeer/caribou), consideration had to be given to the possibility of behavioral variations between Pleistocene and extant members of the same species. Nevertheless, since many of the seasonally specific traits and behaviors depicted in Paleolithic images show a remarkable similarity to those known for extant species (e.g., "testing" of female estrus by males, differences of pelage, presence and absence of antler, calving, and rutting), whatever differences may exist in the specifics of such behavior (such as the exact timing of commencement and termination) probably do not affect the reliability of the observations used to recognize seasonality in visual imagery.

Although the original goal of this study was to systematically examine representations of seasonality in *all* of the images from Lascaux and Le Gabillou, the sample of usable images from the two caves was limited by several factors. First, many of the images, particularly the engravings from Lascaux, are incomplete and did not provide enough information for seasonal interpretation or even positive identification. Second, only images that could be found in published sources could be used. For Gabillou, this was not a problem because the cave has been meticulously documented by Dr. Jean Gaussen (1964). On the other hand, although Lascaux has been well documented in both photographs and drawings, many of the engravings from the Apse and Passage are difficult to identify from these published sources. Engravings in general are difficult to photograph because of the very specific directional lighting required to make the images "stand out" so that they can be seen. However, even with the right lighting, engravings can be very difficult to see in photographs. Drawings provide a means for studying engraved images, but in the case of Lascaux, many of the images are lost in a web of lines that obscure the figures. Leroi-Gourhan and Allain (1979) have reproduced drawings of the engravings from Lascaux which were done by the Abbé Glory, a French prehistorian. Many of the engraved panels, however, have so many random lines that it is often difficult to locate and identify animal representations. Because Glory's drawings were the only available source for these engravings, images that could not be found or identified in his drawings could not be included in this study. Images that could be identified, yet did not allow for interpretation of seasonality (because they were incomplete or indefinite in terms of the season represented) were retained as part of the sample in order to illustrate some of the problems of identifying seasonality in visual imagery.

The sample considered was limited to the six species most often represented in the art at these two caves: reindeer (*Rangifer tarandus*); red deer (*Cervus elaphus*); horse (*Equus przewalski*); bison (*Bison priscus*); ibex (*Capra ibex*); and aurochs (*Bos primigenius*). Each species is presented here individually with a description of the characteristics used to determine seasonality. Although it is not possible to reproduce here all of the information that can be used to interpret seasonality in visual images, the descriptions provided describe the main criteria used in this study.

Reindeer

Seasonality of reindeer (*Rangifer tarandus*) images was assigned based on a number of different criteria. First, the presence or absence of antler clearly indicates season, as does the amount of antler growth exhibited. Because both sexes of reindeer carry antler and the annual seasons of growth and shedding differ between the sexes, interpreting the seasonality in visual imagery from the presence or absence of antler alone may be problematic (Skoog 1968:41). It is often possible, however, to determine the sex of the animal based on the size and complexity of its antlers, as adult male *Rangifer* have antlers that are generally larger and more complex in terms of the number of tines than those of female *Rangifer* (Fig. 1). Sub-adult males, on the other hand, have not yet achieved full antler growth and may not be easily distinguished from females based on antler development alone (Skoog 1968:41; Whitehead 1972:38).

Adult male caribou in Canada shed their antlers shortly after the end of the rut, in late autumn (Skoog 1968:54; Spiess 1979:99; Whitehead 1972:37) and remain antlerless through the winter until early to mid spring, when new growth begins. Adult females, in contrast, keep their antler through the winter, and shed them according to their reproductive condition. Non-breeding females will shed first, in mid May, and new growth will begin shortly after. Pregnant cows shed their antler after calving, in early June, and new growth begins within a week (Spiess 1979:98–99).

Rangifer pelage also exhibits annual changes in consistency and color which correspond to changes of season. Their pelage consists of two different types of hair; long guard hairs, which account for most of the hair by weight, and a thicker underwool, which lies close to the skin

Fig. 1:
Male and female *Rangifer tarandus*. Photo: George Calef, printed with permission of Canadian Arctic Resources Committee.

(Spiess 1979:29; Whitehead 1972:384). During the winter months, the hair is denser and lightens in color. The annual moult, which occurs during the summer months, leaves caribou dark brown in color (although cows are generally lighter in color than bulls), with contrasting white on the tail, perineum, belly, and rings above each hoof (Skoog 1968:65; Whitehead 1972:34).

Certain aspects of *Rangifer* behavior such as rutting, mating, and calving can also be indicators of season, and are often depicted in Upper Paleolithic graphic images (Guthrie 1984). During the summer, males gain weight in anticipation of the autumn rut when there is great competition between males for females. Stored fat in adult males may increase their weight by more than 20% (Skoog 1968:521) resulting in a noticeable difference of stature. The appearance of males during the rut is further distinguished by the development of a shocking white mane with a "dewlap" of long hairs that hang from the neck (Calef 1981:128; Skoog 1968:66; Whitehead 1972:35; Lent 1965:259) (Fig. 2). During the rut, the necks of male *Rangifer* swell, and their antler is at full growth before the winter shedding. Guthrie (1984) has argued that most Upper Paleolithic depictions of reindeer are males in rut pelage and posture. It is possible that the impressive sight created by males at this time left a lasting impression in the minds of those who created graphic images, or that it was at this time that the animals were in their prime for use as a human resource (i.e., high fat yield, large antler which could be used as a raw material, etc.), and were depicted because of their economic as well as symbolic value. Significantly, it must be noted that contrary to Guthrie's argument, there are also several images of female and juvenile reindeer in the Upper Paleolithic, as well as males which are not in rut (see for example the engraved blocks from Limeuil, Tosello 1992).

Other behavioral characteristics indicating season which may be depicted in graphic images of reindeer are mating and calving. During the rut males compete for

Fig. 2: Male *Rangifer tarandus* in full antler with dewlap. Photo: George Calef, printed with permission of Canadian Arctic Resources Committee.

females with which to breed. Often males will follow closely behind a female in order to "test" her estrus state (Lent 1965:260), a behavior common to many species. Scenes such as this may be evidenced in pieces such as the carved batons from the French sites of Laugerie-Basse, Bruniquel, and Teyjat. The gestation period for caribou is generally seven and a half to eight months. Calving begins in mid spring, but most calves are born in late spring/early summer (Banfield 1974:386; Whitehead 1972:37), and are single births.

Reindeer are among the species most often depicted at Le Gabillou (n = 21), and have given the clearest results in terms of overall seasonality (Table 1). Reindeer are often the subjects in Upper Paleolithic portable art, but only rarely are they depicted on cave walls. For this reason, the large proportion of reindeer images at Le Gabillou is quite exceptional (Gaussen 1964:40). The reindeer images can be most frequently assigned to autumn, such depictions comprising 42.9% (Fig. 3). However, images assigned to late summer through early spring are nearly as abundant, comprising 38.1% of the reindeer images. Animals were

Table 1. Seasonality of reindeer images at Le Gabillou

a. Percentages of images assigned to each seasonal category

Season	No. of images*	% of images
Autumn	9	42.9
Late summer/autumn/ winter/early spring	8	38.1
Late summer/autumn	3	14.3
Winter/spring	1	4.7

b. Percentages of images assigned to more broadly defined seasonal categories**

Season	No. of images*	% of images
Autumn	20	95.2
Winter/spring	1	4.8

*All the reindeer images from Le Gabillou are included here (n = 21).
**Where late summer through spring, late summer/ autumn, and autumn are considered to be a single season (autumn).

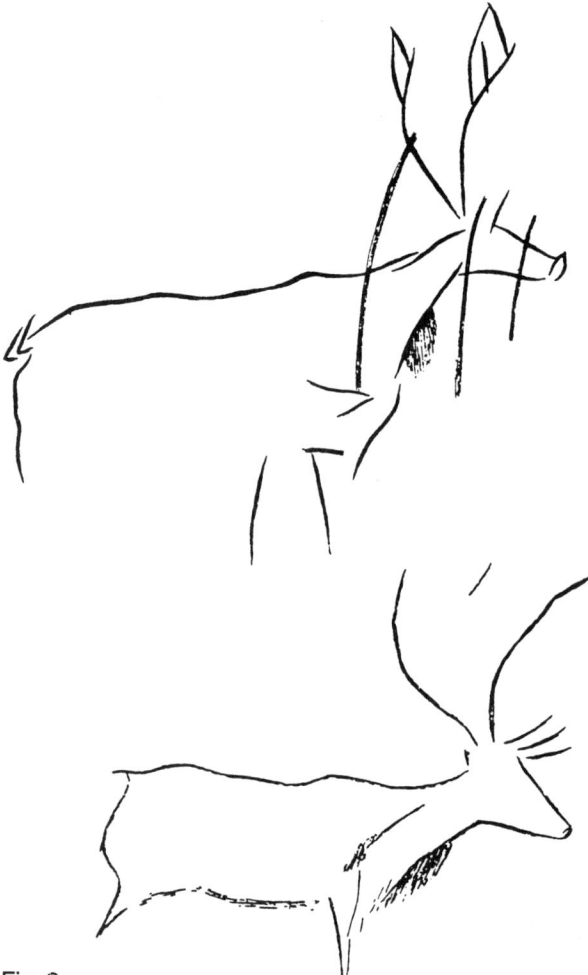

Fig. 3:
Engraved reindeer from Le Gabillou. Drawing: Jean Gaussen. Top reindeer, 15 cm.

Fig. 4:
Engraved reindeer from Le Gabillou. Drawing: Jean Gaussen. Reindeer, 18 cm.

assigned to this broad category of late summer through early spring because they had antlers, but could have been either male or female, and there was no clear sign of sex or autumn seasonality (i.e., rutting appearance or behavior) (Fig. 4). This was a precaution on my part, as it is quite possible that the images are all male reindeer in full antler, and thus represent autumn animals. Table 1b illustrates the resulting distribution if the images so cautiously assigned to late summer through spring were, in fact, all interpreted as autumn images. It is clear that when these images are subsumed into a single seasonal category of autumn, the reindeer images at Gabillou are overwhelmingly composed of autumn animals (95.2%).

At Lascaux, images of reindeer appear to be all autumn or late summer/autumn images (Table 2). The sample size for reindeer at Lascaux is too small (n = 3) and tenuous, however, to permit any meaningful determination of overall seasonality. The reindeer sample may be further limited at Lascaux given the possibility that two of the three images considered here as reindeer may in fact be *Cervus elaphus*. This would leave only one depiction of reindeer in the entire cave of Lascaux.

Red deer

Like most cervids, only male *Cervus elaphus* carry antlers. These antlers are noticeably different in form from those of reindeer, and have different cycles of growth and shedding. Antler growth begins in the early spring, and continues throughout the summer months. By autumn, the velvety covering has been worn off, and the antlers are smooth and polished. Unlike *Rangifer* males, who shed their antlers shortly after the autumn rut, male red deer retain their antlers throughout the winter months, and begin to shed them in late winter/early spring. Yearling stags have antlers which resemble tall spikes growing from the pedicle. The second set of antlers, which grows in the second year of life, is more complex, with three or four points on the rack. Through the years the antlers grow larger, heavier, and more complex, with six points on each side being "normal" adult growth (Banfield 1974:399).

Table 2. Seasonality of reindeer* images at Lascaux

Season	No. of images	% of images
Autumn	1	33.3
Late summer/autumn	2	66.7

*I have interpreted these images as reindeer based on the morphology of their antler. It must be noted that these interpretations are dubious, and the images may represent red deer.

The winter coat of *Cervus elaphus*, like that of *Rangifer*, is composed of long guard hairs and an underfur. It is grayish brown on the back and flanks, and seal brown on the face, neck, legs, and belly. Stags' flanks, which are much lighter than hinds' and yearlings', turn a light straw color in the winter (Banfield 1974:399), and a patch of longer hair on the neck forms a ventral mane. There are two annual moults, one in the autumn which is hardly noticeable, and another in the spring when the heavier winter coat is shed, revealing the lighter-weight summer coat. The summer coat is short and without underfur. It is "sleek, tawny brown, darker on face, belly, neck, and legs, with a large buffy rump patch surrounding the tail and including the buttocks" (Banfield 1974:399).

A number of ethological characteristics of *Cervus elaphus* correspond to annual seasonal changes and the life cycles of the animals. There are several distinct populations of extant red deer and although there are overall similarities in breeding behavior, there is no strict model which is followed by all groups (Clutton-Brock et al. 1982:301). In late summer/early autumn, red deer stags become increasingly intolerant of each other as the rut approaches, and they will begin to compete for females with which to breed. During this time an increase in the testosterone level in males triggers an increase in the size of the testes as well as the development of a mane and large neck muscles (Clutton-Brock et al. 1982:105).

Harems are maintained by dominant males, although the size and duration of maintenance may vary according to the fitness and age of the male (Pike-Tay 1989:109). "Roaring" is also common during the rut, and male red deer will raise their heads and sound out a deep guttural roar as a threat to other males. Other rutting behaviors by male red deer include sniffing and licking of females, wallowing in pools or peat bogs, showing flehmen (when stags raise their heads and curl back their upper lip in response to sniffing a hind or where one has been), chivying (chasing females), and locking antler (Clutton-Brock et al. 1982:107–117).

Breeding occurs in the autumn during the rut. The gestation period for red deer is generally 238–245 days (Gamble 1986:108), and calving, which is highly synchronized, occurs in late May/early June (Clutton-Brock et al. 1982:18; Pike-Tay 1989:109; Gamble 1986:108).

Respective emphases on red deer and reindeer in the visual imagery further distinguish Lascaux and Le Gabillou. At Le Gabillou, there is only one possible depiction of *Cervus elaphus*, and it is female. Because female red deer do not carry antlers, in the absence of ethological information (such as calving) it is impossible to assign a season to this image. At Lascaux, on the other hand, red deer is the second most often represented species (n = 85) in the visual imagery. Because they show no clear signs of autumn seasonality but have antlers, most of the images of red deer at Lascaux have been assigned to the broad seasonal category of late summer through winter (Table 3). However, if all of these images are, in fact, autumn animals (as is possible for reindeer images at Le Gabillou), 100% of the red deer depicted at Lascaux would be autumn images.

Most often, reindeer and red deer are depicted with antlers, both at the sites described here and in the rest of Upper Paleolithic art (Guthrie 1984). Antler may have been depicted because of the seasonal information that it can convey, but more likely it offers information about the species. There is a noticeable difference between the antler form of *Cervus elaphus* and *Rangifer tarandus*, and perhaps antler provided a visual means of distinguishing between different types of deer. Antler may have also been important symbolically, or economically as a raw material (White 1982), and was thus depicted.

Table 3. Seasonality of red deer images at Lascaux

a. Paintings (Rotunda, Axial Gallery, Nave, Chamber of Felines, Shaft)

Season	No. of images identified*	% of images
Late summer/ autumn/early winter	10	90.9
Autumn	1	9.1

b. Engravings (Apse only; those from the Passage were not suitable for seasonal analysis)

Season	No. of images identified*	% from 23 cases able to be assigned to a season
Late summer/ autumn/early winter	15	65.2
Autumn	6	26.1
Autumn/winter	2	8.7
Indeterminate	4	–

c. All red deer images (painted and engraved)

Season	No. of images identified*	% from 34 cases able to be assigned to a season
Late summer/ autumn/early winter	25	73.5
Autumn	7	20.6
Autumn/winter	2	5.9
Indeterminate	4	–

*There is a total of 85 images of red deer recorded at Lascaux (Leroi-Gourhan and Allain 1979:344). Many of the images were excluded from this study because they were incomplete, unclear, or could not be found in published sources.

Horse

It has been argued that several types of *Equus* were depicted in Upper Paleolithic visual representations (Capitan et al. 1924; Windels and Laming 1949:115). The variations seen in Paleolithic representations of horses, which have led some to believe different species were being reproduced, may be due to individual variation, seasonal appearance, style, or inaccuracy (Zeuner 1963:308; Laming 1959:132), rather than to the depiction of different types. It is also possible that several different "ecotypes" (a single species that shows slight variations due to geographic isolation and/or specialization) were being represented (Zeuner 1963:310). Many consider *Equus przewalski* to be very closely related to, if not conspecific with, the horses depicted in Upper Paleolithic visual representations (Kurtén 1968:150; Baffier 1984:149; Sutcliffe 1985:92; Mohr 1971:26; cf. Zeuner 1963:306–311). Because they represent the only truly wild horses, and because of the remarkable likeness between Przewalski's horses and those depicted on the walls at Lascaux and Le Gabillou, I have used *Equus przewalski*, rather than *Equus caballus* (modern horse) as the model for interpreting seasonality in Upper Paleolithic wild horses.

Przewalski's horses have short stiff manes of upwardly directed hair and a "stockier" stature than modern domestic horses (*Equus caballus*). Because of the degree of variation in color between individual Przewalski horses, and variation according to age and season within an individual horse's lifetime, it is impossible to use a single criterion of coloring to classify the species (Mohr 1971:23). Information from studies of Przewalski's horse in captivity as well as painted images from the Upper Paleolithic indicates some variation in color, although there are some standard characteristics of pelage. The summer coat is smooth and short, often with stripes along the shoulders and belly much like the "Chinese horse" from Lascaux (Sutcliffe 1985:92). The mane is dark in color, and there is a dorsal stripe that leads from it along the back and into the dark colored tail. The overall color of the summer coat is light, and "with the exception of foals and the lightest coloured animals, the legs are dark brown in varying degrees; some have only a dark brown ring above the coronet, others are black up to the knee and hocks, although the inside of the legs, especially the forelegs is somewhat lighter" (Mohr 1971:58). On some horses, the lighter-colored belly and darker-colored upper body create an M-shaped pattern of color on the horse's body during the summer months (Fig. 5) (Bahn and Vertut 1988:121). This pattern disappears during the winter months when the horses are generally darker in color and have their shaggy winter coat.

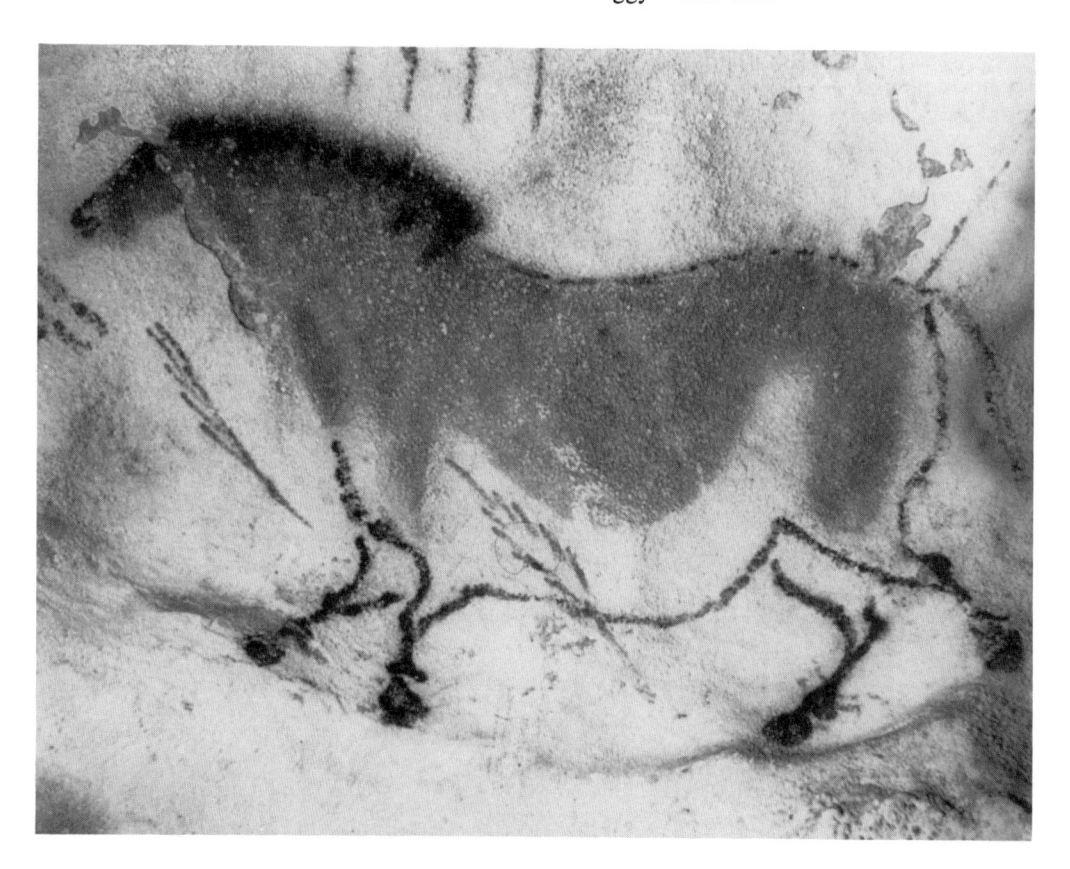

Fig. 5:
Painted "Chinese horse" from Lascaux. Photograph: Doug Mazonowicz. Horse, approx. 140 cm.

Unlike domestic horses, where the mane and tail grow as long as hair on human heads, wild horses have a periodic, annual change of hair in the mane and tail. Animals in their winter coat are easily recognized by the length and thickness of their hair. The thick winter coat adds volume to their body mass, making them appear considerably larger than in the summer. Winter hair grows especially long on the chin, creating a very distinct "beard" (Figs. 6 and 7), as well as a fringe around the hoofs and on the belly (Sutcliffe 1985:92; Mohr 1971:58). Many of the horse depicted at both Lascaux and Le Gabillou are clearly in their winter coats and have easily recognizable beards.

Fig. 6:
Przewalski's horse in summer coat. Photograph: Lee Boyd.

Fig. 7:
Przewalski's horse in winter coat. Photograph: Lee Boyd.

Horse bands are usually small, consisting of either bachelor groups or harems of one stallion with several females and their offspring (Olsen 1989:317). In the harem group, it is the single stallion that acts as defender of the herd. It is well known that wild horses, especially when trying to avoid danger, will travel in single file (Mohr 1971:67; Spiess 1979:258). When danger arises the stallion will show by his movement that he is uneasy and will run alongside the group, or in front if there are no foals present, thus controlling the direction of the group's movement and acting to herd the band (Mohr 1971:67) to safety.

Depictions of horse at Le Gabillou (Table 4) show a close distribution between cold season (45.2%) and warm season (54.8%) images (Figs. 8 and 9). The categories of "warm season" and "cold season" were used for those species (such as horse and aurochs) that show seasonality based on gradual changes in pelage. It would be impossible for me to determine if the beard on a horse represents early winter (when the winter coat has just developed), or spring (just before the coat is shed). Similarly, it would be impossible to determine whether a horse without shaggy pelage was one in the spring (when the winter coat has just been shed), or in the early fall (when it is just beginning to grow). At Lascaux, painted depictions of horse show an even distribution between warm and cold season animals, whereas the engravings exhibit a bias toward warm season (Table 5). The combined seasonality of painted and engraved horses at Lascaux also shows a bias toward warm season animals.

Aurochs

The last truly wild individual of the species *Bos primigenius* died out in 1627, leaving only a handful of half-wild animals which died out before 1652 (Towne and Wentworth 1955:16). For this reason, a great deal of what we know about the appearance of these animals comes from Upper Paleolithic engravings and cave paintings themselves, particularly the polychromes from Lascaux. From these images it can be noted that there is a difference between bulls and cows in terms of size and coloration, with bulls being noticeably larger and generally darker in color. Bulls are often depicted as black, and cows as red, although apparently the cows were reddish brown and the bulls much darker (Sutcliffe 1985:189).

An experiment published in 1951 by Heinz Heck, director of the Tierpark Hellabrun in Munich, was apparently successful in "breeding back" cattle to recreate the primitive characteristics of the aurochs (Heck 1951). Heck's work has provided the only firsthand information on not only the appearance, but also the behavior of these animals. Of their appearance Heck writes

> The adult Aurochs bull was black with a yellow-white stripe along the back, while the cow was red-brown in colouring with a darker neck . . . Both sexes were alike in the white colouring around the

Table 4. Seasonality of horse images at Le Gabillou

Season	No. of images identified*	% from 42 cases able to be assigned to a season
Warm	23	54.8
Cold	19	45.2
Indeterminate	4	–

*The total number of horses depicted at Le Gabillou is 56. Although 46 images were identified as horse for this study, only 42 cases were able to be assigned to a particular season.

Table 5. Seasonality of horse images at Lascaux

a. Paintings (Rotunda, Axial Gallery, Nave, Chamber of Felines, Shaft)

Season	No. of images identified*	% from 40 cases able to be assigned to a season
Warm	20	50
Cold	20	50
Indeterminate	9	–

b. Engravings (Passage and Apse)

Season	No. of images identified*	% from 55 cases able to be assigned to a season
Warm	40	72.7
Cold	15	27.2
Indeterminate	9	–

c. All horse images (painted and engraved)

Season	No. of images identified*	% from 95 cases able to be assigned to a season
Warm	60	63.2
Cold	35	36.8
Indeterminate	18	–

*The total number of horse images recorded at Lascaux is 355 (Leroi-Gourhan 1979:344). Many of these images have been excluded from this study because they are only identifiable parts of horse (i.e., manes, tails, heads, etc.), and could not be used to determine seasonality.

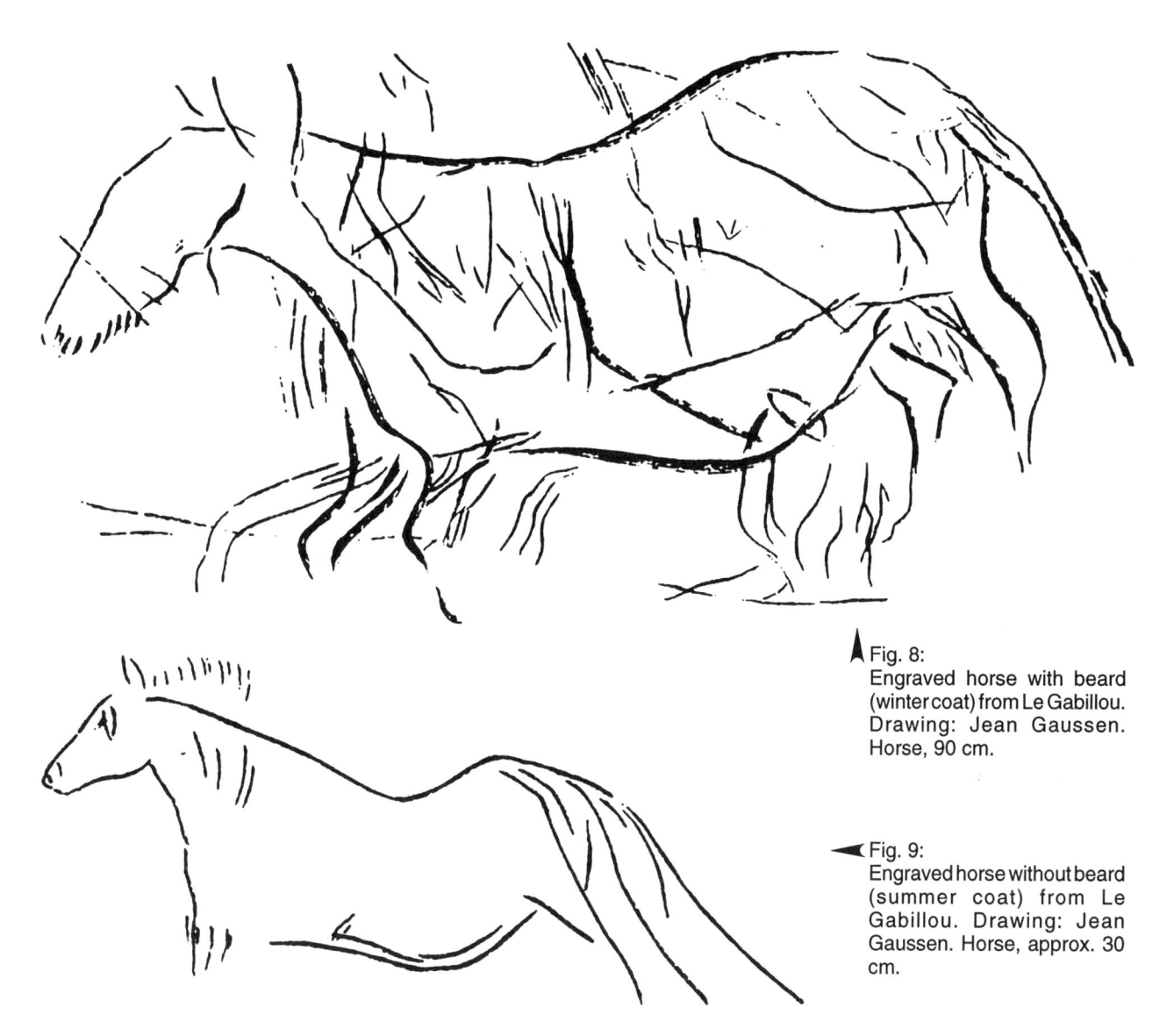

Fig. 8:
Engraved horse with beard (winter coat) from Le Gabillou. Drawing: Jean Gaussen. Horse, 90 cm.

Fig. 9:
Engraved horse without beard (summer coat) from Le Gabillou. Drawing: Jean Gaussen. Horse, approx. 30 cm.

muzzle and both had long, strong, pale horns with black tips. We know how they were coloured because there are in existence a considerable number of contemporary paintings depicting it [sic], and also some detailed descriptions. (Heck 1951:118–119)

Heck also notes that the summer coat of aurochs was smooth and short whereas the winter coat was long and shaggy. The color of calves at birth is uniformly brown although after a few months the color begins to appear adult in pattern with both sexes developing a white muzzle, and males turning black, and females turning red-brown. Bulls become increasingly darker as they age, losing their back stripe so as to appear uniformly black. The white area on the muzzle also decreases in size and in older animals remains only on the lower jaw. It must be noted that although the color of aurochs is consistent within specified cohorts, the shade of coloring sometimes varies between animals of the same age and sex so that some aurochs appear darker and others lighter in color (Heck 1951:120–121).

Female *Bos primigenius* and their offspring, including young bulls, formed small herds which were headed by a dominant cow. The bulls lived alone for most of the year, although sometimes in the company of one or two other bulls of the same age class. During the rutting season (late summer/ early autumn) the bulls joined the females in order to mate.

As for horses, seasonality of aurochs was based on annual changes in pelage (Heck 1951:119). Depictions of aurochs at Le Gabillou (Table 6) are mostly warm season, but the sample is small (n = 13), and thus somewhat unreliable. The sample of aurochs from Lascaux is also small (n = 18 painted and engraved images), but the seasonality for this species also tends toward warm season depictions at that site (Table 7).

It is possible that the bias toward warm season depictions results from the failure of the "artists" to add those char-

Table 6. Seasonality of autochs images at Le Gabillou

Season	No. of images identified*	% from 8 cases able to be assigned to a season
Warm	6	75
Cold	2	25
Indeterminate	5	–

*The total number of aurochs images at Le Gaillou is 13.

Table 7. Seasonality of aurochs images at Lascaux

a. Paintings (Rotunda, Axial Gallery, Nave, Chamber of Felines, Shaft)

Season	No. of images identified*	% from 11 cases able to be assigned to a season
Winter/spring/ early summer	4	36.4
Warm	7	63.6
Indeterminate	2	–

b. Engravings (Apse only; those from the Passage were not suitable for seasonal analysis)

Season	No. of images identified*	% from 1 case able to be assigned to a season
Cold	1	100
Indeterminate	4	–

c. All aurochs images (painted and engraved)

Season	No. of images identified*	% from 12 cases able to be assigned to a season
Winter/spring/ early summer	4	33.3
Warm	7	58.3
Cold	1	8.3
Indeterminate	6	–

*The total number of aurochs images recorded at Lascaux is 87 (Leroi-Gourhan and Allain 1979:344). Many of these images have been excluded from this study because they are not available in a published source, or because they are only identifiable as parts of bovids and are not suitable for seasonal analysis.

acteristics that would indicate cold season (long hair). In other words, a picture of an aurochs shows characteristics of a warm season animal (lacking a shaggy coat), until cold season characteristics are added. While it is possible that warm season animals simply lack the addition of cold season characteristics, the fact that other species are undoubtedly depicted at the same site in *both* warm and cold season pelage suggests that this constitutes a choice on the part of the "artist."

Bison

While wild populations of European bison (*Bison bonasus*) offer information about the ethology of their ancestors, a great deal of what is known about the appearance of Pleistocene bison (*Bison priscus*), as with aurochs, comes from Upper Paleolithic graphic images, particularly the polychrome paintings from Lascaux (Dordogne), Font de Gaume (Dordogne), and Altamira (Santander).

In concurrence with Geist (1971), Guthrie (1990:117–118) has argued that the hair pattern of European Pleistocene bison, as portrayed in parietal representations, was unlike that of extant species of bison. Guthrie has reconstructed the appearance of Paleolithic bison pelage based on cave paintings, and the remains of a mummified Pleistocene bison which was discovered in 1979 ("Blue Babe," see Guthrie 1990). Unlike skeletal features, pelage is quite variable among geographically isolated populations of the same species, as its patterning is related to social behavior rather than environmental constraints (Guthrie 1990:123). Modern European bison (*Bison bonasus*) is homogeneously colored a dark rusty brown, but *Bison priscus*, prehistoric bison, appears to have had a dark reddish bodily interior with darker (near black) color on the cervical and thoracic hump, the tail, legs, and face (Guthrie 1990:124–126). This coloration is evident in paintings at Lascaux, although the dark red interior patch has also been interpreted as exposed underfur during a seasonal moult (Ruspoli 1986:33).

Female *Bison bonasus* can weigh between seven hundred and twelve hundred pounds and males are considerably larger, weighing up to a ton and standing six feet high (Hinrichsen 1990:38). Faunal evidence suggests that *Bison priscus* was larger in body size than extant European bison, and had horns which were almost twice as large. Sexual dimorphism in *Bison priscus* was the greatest of any bison species (McDonald 1981) suggesting that the males stayed apart from the group for most of the year, and had access to better forage (Guthrie 1990:158). Despite their lumbering appearance bison are quite fast, and can charge at speeds up to twenty five miles an hour with enormous force (Guthrie 1990:158). One of the most well known images from Lascaux, the "well scene," depicts a wounded bison charging at a man.

For most of the year male bison remain separate from the rest of the population, rejoining the herd only for a short time during the rut (from mid August through October) (Krasinski 1990; Hinrichsen 1990). During the rut, males engage in head-to-head combat to secure breeding privileges. Usually only the largest males participate in actual combat, having scared off the smaller males who are unable to successfully compete. The large horns of *Bison priscus*, as with extant species of bison, were used as social display to ward off competition, as well as to engage in actual combat with males not deterred by the display.

When the rut is over, the males reband in their bachelor herds and the females and their offspring form a separate band which will fend for itself throughout the rest of the year (Hinrichsen 1990). Breeding for *Bison bonasus* (European bison) occurs in early to mid autumn, during the rut. The gestation period is 261–283 days, and calving (single birth) occurs in late spring (May through June) (Gamble 1986:108; Hinrichsen 1990).

Seasonality in depictions of bison at Gabillou is indeterminate. This species is particularly difficult to judge season based on observed characteristics in the images. Although bison grow a thick winter coat (Guthrie 1984:45–46), they have beards and "bonnets" year-round and the change in pelage is not as noticeable as that, for example, of horse. At Le Gabillou the depiction of bison with beards and "bonnets" may be a convention for representing that animal, rather than an attempt to depict a particular season (such as winter when these features are slightly more pronounced but difficult to see because of increased hair growth over the entire body) (Fig. 10). At Lascaux, seasonality of bison images is also difficult to judge (Table 8), but the juxtaposition of some images (Fig. 11) suggests the seasonally influenced act of rutting (Ruspoli 1986:141). Again, the total sample for this species is small (n = 9), but all images that could be assigned to a season (n = 4) were assigned to autumn.

Ibex

There are two living forms of European ibex, *Capra ibex ibex* (alpine ibex) which is geographically restricted to the Alps and Tatra Mountains, and *Capra ibex pyrenaica* (Spanish ibex) which is probably already extinct in the Pyrenees, but still surviving in other high Spanish mountains (Sutcliffe 1985:96). Modern ibex are high mountain dwellers that rarely descend below 1500 feet, but it is likely that they inhabited much lower altitudes during the Pleistocene (Spiess 1979:262). Migrations occur between high and low altitudes, with ibex descending to lower altitudes during the spring when snow cover begins to melt and new green shoots appear which can be eaten (Couturier 1962:123–124).

The two species of ibex can be distinguished archaeologically by shape of their horns (Delpech 1983:193). Alpine ibex have horns which are rectangular in cross section, and Spanish ibex have horns which are triangular in cross section. Sutcliffe (1985:97) has argued that although in some of the better done Paleolithic images

Fig. 10:
Engraved bison from Le Gabillou. Drawing: Jean Gaussen. Bison, 28 cm.

it may be possible to make identifications as to whether the figure depicted is alpine or Spanish ibex, the similarity of appearance and geographic overlap of the two species makes such identification tenuous at best. It is best, therefore, to consider here a more generalized pattern of ibex behavior rather than that specific to either geographic population.

Male ibex are characterized by their large curved horns which can reach lengths of one meter or more (Kurtén 1968:181). The anterior surface of the horns, although relatively flat, is broken by a series of distinct transverse ridges (Fig. 12) (Schaller 1977:26). Female ibex also have horns, but there is marked sexual dimorphism and after the second year of life females' horns become noticeably smaller than those of males as does their overall body size (Couturier 1962:400).

Male ibex have beards which begin to grow during the second year of life. The length of the beard is not proportionate to the age of the ibex, but there is a slight seasonal variation in length (i.e slightly longer in the winter) (Couturier 1962:93). This change in beard length is negligible, however, and cannot be used in this study as a reliable criterion for determining seasonality of visual images.

Capra ibex have pale colored pelage with white abdomen and dark, blackish flanks. Ibex have only one seasonal moult which occurs in the spring when the darker, thicker winter coat is shed. At the start of the moult the color of hair fades and becomes a whitish hue (Couterier 1962:103). As

Fig. 11:
Painted "crossed bison" from Lascaux. Photograph: Doug Mazonowicz. Bison, approx. 240 cm.

Table 8. Seasonality of bison images at Lascaux

a. Paintings (Rotunda, Axial Gallery, Nave, Chamber of Felines, Shaft)

Season	No. of images identified*	% from 2 cases able to be assigned to a season
Autumn	2	100
Indeterminate	4	–

b. Engravings (Apse only; those from the Passage were not suitable for seasonal analysis)

Season	No. of images identified*	% from 2 cases able to be assigned to a season
Autumn	2	100
Indeterminate	1	–

c. All bison images (painted and engraved)

Season	No. of images identified*	% from 4 cases able to be assigned to a season
Autumn	4	100
Indeterminate	5	–

*The total number of bison images recorded at Lascaux is 20 (Leroi-Gourhan and Allain 1979:344). Many of these have been excluded because they are not suitable for seasonal analysis, or could not be found in published sources.

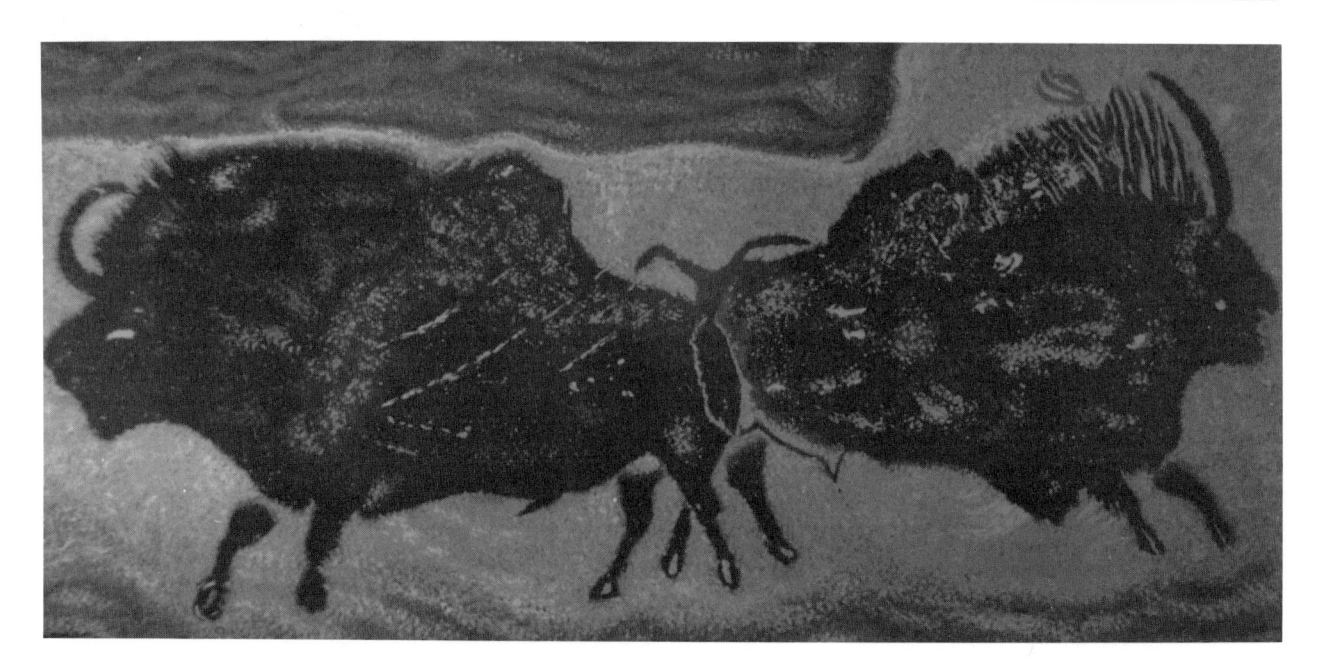

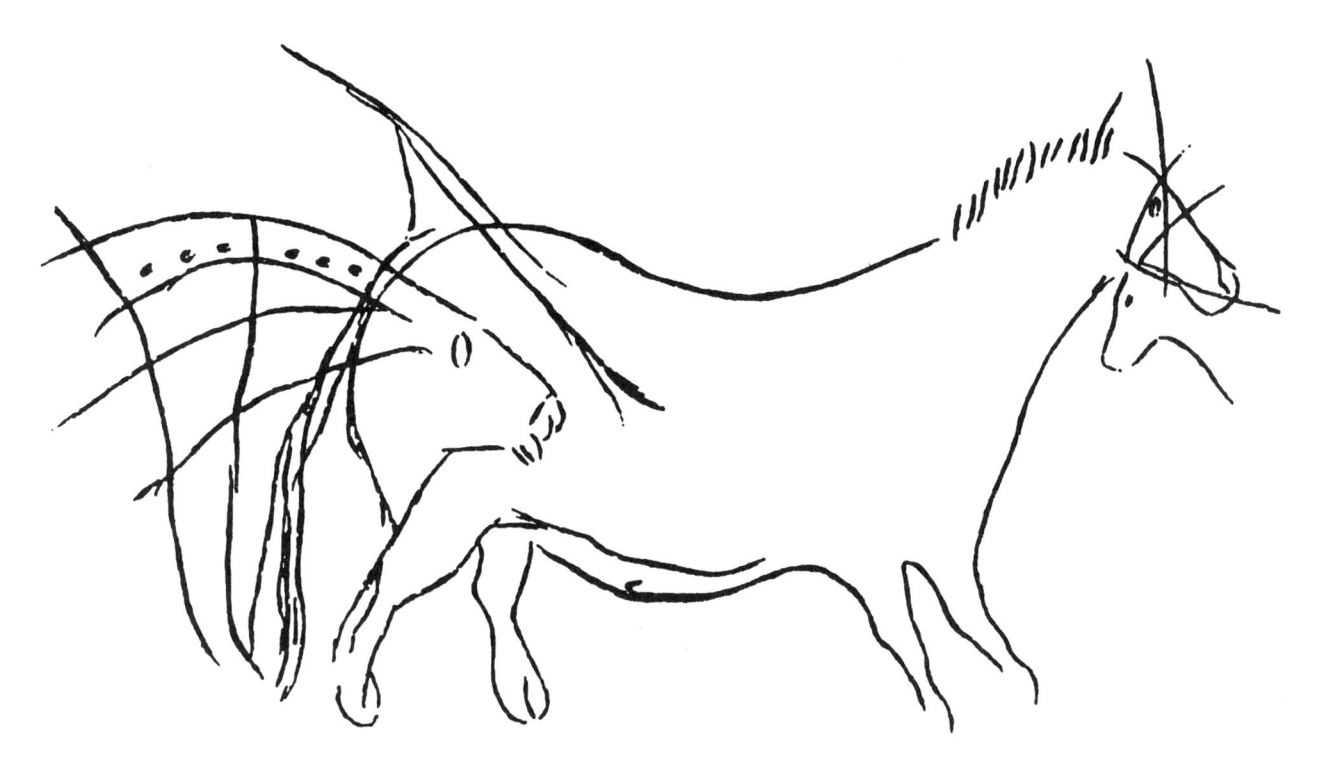

Fig. 12:
Engraved ibex from Le Gabillou. Drawing: Jean Gaussen. Horse, 75 cm.

the hair begins to fall out the animals rub up against rocks and trees to shed the thick coat. When the winter coat is shed, a shorter, sleeker summer coat replaces it. Although the moult begins in the spring, it may not be complete (i.e., all winter hair has been shed) until early summer.

The rutting season occurs in December and January, and consists of aggressive fights between males competing for females with which to breed. Males participate in aggressive battles in which they charge at each other and knock horns. Successful males win breeding privileges, and mating occurs around this time. The gestation period for ibex is 165–170 days (Schaller 1977:120, 364; Couterier 1960:63), and single births occur in May to June.

As with bison, seasonality of ibex is indeterminate at Le Gabillou. At Lascaux (Table 9), interpretations of seasonality are based on ethologically suggestive compositions, although the sample is small (n = 10), and seven of the ten figures used comprise a single composition. This group of seven ibex is interpreted as a bachelor band (spring/summer/autumn) based on seasonal variation in herd composition. Males are separate from the females for most of the year, and join them only in the winter, during the rutting season, in order to mate (Schaller 1977; Couturier 1960, 1962). The remaining two images of ibex at Lascaux have been interpreted both here, and elsewhere (Delluc and Delluc 1986:176), as confronted males during the winter rut.

Table 9. Seasonality of ibex images at Lascaux, paintings only (Rotunda, Axial Gallery, Nave, Chamber of Felines, Shaft). None of the engravings from the Apse and Passage were suitable for seasonal analysis.

Season	No. of images identified*	% from 9 cases able to be assigned to a season
Winter	2	22.2
Spring/summer/autumn	7	77.7
Indeterminate	1	–

*The total number of ibex images recorded at Lascaux is 35 (Leroi-Gourhan and Allain 1979:344). Many have been excluded from this study because they are not suitable for seasonal analysis, or could not be found in published sources.

Discussion

Problems

Determining the seasonal content of visual imagery may be valuable to our understanding of the broader economic and social context of the images themselves. Despite this potential, interpreting seasonality in the visual record continues to be problematic. First, there are obvious sampling problems. The two caves used here offered a large sample of visual images, but only a portion of these was actually usable. For some species (ibex, bison, and perhaps aurochs), the sample of usable images was so small as to be unreliable for interpreting overall seasonality. Sample size, in terms of the ability to assign season, varies a great deal by species and by site. It is also clear that certain species are better suited to an analysis of seasonality represented in visual imagery. Of the six species used in this study, horse, red deer, and reindeer are the most amenable to seasonal interpretation. For cervids, specific seasons can be assigned according to the known growth/shedding pattern of antler. Horses must be assigned to broad seasonal categories, but this does not render them useless in terms of understanding seasonal context. These broad categories still break the year into two temporal units (cold season and warm season), and this information can then be used to compare seasonality of horse images to seasonality of other species, as well as to the seasonality of associated archaeological fauna.

Interpreting seasonality in images of bison and ibex is much more difficult than for horses and cervids. Both male and female ibex have horns, but there is not a growth/shedding pattern that can be used to interpret seasonality, as there is for cervids which shed their antlers annually. Ibex pelage gets thicker and more dense in the winter months, but visually the change is not as evident as the change in horse pelage. Bison also have an increased growth of hair in the winter months, but this change is also not as discernable as it is for horse.

Ethological information contained in visual representations of ibex and bison can offer evidence of seasonality, but this is a much more speculative interpretation than those involving observations of actual physical variation. Because ethological interpretations first require an interpretation of images as a "composition," physical traits, such as a shaggy coat and beard on a horse are a much more reliable indication of season than is an ethological interpretation based on herd composition. For example, the person who created the frieze of seven ibex at Lascaux, interpreted here as a bachelor band (spring/summer/autumn), may have not done so with the intention of depicting a bachelor band of ibex. The ibex may have been grouped as they are in order to depict the repetitious pattern created by the row of large male horns, rather than to depict the specific seasonal event of male ibex separating from the females. Ironically, the visual effect of multiple large horns seen in an all male herd of ibex in nature, may have inspired the artist to create the same visual effect in a permanent graphic image.

There is no question that Upper Paleolithic people had a thorough and precise understanding of seasonal variation in both the appearance and behavior of the animals they hunted and painted/engraved. This detailed knowledge of animal appearance and ethology is evident in the images themselves. More difficult to interpret is the intention of rendering animals in different seasonal conditions. Although the method used here does not address issues concerning the intent of Paleolithic "artists" in depicting seasonal variation in animals, it does serve to contextualize Upper Paleolithic art in terms of seasonality. This is clearly an important issue in Upper Paleolithic research, given the strong influence of seasonality both economically, in terms of resource procurement and scheduling, and socially, in terms of aggregation and information exchange. It is only after we understand how seasonality is represented symbolically through visual imagery that we can begin to incorporate this information into wider archaeological frameworks, both social and economic.

Research applications

Ethnographic studies have also shown that seasonal aggregations may be closely related to resource procurement (Stuart 1977), and that communal hunting is an effective strategy for the procurement of large migrating herds such as caribou (*Rangifer tarandus*) (Spiess 1979; Driver 1990). For the Upper Paleolithic, White (1985) has suggested that four large sites (Limeuil, Laugerie-Basse, La Madeleine, and Rochereil), in the Périgord region of southwest France, were used as aggregation loci where not only was information exchanged but herds of migrating reindeer were communally hunted. These four large sites all contain large amounts of visual imagery in the form of bone, antler, and ivory objects that have been carved and engraved, most often with images of animals. Many of the images also exhibit seasonally variable physical and ethological traits. A systematic examination of seasonality in the images recovered from proposed aggregation sites may reveal patterning in how the relationship between hunters and prey is manifest in a symbolic context in the form of permanent graphic images.

Nearly all of the images from these sites, however, are found on portable objects (engraved bone, antler, ivory, etc.), and are therefore slightly problematic. Because they are portable, they can be moved to, from, and between sites, and it is not possible to know for certain if objects were created at a site, or carried there from another location. Modern excavation techniques that employ fine mesh screening to allow for the recovery of production debitage from the creation of these objects would aid in addressing this question. Unfortunately, the majority of European Upper Paleolithic portable imagery was recovered through excavations that employed recovery techniques insensitive to the retrieval of small artifactual material. Nevertheless, it would be interesting to see if patterning exists in the seasonality represented in the visual imagery recovered from these sites (whether created on site, or carried there from elsewhere).

Another application of this research is to re-examine hypotheses concerning "scenes" in Upper Paleolithic art. Kehoe (1990) has suggested that communal hunting is evidenced in the parietal art of some Upper Paleolithic cave sites. He has argued that scenes painted on the walls at both Lascaux and Altamira depict communal hunting events, specifically animals being driven through the use of brush and/or stone barriers into corrals. Using data on how different seasons are depicted in visual imagery, I have re-examined one of the corralling scenes described by Kehoe (1990:34–38) from the south wall of the Axial Gallery at Lascaux.

Kehoe has interpreted two rows of black dots that converge at a rectangular shape as a drive lane through which game passes before being trapped in a corral (the rectangular shape). Although corralling is well known ethnographically (Kehoe 1990), a direct ethnographic analogy may not be appropriate for interpreting Upper Paleolithic art. The three horses called the "Chinese horses," and the animals in the "frieze of little ponies" at Lascaux are described by Kehoe as part of a scene which depicts horses being driven into the above-mentioned corral, although they appear to represent horses during different seasons of the year. I have interpreted two of the "Chinese horses" (#43 and #45, Windels and Laming 1949) as warm-season images based on the absence of a shaggy coat, and the presence of an M-shaped pattern which is only visible when horses are in their short summer coats (Fig. 5). The third "Chinese horse" (#42, Windels and Laming 1949), however, has a fringe of hair on its belly suggesting a long winter coat. The horses in the "frieze of little ponies" (Fig. 13) also appear to be animals in their winter coats (Schmid 1984:155). Clearly, if the seasonal interpretations proposed here are correct, the above-mentioned horses cannot represent a single herd being corralled.

Historically, ethnographic analogy has been an important tool for understanding all aspects of prehistoric life. Many of the classic interpretations of Upper Paleolithic images such as hunting magic and depictions of shamans were based on information taken from direct ethnographic sources. Although ethnographic information continues to be an important aspect of archaeological research it must be supplemented, and if possible tested, by objective research methods.

Prospects for future research

I have attempted to illustrate in this paper the possibility of creating a seasonal context in which to view prehistoric visual imagery. Although it constitutes a potentially informative data base, many archaeologists feel that prehistoric visual imagery is in the realm of the "unknowable" (Hawkes 1954; Wylie 1981 cited in Conkey 1987:65), and have largely ignored it in favor of those things considered more reliably interpreted through the archaeological record, such as subsistence economy. The problem, however, is not that the content of Upper Paleolithic art is permanently inaccessible, but that there is a paucity of objective methods, and a fear of assigning meaning to something so far removed from the present. Although this fear is well justified, archaeologists must explore new and methodologically sound ways of examining all potentially informative sets of data, including visual imagery.

I hope that the method described here for identifying seasonality in visual imagery is a first step toward a better

Fig. 13:
Painted "frieze of little ponies" from Lascaux. Photograph: Doug Mazonowicz. Frieze of horses, approx. 170 cm.

understanding of the entire body of Upper Paleolithic art and its relationship to broader social and economic issues. This method can be expanded and fortified by studies on the seasonality of the fauna found at sites containing visual imagery. A number of scientific techniques have been developed to determine seasonality of archaeofauna, and work continues to be done to improve our understanding of seasonal exploitation of prey in Europe during the Upper Paleolithic. A valuable research trajectory would employ methods of determining seasonality in archaeological fauna, and compare the results obtained to seasonality interpreted in visual images at the same site. Although well beyond the scope of this thesis, such an investigation would offer valuable information on the relationship between what people hunted, and what they recorded in graphic images.

New techniques for analyzing pigments (Bahn 1990; Clottes et al. 1990) may also add to our knowledge of the creation of visual images. Lascaux, for example, contains a great deal of superimpositioning of painted images. This overlapping may have occurred because the images were painted during different episodes. If these episodes could be temporally isolated by pigment analysis, an interpretation of the seasonality depicted for each episode may, when combined with faunal studies, offer information about the seasonal re-occupation of a site.

In the last hundred years, our understanding of Upper Paleolithic "art" has become increasingly sensitive to its inherent complexities. In order to continue this trend, we should not abandon such a valuable database, but rather should expand our methods to deal with it systematically and objectively. Our knowledge of seasonality in hunter-gatherer subsistence and settlement systems allows us to infer that seasonality played an important role in hunter-gatherer settlement systems and resource exploitation in the Upper Paleolithic. Seasonality not only influenced the subsistence and settlement systems of these groups, it also was reflected symbolically in the form of visual images that have survived in the archaeological record.

Acknowledgments

I am grateful to the Canadian Arctic Resources Committee for allowing me to publish photographs from George Calef's amazing book, *Caribou and the Barren-lands*; and also to Lee Boyd for generously providing me with photographs of Przewalski's horse. My thanks to Doug Campana and two anonymous reviewers for reading previous drafts of this paper and for offering useful suggestions on how to improve it. Of course any errors in this work are my own. Finally, I would like to thank David Parry for his editorial help and eternal support.

References

Baffier, D. 1984. Les caracteres sexuels secondaires des mammiferes dans l'art parietal paleolithique franco-cantabrique. In *La contribution de la zoologie et de l'ethologie a l'interpretation de l'art des peuples chasseurs prehistoriques*, ed. H. G. Bandi, W. Huber, M.-R. Sauter, B. Sitter, pp. 143–154. Editions Universitaires Fribourg, Suisse.

Bahn, P. 1977. Seasonal Migration in South-West France During the Late Glacial Period. *Journal of Archaeological Science* 4:245–257.

_____ 1990. Pigments of the Imagination. *Nature* 347:426.

Bahn, P., and J. Vertut. 1988. *Images of the Ice Age*. Facts on File, New York.

Banfield, A. W. F. 1974. *The Mammals of Canada*. University of Toronto Press, Toronto.

Binford, L. R. 1983. *In Pursuit of the Past*. Thames and Hudson, New York.

Burch, E. S. 1972. The Caribou/Wild Reindeer as a Human Resource. *American Antiquity* 37(3):339–368.

_____ 1991. Herd Following Reconsidered. *Current Anthropology* (32)4:439–444.

Calef, G. 1981. *Caribou and the Barren-lands*. Canadian Arctic Resources Committee, Ottawa. Firefly Books.

Capitan, L., H. Breuil, and D. Peyrony. 1924. *Les combarelles aux Eyzies (Dordogne)*. Masson, Paris.

Casey, S. 1993. Seasonal Context in Upper Paleolithic "Art": An Examination of the Images from Le Gabillou (Dordogne) and Lascaux (Dordogne). M.A. thesis, Department of Anthropology, New York University.

Clottes, J., M. Menu, and P. Walter. 1990. New Light on the Niaux Paintings. *Rock Art Research* (7):21–26.

Clutton-Brock, T. H., S. D. Albon, and F. Guiness. 1982. *Red Deer: Behavior and Ecology of Two Species*. Chicago University Press, Chicago.

Conkey, M. W. 1978. Style and Information in Cultural Evolution: Toward a Predictive Model for the Paleolithic. In *Social Archaeology, Beyond Subsistence and Dating*, ed. C. L. Redman, M. J. Berman, E. Curtin, W. T. Langhorne, Jr., N. Versaggi, and J. Wanser, pp. 61–85. Academic Press, New York.

_____ 1980. The Identification of Prehistoric Hunter-Gatherer Aggregation Sites: The Case for Altimira. *Current Anthropology* 21(5):609–630.

_____ 1987. Interpretive Problems in Hunter-Gatherer Regional Studies: Some Thoughts on the European Upper Paleolithic. In *The Pleistocene Old World*, ed. O. Soffer, pp. 63–77. Plenum, New York.

Couturier, M. 1960. Ecologie et protection du bouquetin (*Capra aegagrus ibex ibex* L.) et du chamois (*Rupicapra rupicapra rupicapra* L.) dans les Alpes. In *Ecology and Management of Wild Grazing*

Animals in Temperate Zones, ed. F. Bourlière, pp. 54–73. U.I.C.N., Warsaw.

———. 1962. *Le bouquetin des Alpes*. Privately printed, Grenoble.

Delluc, B., and G. Delluc. 1986. Chronology and the Analysis of Styles. In *Lascaux: The Final Photographs*, ed. M. Ruspoli, pp. 195–197. Abrams, New York.

Delpech, F. 1983. *Les faunes du Paléolithique supérieur dans le Sud-Ouest de la France*. Cahiers du Quarternaire 6. Centre National de la Recherche Scientifique, Paris.

Driver, J. C. 1990. Meat in Due Season: The Timing of Communal Hunts. In *Hunters of the Recent Past*, ed. L. B. Davis and B. O. K. Reeves, pp. 11–33. Unwin Hyman, London.

Gamble, C. 1986. *The Paleolithic Settlement of Europe*. Cambridge University Press, Cambridge.

Gaussen, J. 1964. *La Grotte Ornée de Gabillou (près Mussidan, Dordogne)*. Imprimeries Delmas, Bordeaux.

Geist, V. 1971. The Relation of Social Evolution and Dispersal in Ungulates During the Pleistocene with Emphasis on the Old World Deer and the Genus *Bison*. *Quarternary Research* 1:283–315.

Gordon, B. 1988. *Of Men and Reindeer Herds in French Magdalenian Prehistory*. BAR International Series 390. British Archaeological Reports, Oxford.

Gutherie, R. D. 1984. Ethological Observations from Paleolithic Art. In *La contribution de la zoologie et de l'ethologie a l'interpretation de l'art des peuples chausseurs prehistoriques*, ed. H. G. Bandi, W. Huber, M.-R. Sauter, B. Sitter, pp. 35–73. Editions Universitaires Fribourg, Suisse.

———. 1990. *Frozen Fauna of the Mammoth Steppe: The Story of Blue Babe*. University of Chicago Press, Chicago.

Hawkes, C. 1954. Archaeological Theory and Method: Some Suggestions from the Old World. *American Anthropologist* (56)155–168.

Heck, H. 1951. The Breeding Back of Aurochs. In *Oryx*, pp. 117–122. London.

Hinrichsen, D. 1990. How Poland Rescued Europe's Largest Mammal. *International Wildlife* (20)4:36–39.

Jochim, M. 1976. *Hunter Gatherer Subsistence and Settlement: A Predictive Model*. Academic Press, New York.

Kehoe, T. F. 1990. Corraling Evidence From Upper Paleolithic Cave Art. In *Hunters of the Recent Past*, ed. L. B. Davis and B. O. K. Reeves, pp. 34–46. Unwin Hyman, London.

Krasinski, Z. 1990. The Border Where the Bison Roam. *Natural History* 6:62–63.

Kurtén, B. 1968. *Pleistocene Mammals of Europe*. Aldine, Chicago.

Laming-Emperaire, A. 1959. *Lascaux Paintings and Engravings*. Pelican, Harmondsworth.

Lent, P. C. 1965. Rutting Behavior in a Barren-ground Caribou Population. *Animal Behavior* 13:259–264.

Leroi-Gourhan, A., and J. Allain (eds.). 1979. *Lascaux inconnu*. Gallia préhistoire, 12th suppl. Centre National de la Recherche Scientifique, Paris.

Marshack, A. 1972. *The Roots of Civilization*. Weidenfeld and Nicholson, London.

———. 1989. Methodology in the Analysis and Interpretation of Upper Paleolithic Image: Theory Versus Contextual Analysis. *Rock Art Research* (6)1:17–53.

Mauss, M. 1904. Essai sur les variations saisonières des société Eskimos: étude de morphologie sociale. *Année Sociologique* 9:39–132.

McDonald, J. N. 1981. *North American Bison: Their Classification and Evolution*. University of California Press, Berkeley.

Mellars, P. 1973. The Character of the Middle–Upper Paleolithic Transition in South-West France. In *The Explanation of Culture Change*, ed. C. Renfrew, pp. 255–276. Duckworth, London.

Mithen, S. 1988. Looking and Learning: Upper Paleolithic Art and Information Gathering. *World Archaeology* 19(3):297–327.

———. 1990. *Thoughtful Foragers: A Study of Prehistoric Decision Makers*. Cambridge University Press, Cambridge.

Mohr, E. 1971. *The Asiatic Wild Horse*. J. A. Allen and Co., London.

Monks, G. 1981. Seasonality Studies. In *Advances in Archaeological Method and Theory*, Vol. 4, ed. M. Schiffer, pp. 177–240. Academic Press, New York.

Olsen, S. 1989. Solutré: A Theoretical Approach to the Reconstruction of Upper Paleolithic Hunting Strategies. *Journal of Human Evolution* 18:295–327.

Pike-Tay, A. 1989. *Red Deer Hunting in the Upper Paleolithic of South-West France: A Seasonality Study*. Unpubl. Ph.D. diss., Department of Anthropology, New York University, New York.

Quimby, G. 1962. A Year with a Chippewa Family. *Ethnohistory* 9(3):217–239.

Ruspoli, M. 1986. *Lascaux: The Final Photographs*. Abrams, New York.

Schaller, G. 1977. *Mountain Monarchs: Wild Sheep and Goats of the Himalaya*. University of Chicago Press, Chicago.

Schmid, E. 1984. Some Anatomical Observations on Paleolithic Depictions of Horses. In *La contribution de la zoologie et de l'ethologie a l'interpretation de l'art des peuples chausseurs prehistoriques*, ed. H. G. Bandi, W. Huber, M.-R. Sauter, B. Sitter, pp. 155–160. Editions Universitaires Fribourg, Suisse.

Sieveking, A. 1976. Settlement Patterns of the Later

Magdalenian in the Central Pyrenees. In *Problems in Economic and Social Archaeology*, ed. G. de G. Sieveking, I. H. Longworth, and K. E. Wilson, pp. 583–603. Duckworth, London.

Skoog, R. 1968. *Ecology of the Caribou (Rangifer tarandus granti) in Alaska*, Pts. 1 and 2. Microfilms International, Ann Arbor, MI.

Speth, J. 1983. *Bison Kills and Bone Counts: Decision Making By Ancient Hunters*. University of Chicago Press, Chicago.

Spiess, A. E. 1979. *Reindeer and Caribou Hunters: An Archaeological Study*. Academic Press, New York.

Stuart, D. 1977. Seasonal Phases of Ono Subsistence, Territorial Distribution, and Organization: Implications for the Archaeological Record. In *For Theory Building in Archaeology*, ed. L. Binford, pp. 251–283. Academic Press, New York.

Sturdy, D. A. 1975. Some Reindeer Economies in Prehistoric Europe. In *Paleoeconomy*, ed. E. Higgs, pp. 55–95. Cambridge University Press, Cambridge.

Sutcliffe, A. 1985. *On the Track of Ice Age Mammals*. Harvard University Press, Cambridge, MA.

Tosello, G. 1992. Magdalenian Engraved Blocks from Limeuil: The Logan Museum of Anthropology Collection. In *French Paleolithic Collections in the Logan Museum of Anthropology*, ed. R. White and L. B. Breitborde, pp. 277–345. *Logan Museum Bulletin* (n.s.) 1(2).

Towne, C. W., and E. N. Wentworth. 1955. *Cattle and Men*. University of Oklahoma Press.

White, R. 1982. Rethinking the Middle/Upper Paleolithic Transition. *Current Anthropology* 23(2):169–192.

———— 1985. *Upper Paleolithic Land Use in the Périgord: A Topographic Approach to Subsistence and Settlement*. BAR International Series 253. British Archaeological Reports, Oxford.

———— 1989. Husbandry and Herd Control in the Upper Paleolithic. *Current Anthropology* 30(5):609–632.

Whitehead, G. K. 1972. *Deer of the World*. Viking Press, New York.

Windels, F., and A. Laming 1949. *The Lascaux Cave Paintings*. Viking Press, New York.

Winters, H. D. 1969. *The Riverton Culture*. Illinois State Museum Reports of Investigations no. 13. Springfield.

Wylie, M. A. 1981. *Positivism and the New Archaeology*. Unpubl. Ph.D. diss., Department of Philosophy, State University of New York, Binghamton.

Zeuner, F. 1963. *A History of Domesticated Animals*. Harper Row, New York.

SOCIAL HUNTING AND MULTIPLE PREDATION

Jonathan C. Driver

Department of Archaeology, Simon Fraser University, Burnaby, British Columbia, Canada V5A 1S6

Introduction

Paleoanthropologists and archaeologists have stressed the importance of hunting large game in societies without domesticates because hunting implies a range of other behaviors. The ability to hunt large animals has been linked to the development of bipedalism, to the evolution of technology, to intelligence, to aggression, to division of labor, to sharing, and to the emergence of social systems. Since the 1960s a number of developments in archaeological method and theory require that we adopt a more critical attitude to the archaeological evidence for hunting and its implied preeminence in hunter-gatherer societies. First, reviews of ethnographic data have shown that hunting is not as important in hunter-gatherer subsistence as was once thought, except in higher latitudes (e.g., Lee 1968; Hayden 1981). These data, though, serve to emphasize the social importance of hunting, in particular the prestige that may accrue to successful hunters. Second, the Cambridge school of "palaeoeconomists" has suggested that there was a wide range of human-animal interactions prior to the isolation of domestic populations (e.g., Wilkinson 1972; Sturdy 1975), and that the term "hunting" has been used too simplistically, masking a great variety of subsistence strategies. Third, the archaeological application of taphonomy and the development of a more critical "middle-range theory" have prompted the reassessment of archaeological evidence for hunting and more cautious interpretation of faunal data (e.g., Binford 1981, 1985; Brain 1981; Lyman 1994).

This paper deals with social hunting of multiple prey, with an emphasis on large terrestrial mammals. In view of the developments discussed above, it is concerned with the problems of recognizing social hunting and multiple predation in the archaeological record, with documenting the occurrence of such activity, and with explaining the emergence of social hunting as a component of both subsistence and social organization.

Social hunting

In attempting to classify and identify prehistoric hunting systems, there are three attributes that have to be considered: organization of the hunters; number of animals killed; and hunting technology. In a previous article I defined communal hunting rather broadly to encompass almost any hunting method that required the cooperation of more than two hunters (Driver 1990a:12). Vivian and Hanna (1993) have criticized this definition, suggesting that "communal" implies large-scale organization and the cooperation of most of the members of a society. They propose that "cooperative" hunting be used for relatively small hunting parties (two to six people), and that "communal" be reserved for events on the scale of historic Plains Indian bison drives. In this definition they follow Hayden (1981:421). However, in my opinion, it is not the size of the hunting party that is important but the extent to which a hunting event requires the participation of a significant proportion of the population of a local group or community. One can distinguish between cooperative hunting and communal hunting in the following way. Cooperative hunts involve more than one hunter, rarely involve people who do not also hunt as individuals, and do not include the majority of people in a community. Communal hunts involve more than one hunter, include people who do not normally participate in other types of hunting, and include a majority of people (or at least adults) in the community. As with most qualitative definitions, there will be ethnographic examples that do not fit clearly into either of the above categories.

Steele and Baker (1993) have reviewed human hunting strategies, and have proposed that one must consider the number of prey taken and the size and organization of the hunting party as separate issues. They point out that multiple predation (killing of more than one individual prey in a single hunting episode) is a common human strategy, but relatively rare in other terrestrial mammalian predators (Steele and Baker 1993:18). They distinguish three predation strategies used by humans. Single predation occurs when one prey specimen is killed. Sequential predation is defined by a series of separate but associated hunting episodes in each of which a single prey specimen is killed.

Mass predation occurs when multiple prey specimens are taken in the same hunting episode. Sequential and mass predation are both examples of multiple predation. All three predation strategies can be undertaken by solitary hunters or groups of hunters (Steele and Baker 1993:fig. 2-1).

One can also consider the technology of hunting, which I consider here to include both weapons and hunting tactics. When considering weapons, and especially when considering ethnographic data, it is important to identify hunting methods that use modern firearms, as these can drastically alter hunting success. Prior to the invention of firearms most hunting methods required hunters to get fairly close to their prey. In addition to obvious hunting weapons (bow and arrow, spear, club) one should also remember passive technologies such as traps, snares, and poisons. Humans have employed a wide range of hunting tactics, including stalking, intercepts and ambushes, running, and driving.

Given these various attributes of human hunting, one can construct a matrix which combines social organization of the hunters with predation type, and consider the hunting technology most appropriate to the various combinations (Table 1). Note that this table deals only with terrestrial hunting, and does not include passive technologies such as traps, because these generally take single individuals. (Some multiple predation did involve snaring animals by driving them towards fences in which snares were set). Single hunters are expected to hunt most frequently for single animals. Tactics could include stalking, intercept (when the hunter waits for animals to appear in predictable locations) or running down (for example on snow shoes in deep snow). Single hunters are unlikely to hunt sequentially. Under some conditions prey may be immobilized, in which case sequential hunts are possible. Examples might include hunting seal pups on beaches or animals trapped in snowdrifts. The use of efficient firearms would also allow a single hunter to conduct sequential kills. Mass predation by single hunters is likely to be very rare, and would almost always require modern technology.

Cooperative hunters may hunt single prey individuals in ways similar to single hunters. Group participation may be required to increase the chances of locating an animal or to kill a large or aggressive individual (Johnson et al. 1980). A somewhat specialized form of cooperative hunting is to run down a single animal through a relay system (e.g., Anell 1969:43). Most examples of sequential predation by cooperative groups involve intercept hunting, in which groups of hunters wait for animals to arrive at locations suitable for slaughter. Good examples are found throughout northern North America, where caribou were often hunted from kayaks and canoes as they crossed lakes during migrations (e.g., Anell 1969:15). Such episodes may be associated with the construction of fences or cairn lines to guide animals to desired crossing points. Cooperative

Table 1. Social organization of hunters, predation type, and hunting tactics in terrestrial hunting. Brackets indicate rare hunting tactics. See text for details.

Social organization	Predation Type		
	Single	Sequential	Mass
Single	Stalking Intercept Running down	[Immobile] [Firearms]	[Firearms]
Cooperative	Stalking Intercept Relay running	Intercept	Driving
Communal	[Stalking] [Driving]	[Driving] [Intercept]	Driving

hunting groups also undertook mass predation, primarily through some form of driving to concentrate groups of animals (see Anell 1969; Driver 1990a; Steele and Baker 1993 for detailed examples). Some driving technologies also used fences or cairns to move animals in desired directions, and some used nets or corrals to trap the animals.

Communal hunts, as defined above, require significant levels of organization in order to concentrate the prey in a confined area where predation can occur. Such events are very rare for single or sequential predation, and usually involve some form of driving to artificially concentrate the prey individuals for the purposes of mass predation. Some sequential hunts which use intercept or driving tactics may involve communal organization, usually if the human community is small, such as one might find in northern latitudes. Communal hunts involving large numbers of people are most frequently associated with mass predation.

This paper is concerned with episodes of multiple predation. As modeled in Table 1, these are most likely to be associated with either cooperative or communal hunting, usually employing intercept or driving tactics which are designed to place hunters in the proximity of numerous prey individuals. Cooperative and communal hunts may be undertaken to kill individual animals, and in very rare cases it is possible that single hunters could obtain multiple prey. By focusing on social hunting of multiple prey, the paper focuses on two phenomena: (1) the ability to acquire significant quantities of meat in a single hunting episode; and (2) the fact that human groups can organize numerous individuals to accomplish a common goal. Both of these phenomena have relevance to understanding the evolution of human behavior.

For this paper, "social hunting" implies the active cooperation of a group of hunters to confine and slaughter larger numbers of animals than could normally be obtained by each hunter acting individually. Although technqiues of hunting varied, most methods minimally involved the following:

1. Hunters acted according to a preconceived plan, which usually involved many people working together (Frison 1987). "Many" is used relative to the normal size of the residential group. Thus, in a small band, a cooperative hunting group of five people might constitute a significant portion of the population. While ethnographic data suggest that social hunting groups were often composed exclusively of men, we should bear in mind that women and children were participants in hunts for large mammals, as on the North American Plains (Verbicky-Todd 1984), and for a wide variety of small game or fish. There is ample ethnographic data to suggest that communal hunts frequently required help from non-hunters to process the meat acquired, and this incorporated an even greater proportion of the total community in the event.
2. Before the hunt began the prey was often more aggregated than usual, as a result of either migration or other environmental variables (e.g., forage availability, snow depth, etc.). This is not universal, though. Certain well-known social hunts, such as rabbit drives in the American Southwest, used human "beaters" to concentrate the population artificially.
3. The social hunt was designed to further concentrate animals in a location where they could be confined, hindered, or impeded in order to make their slaughter more easy. Disabling stampedes over cliff faces are quite rare in the ethnographic record, and most social hunts required hunters to place projectiles accurately.

Social hunting of large animals occurred widely throughout the world prior to the wholesale destruction of game species caused by industrialized hunting, habitat loss, and the widespread introduction of firearms to cultures previously equipped with less efficient means of long-range killing. Well-known examples include bison hunts of the Plains Indians, or Shoshone pronghorn drives. Social hunting was practiced in most of the major biogeographic zones and was undertaken by societies with social organizations ranging from simple bands to agricultural states (Driver 1990a; Forbis 1978).

This paper will deal only with social hunts for large game (usually over 50 kg) undertaken by hunter-gatherers. This excludes not only horticultural, agricultural, and pastoral societies, but also hunter-gatherer societies that hunt socially for smaller species. Thus, Great Basin grasshopper or rabbit drives would be excluded, as would many of the social net-hunts known from Africa or social fishing in temperate rivers. Although a previous review of social hunting (Driver 1990a) utilized data from a wide range of societies, the economic and ecological circumstances of agriculturalists and hunter-gatherers are different. Agriculturalists in many parts of the world hunt to provide protein as a supplement to carbohydrate-rich diets, whereas many hunter-gatherer groups hunt to supply calories (from fat) as well as protein. Many agricultural groups live in larger social units than many (although not all) hunter-gatherers, and this means that hunters in agricultural societies are often aggregated for much of the year. In contrast, many hunter-gatherer groups must form short-term aggregations for the purpose of conducting social hunts.

There are a number of reasons for confining this study to large mammal social hunts. First, social hunting of large game has the potential to provide massive quantities of meat to human groups. Social hunts of large mammals must have had considerable significance to societies in which they occurred. If successful, they provided a store of food which could be used over a number of weeks or months. They also allowed aggregation of scattered groups of people for social and ritual events. Second, the archaeological record has sparse records of kill sites for some species of large mammals, but no kill sites for smaller game. Third, as will be seen below, evidence for social hunting is often based on age and sex ratios of the hunted species or analysis of body part representation and butchery methods. Studies of smaller game have not yet revealed well-defined patterns which might help distinguish social hunts from other forms of small game procurement. Last, when comparing humans to other mammalian predators, the type of social hunting practiced by people differs from that of most other animals. Other mammals hunt socially (e.g., lions, wolves) but the weight of prey is usually lower than the combined weight of the predators. There are some exceptions to this: for example, sabertooth cats may have hunted the largest Pleistocene megafauna (Marean 1989). However, humans typically obtain many times their own weight in meat in social hunting of large mammals, and this distinguishes such events from predation on smaller prey.

There are a number of reasons for pursuing the study of social hunting as an important prehistoric human behavior. Social hunting requires cooperation, sophisticated communication, and planning, both to organize a hunt and to benefit from the surplus of meat procured if the hunt is successful. Identification of social hunting during the Pleistocene should provide evidence for the development of various facets of human social behaviour. Social hunting may also be an important part of an annual economic cycle. For example, Reeves (1990) has commented on the importance of social hunts for the production of pemmican in the "Classic" prehistoric bison hunting society of the northwestern Plains, and Soffer (1989) has discussed the implications of meat surpluses in Pleistocene Europe. We should also bear in mind the social and ritual activities which often accompanied social hunting aggregations. Conkey (1980) has discussed the hypothesis that some large painted caves in western Europe represent aggregation sites; aggregations of this nature require an economic base, and social hunting is one of a number of ways of providing food for periods of ritual and social intensity. Finally, it appears that while social hunting is widespread it is by no means the most common human hunting technique. We should therefore attempt to understand under what conditions it is likely to occur.

Parameters of social hunting

In a review of ethnographic data concerning social hunting (Driver 1990a), it has been shown that social hunts of large mammals are usually initiated by concentrations of game animals, although social hunts for solitary species such as moose (Nelson 1973) may also occur. Aggregations of animals are often the result of seasonal migrations, but may be due to a variety of other factors, such as drought, floods, snow depth, or forage quality. It is notable that in higher latitudes migrations are of particular importance in defining times of game aggregation, and that as one moves to lower latitudes a greater variety of circumstances may cause game to aggregate and disperse (Driver 1990a).

Elsewhere (Driver 1990a) I have discussed possible reasons for conducting social hunts. In many cases, social hunting involves the ability to kill more animals than hunters working as individuals could normally obtain (Frison 1987:179). For example, Plains bison hunters or northern Athabascan and Inuit caribou hunters often trapped and slaughtered large numbers of animals using techniques which could not be operated by individuals. In such cases it appears likely that the productivity (kills per hunter per day) was high, and the production of storable meat supplies was often the result. In other cases, it would seem that the greater chance of a kill when using social techniques is important, even though the overall productivity of meat per hunter might be lower. In other words, under certain circumstances, it is better to reduce risk of starvation than maximize food production. For example, Kutchin social winter hunts for moose seem to be undertaken by a group to raise the chances of killing an individual animal, an important consideration during the winter when lack of food would cause critical problems (Nelson 1973). Similarly, most ethnographically known whaling was by social techniques, probably because a social effort is required to supply the manpower to get to the whale and retrieve it after it has been killed. Generally, the extra effort expended in social hunting is justified either by higher meat returns per hunter or by greater reliability of meat procurement.

One should also note that social hunting tends to decline when firearms are introduced (Driver 1990a), suggesting that social techniques conferred advantages to hunters using relatively simple weapons. The most important advantage was probably decreasing the distance between the hunter and the prey, thus ensuring a better chance of making a kill. Biologists have also noted that cooperative hunting by non-human predators is likely to occur when cooperation increases the likelihood of a kill (Packer and Rutton 1988). It is debatable whether prehistoric technological changes had a great effect on the incidence of social hunting. Pike-Tay (1991) has suggested that the introduction of the spear-thrower during the Upper Paleolithic in western Europe resulted in a reduction of social hunting of red deer, because longer-range projectiles allowed individual animals to be killed by hunters who stalked them. On the other hand, the introduction of the bow and arrow to the North American Plains seems to have increased the ability of hunters to kill large numbers of bison during social hunts and there is no evidence that social hunting declined after the introduction of the new technology (Reeves 1990:170–171).

Emphasis on social hunting as a major subsistence strategy appears to be correlated with environments that lack reliable plant and fish resources, with a markedly seasonal climate, and with a low diversity of large game, usually migratory. In such situations social hunting was probably important because it was a reliable way of procuring adequate supplies of calories in a risky environment, for the following reasons:

1. As migratory animals are likely to move out of an area, procurement and storage of large quantities of meat via social hunts ensures that a supply of the migratory species remains after a migration takes place. This is probably why environments dominated by one or two big game species (e.g., the Arctic, temperate grasslands) are strongly associated with social hunting. This would also explain why social kills of non-migratory guanaco are absent from the Fuego-Patagonia region of South America (Borrero 1990).
2. Low species diversity, and especially a lack of edible plants or anadromous fish, increases the chances of starvation if an important constituent of the edible biomass moves out of the area.
3. Social hunts allow hunters to obtain prime animals in large numbers. Fat levels and hide quality were of great importance to hunters (Hayden 1981; Speth and Spielmann 1983), and it was necessary to obtain high-quality products in large quantities in environments where one or two species were economic mainstays.

We know that seasonality was well marked in many temperate areas, but resource diversity was higher than in subarctic and arctic regions, and other more reliable resources such as fish and nuts may have been preferred. The extent to which social hunts were undertaken by prehistoric temperate hunter-gatherers is likely to vary with the nature of the overall resource base, and especially with predictable, storable plant foods or marine resources such as anadromous fish. Reliance on social hunting seems unlikely in temperate forests or along temperate coasts. On the other hand, temperate grasslands were probably important areas of prehistoric social hunts because of low resource diversity and the migratory tendencies of most large mammals in grassland environments.

When considering the prehistoric reliance on social hunting, it is worth noting that this activity is generally ranked low as a subsistence strategy in societies where alternative resources are available. This seems to be because of the labor-intensive nature of social hunting, the greater reliability of other resources, and the amount of organization required to implement a social hunt. Ethnographic data demonstrate widespread use of social hunts (Driver 1990a), but in many cases the hunts are scheduled around more important activities, both in hunter-gatherer and agricultural societies. These activities include gathering wild plants, fishing, and agriculture. Thus, one should not expect social hunts to be an important component of hunter-gatherer subsistence strategies except in the types of environment outlined above, i.e., those with migratory large mammals, relatively low diversity of other edible species, lack of alternate foods, and pronounced seasonality.

Social hunting also has a social dimension. For many hunting societies it provides a chance for social aggregation to occur. However, most associations of hunters for the purposes of social hunting are impermanent. In many environments animals are only aggregated for particular times of the year; as soon as animals begin to disperse, social hunting is no longer as efficient as individual hunting (Driver 1990a). Thus, while there are some societies which seem to have relied heavily on social hunting (many of the Plains Indian groups and northern caribou hunters would be prime examples), the opportunities for efficient social hunting were never frequent enough to maintain a permanent organization for this purpose. Again using Plains Indian groups as an example, references to the close control of social hunts (Verbicky-Todd 1984:25–32) suggest that any society that relied on social hunting for its year-round subsistence would have to develop permanent social controls and institutions to regulate the hunt. There do not seem to be any ethnographic accounts of hunter-gatherer societies where social hunting was so pervasive as to result in this sort of permanent organization. Instead, one finds that certain individuals may be temporarily promoted to positions of importance during the planning and execution of the hunt (Frison 1987:209).

It seems unlikely that a complex social organization could develop in societies where social hunting of large game provided the major source of food. Complex hunting and gathering social organization is usually tied to low residential mobility for least part of the year and highly predictable, storable resources (see various examples in Price and Brown 1985). In temperate and higher latitudes large mammals usually exhibit seasonal cycles of aggregation and dispersal, and often migration. Often this necessitates a mobile annual round on the part of hunter-gatherers, and this involves cycles of aggregation and dispersal of human population, reducing the chances of permanent complex social controls developing. Furthermore, although large mammals make regular movements, it would be incorrect to state that these are highly predictable. In many cases, movement is dependent on local variables such as weather, snow depth, forage availability and quality, or even fire. Even the very regular movements of the great herds of barren-ground caribou in Canada may fluctuate from year to year, although the frequency of such fluctuations may have been over-emphasized (Gordon 1990).

One possible exception to this general pattern has been postulated from prehistoric data. Soffer (1985, 1989) suggests that while evidence for storage and sedentism is rare in much of Pleistocene Eurasia, Upper Paleolithic cultures on the Russian Plain appear to have practiced meat storage on a large scale and to have maintained aggregated populations for most of the year, leading to the development of social inequalities (Soffer 1989:727). There is relatively little data to suggest that these societies were year-round social hunters, although one would expect social hunting to be a viable strategy in the late Pleistocene environments of the region, and possibly also in some western European locales.

In summary, social hunts were probably widespread in prehistoric hunter-gatherer societies, but were probably only a significant component of subsistence strategies in environments with fairly specific characteristics: low diversity of edible species; large mammal community dominated by one or two species; few reliable, abundant plant or fish resources; strongly seasonal environments encouraging migration of large game and fostering cyclical changes in meat and hide quality.

Identifying social hunting in the archaeological record

As with many human behaviors, the "signature" of social hunting in the archaeological record is not easily read. North American archaeologists are familiar with the idea of a "buffalo jump" as a readily recognized attribute of a social hunt. However, in many other parts of the Americas and in most of the Old World, direct evidence for social hunting is more difficult to detect in the archaeological record.

In order to investigate the prehistory of social hunting, one must develop criteria for its identification. A number of approaches to this have been suggested, and are summarized below.

Artificial and natural facilities

Deliberately constructed facilities for social hunting are known ethnographically from many parts of the world (e.g., Anell 1969; Barth 1983; Blehr 1990; Brink and Rollans 1990; Frison et al. 1990; Gordon 1990; Spiess 1979; Verbicky-Todd 1984). They include various methods for moving animals to locations where they can be more easily killed, or for concentrating animals into dense groups. Such facilities may leave fairly permanent traces in the archaeological record. For example, drive lanes consisting of piles of stones have been recorded on the North American Plains (Brink and Rollans 1990) and similar structures are known from the arctic areas of North America and Scandinavia (Blehr 1990; Gordon 1990). However, many of these structures are relatively impermanent, such as drift fences constructed from dead wood, and are unlikely to survive for long.

To the best of my knowledge, most deliberately constructed prehistoric facilities are known from North America, generally associated with bison and pronghorn hunting on the Plains and adjacent areas (Arkush 1986; Frison 1978), bighorn sheep hunting in the Rockies (Morris 1990; Frison et al. 1990) and caribou hunting in the Arctic (Gordon 1990). In the Old World, most examples are associated with reindeer hunting in northern regions (Barth 1983; Blehr 1990; Gordon 1990).

In any area where there has been substantial sediment deposition since the construction of facilities, such features are unlikely to be found, except by chance. For example, the extensive loess deposits in the Ukraine (Klein 1973) have probably buried any facilities associated with Upper Paleolithic social hunting. Similarly, areas of the world that have undergone extensive surficial modification (e.g., by ploughing) are unlikely to preserve artificial facilities.

Facilities need not be deliberately constructed. Many social hunts took advantage of topographic or locational features of the landscape to enhance the hunting methods. Good examples of this would include the variety of natural traps documented for bison on the North American Plains and adjacent areas (Frison 1978), and the common practice of killing caribou at water crossings (Gordon 1990). Such natural facilities are likely to survive better in the archaeological record, provided that major landscape changes do not take place. Many examples of such sites are known in North America (see papers in Davis and Reeves 1990; Frison 1978), and a few from the European Paleolithic (e.g., Olsen 1989). Much of the discussions about early hominid hunting centered at one time on the concept that animals could be "mired" and then killed more easily, although many of these early sites have since been reassessed as non-cultural kills, and Frison (1991:19) has noted the improbability of miring as an effective hunting strategy.

Bone beds

Killing and butchering animals in large numbers may leave extensive deposits of bone (Frison 1987:180). Again, the North American Plains provide the best known examples of these. Many bison bone beds are preserved in natural sediment traps, such as ponds (Reher and Frison 1980), arroyos (Frison et al. 1976; Wheat 1972), sand dunes (Frison 1974), and bogs (Landals 1990). In these situations, preservation is likely to be good because of relatively rapid sedimentation. However, not all kill sites are found associated with natural facilities (Stanford 1978; Todd 1987), and bone beds may be preserved under relatively shallow deposits. Todd (1987) has examined the formation of bone beds in some detail, and has demonstrated their potential for analysis of human behavior. He cautions that not all bone beds are necessarily formed through social hunting, although analysis of bones and associated artifacts should enable one to identify a social kill.

The presence of bone beds with associated artifacts does not necessarily demonstrate that humans were involved in killing the animals. The debate about some early "kill sites" such as Torralba has received much exposure (e.g., Binford 1987; Freeman 1981; Villa 1990), but other examples also can be found in later periods. For example, Wilson (1983) discusses the large bison assemblage from the Hitching Post Ranch site in Alberta, and concludes that the assemblage is the result of natural catastrophic processes, rather than deliberate human social kills. The massive deposits of cave bear bones in European Late Pleistocene deposits have been reinterpreted as natural deaths (Gamble 1986:318). An Upper Paleolithic mammoth "kill" at Hallines in Belgium has been reinterpreted as a natural death followed by scavenging (Dennell 1983:132). In all cases deposits of bone were associated with artifacts, but there is little evidence for deliberate social killing.

Age and sex profiles

Most social hunts of herd species destroy significant portions of social units. As social units of large game animals are often characterized by distinctive age and sex composition, it has been argued that the population characteristics of faunal assemblages should provide clues to cause of death. Although sex ratios have been calculated for some studies (e.g., Bedord 1974; Speth 1983), most attention has been directed towards age, and specifically to the concept that mortality patterns of socially hunted prey should reflect catastrophic rather than attritional kills (Klein et al. 1983; Levine 1983; Reher 1973; Wilson 1980). There has been relatively little critical assessment of the polarity of catastrophic and attritional mortality, and this subject should receive attention in future studies. Stiner (1990, 1991; Stiner and Kuhn 1992) has drawn attention to the fact that Holocene human hunters typically selected prime adults as prey, rather than the pattern of juveniles and old adults more typically selected by other mammalian carnivores. Stiner (1990) has also made the important observation that social hunting does not necessarily result in a "catastrophic" mortality pattern in which the age structure of the death assemblage resembles the age structure of the living assemblage, because in many social hunts the hunters still are able to target individual animals, and are not required to slaughter entire social units. It is also doubtful whether humans engaged in individual stalking would select juvenile and senile animals. In fact there is ethnographic data to suggest that prime adults would be selectively stalked, especially if fat content of meat was an important consideration. The following section looks at various problems in using age and sex structure as an indicator of social hunting.

In the first place, some studies have suggested that a sequence of catastrophic kills might not produce a classic "catastrophic" mortality curve if each catastrophic kill culled different portions of a herd or occurred at different seasons (Wilson 1980). For example, a kill of a cow/calf herd followed by two bachelor herds would produce a death assemblage which would not resemble the catastrophic death of a well-defined social unit. Thus, while catastrophic mortality would certainly suggest social hunting, absence of a well-defined pattern need not preclude it.

Second, taphonomic processes may alter the original age and sex structure through selective destruction of certain bones. The bones of young animals are likely to suffer greater destruction than adults. This phenomenon is widely recognized in Plains bison kill sites, where in many cases the younger members of a herd appear to be missing from bone beds (Reher 1973; Reher and Frison 1980). Levine (1983) has documented a similar situation in horse assemblages from Paleolithic European sites. Although it is tempting to conclude that a considerable reduction in the expected number of young animals is the result of natural processes such as scavenging or weathering, closer examination of the data is probably warranted, but this topic cannot be addressed in detail here. For North American bison kills it can be shown that there is a lot of variation in the frequency of young animals, and that at sites with good preservation it is unlikely the younger animals are under-represented as a result of differential preservation (Driver 1983). Furthermore, Stiner's hypothesis that humans select prime adults as prey casts considerable doubt on the working hypothesis of most Plains archaeologists that social hunts produced catastrophic mortality profiles which were then altered by taphonomic processes.

Levine (1983) has reviewed the age structure of some Middle Paleolithic horse assemblages and her work provides the most comprehensive discussion of the problem of under-represented juveniles. In developing mortality profiles for these assemblages she introduced a correction factor, based on the presumption that deciduous teeth would preserve less well than permanent teeth. This was done because deciduous teeth appeared to be under-represented in most assemblages. Olsen (1989) has also noted fewer than expected deciduous teeth in the Upper Paleolithic assemblages at Le Solutré but does not invoke differential preservation to account for it, stating that deciduous teeth differ little from permanent teeth in their resistance to decay processes (Olsen 1989:301).

Levine (1983) presents data for the tooth:bone ratio for a number of assemblages, and provides graphs for the distribution of age classes of horse for the larger assemblages. There are seven assemblages from archaeological sites where both the tooth:bone ratio and the age distribution are presented. In order to investigate the relationship between deciduous tooth representation and general preservation conditions, one can plot the ratio of teeth to bones against the percentage of teeth falling in the 0 to 3-year range before the correction factor is applied (Table 2). (This percentage was chosen because Levine's adjustment formula for the supposedly "missing" juvenile teeth generally affects the 0 to 3-year age group. In most of the presented graphs, the shape of the frequency distribution for animals ages 4 years and greater is not significantly affected by the correction factor). The relationship between percentage of juvenile teeth and teeth:bone ratios is curious. One would expect that assemblages characterized by high tooth:bone ratios would be the most poorly preserved, and that they would have the lowest frequencies of juveniles. In fact the opposite appears to be the case. Assemblages with the lowest tooth:bone ratios have the lowest percentages of juvenile teeth. With the exception of Combe Grenal Layer 14 (which is so badly preserved that virtually no bone survives), the assemblages with the highest tooth:bone ratios (Combe Grenal layers 22 and 23) also have the highest percentages of teeth in the 0 to 3-year age range.

There appears to be no basis for Levine's suggestion that lower frequencies of juvenile teeth can be explained by poor preservation. What is particularly interesting about Levine's study is the Solutré situation. These Upper Paleolithic assemblages are considered the best preserved of any she studied; they are from what is almost certainly a social kill; and yet there is a strikingly low number of juvenile animals (especially 0, 1, and 2-year-olds) in two assemblages from the site (Levine 1983:figs. 4.20 and 4.21). In other words, the classic Old World Paleolithic social kill site does not contain a "catastrophic" mortality pattern, just like most of the classic New World bison kill sites (Driver

Table 2. Ratio of teeth to bone and percentage of 0 to 3-year-old horse teeth from selected Paleolithic sites. Data from Levine (1983).

Assemblage	Teeth: bone	% of 0 to 3-year-olds
Combe Grenal 14	145:1	15.5
Combe Grenal 22	5.9:1	35.5
Combe Grenal 23	10.2:1	38.0
Gonersdorf 06	0.8:1	25.0
Arlay 01	2.9:1	26.0
Le Solutré 2L	0.6:1	17.5
Le Solutré 3P	0.7:1	17.0

1983). Combining these empirical data with Stiner's data and hypothesis, it is unlikely that social kills are necessarily represented by catastrophic mortality profiles. Where such profiles do occur they are probably good evidence for social hunting, but their absence does not necessarily preclude social strategies. It is possible that in some sites poor preservation conditions have resulted in the loss of young individuals. At other sites this explanation does not seem tenable, and we may be seeing evidence for some selectivity on the part of humans. Such selectivity might result from deliberate avoidance of young animals, either as a conservation measure or because meat quality was lower. We should also consider the possibility that social hunts may have taken place more frequently during times of short-term environmental stress, and that these natural stressors reduced juvenile populations prior to social hunting taking place (Driver 1983).

Third, cultural activities following a kill might similarly affect age and sex structures. Relatively little work has been done on this, although Speth (1983) has shown differential butchery and removal of bones based on age and sex of the slaughtered animals.

Fourth, in the absence of well-defined kill sites, the structure of assemblages at processing, caching, or habitation sites of various types and permanency is also likely to be affected by cultural and taphonomic processes, making it difficult to decide whether age and sex structures result from social or individual hunting. For example, the population structure of pronghorn antelope recovered from late prehistoric pueblos in the Sierra Blanca, New Mexico suggests social hunting in the spring, based on the presence of late fetal/neonatal specimens and specimens reaching the end of their first year (Driver 1985). While social hunting is one interpretation, other scenarios are possible. It may be that pronghorn were hunted by individual hunters in the spring (perhaps because of scheduling decisions), resulting in an assemblage which resembles catastrophic mortality.

Representation of skeletal parts

Binford's work with the Nunamiut initiated more detailed consideration of element frequencies as indicators of site function and subsistence strategies (Binford 1978; 1981). Binford suggested that one can construct utility indices to classify parts of the skeleton according to their overall usefulness to a hunter. Bones with high utility indices are likely to be transported away from a kill site—to a processing area, a temporary hunting camp, a cache, or a more permanent settlement. Consequently, one would expect that kill sites would generally show an overabundance of low utility bones, whereas other sites would show progressively higher utility elements as distance from the kill (measured either by space or time) increases. This has been hypothesized for pueblo sites in New Mexico (Driver 1990b), where long-distance transportation of bison results in an assemblage dominated by bones associated with highly desirable cuts of meat. However, as selective transportation is likely to occur from either social or individual kills, it cannot be used as definitive evidence for social killing.

It is also possible that one might detect an overabundance of meat if animals appeared to be lightly butchered, or if only highly valued cuts of meat were removed from a kill. There are two problems with such assumptions. First, if meat storage was a primary goal of multiple predation, one might find very intense processing of animals. This appears well documented at many North American Plains sites. Second, animals in poor condition may undergo relatively selective butchery in situations where selection is made for parts of the body which retain the highest fat levels (Speth 1983). However, selection for body parts that could be expected to undergo fat depletion in animals in poor condition might well be a sign that humans had obtained an abundance of prime condition animals, probably through multiple predation.

Artifact:bone ratios

Studies of North American social kills have revealed low artifact:bone ratios when contrasted with other site types. Kill sites also tend to have relatively few types of artifacts represented, with little evidence for primary manufacture of lithics. This is well demonstrated by Frison's (1973) study of the lithic assemblages from the Wardell kill and processing area.

Numbers of animals and numbers of species

The archaeological literature of the Middle and Upper Paleolithic of Europe and Asia makes frequent reference to social killing, and one of the most commonly cited pieces of evidence in support of this behavior concerns the low diversity of faunas and the large numbers of bones of particular species recovered (e.g., Chase 1986, 1989; Vereshchagin 1967; White 1985). Neither of these criteria is necessarily a valid signature of social hunting. Specialization on a particular species appears to begin within the Middle Paleolithic (Chase 1986; Gaudzinski 1995; Mellars 1989), and there are many examples from Upper Paleolithic sites of occupations dominated by one species (e.g., Boyle 1990). However, it is quite possible for one species to dominate assemblages which were not obtained through social hunting. In any environment in which one large ungulate is a dominant species, most sites will contain high percentages of that species regardless of the hunting strategy employed. A number of archaeologists have used the sheer numbers of animals from some sites as evidence for social hunting and mass kills. However, at most sites there is very little indication of the length of time it took for the assemblages to form, and this too cannot be considered a valid criterion. On the other hand, if one can demonstrate that large monospecific faunal assemblages are not habitation sites but kill locations, the argument for social hunting is more supportable.

Based on the above discussion, we can identify two major criteria for the identification of a social kill in the prehistoric record. First, there must be evidence for the slaughter of fairly large numbers of animals in a single event. Although we know ethnographic examples of social hunts for single individuals, these could probably not be recognized as social from the sites (if they were even preserved). The best evidence will be the presence of a bone bed, coupled with mortality data indicating a catastrophic kill, or evidence for restricted seasonality of death. Secondly, there must be evidence for deliberate human involvement in the slaughter. If artificial facilities are present, the evidence is strong. In the absence of facilities, one must test the hypothesis for human involvement quite carefully. The following types of data would be significant: evidence for an effective weapons system, preferably coupled with wounds, embedded projectile points (e.g., Frison 1978:fig. 5.31), or the association of projectiles with anatomically relevant areas such as the rib cage (e.g., Frison 1978:fig. 5.35); evidence for systematic butchery, especially butchery that appears to result from the coordination of effort of a number of people, such as bone stacking (Wheat 1972; Frison 1978); evidence for large-scale processing of meat, such as the presence of boiling pits and firecracked rock.

In the absence of a putative kill site, support for a social kill hypothesis becomes difficult to sustain. Certain age, sex, and seasonality data may suggest social hunting as one hypothesis to account for faunal remains of a particular species at a non-kill site. Element frequencies might also suggest this. However, such data should really form the impetus for further hypothesis testing, rather than "proof" of social hunting episodes.

Paleolithic social hunting

It is of interest to examine evidence for social hunting during the Paleolithic, because, as discussed earlier, the ability to organize social hunts tells us something about the evolution of human and pre-human technology and social organization. This review concentrates on published evidence from Europe, although Asian and African material is also mentioned. Most of the sites discussed below are either frequently discussed in the literature, or have well-reported faunal assemblages. This section does not deal with social hunting after the end of the Pleistocene, mainly because most of the evidence derives from North America, and has been discussed extensively elsewhere.

The recent reinterpretations of many stone tool and animal bone associations from East Africa has cast doubt on the existence of any organized hunting during Oldowan times (Binford 1985). Sites which have been claimed as social kills include the *Pelorovis* assemblage from Olduvai, but this is not now generally accepted as evidence for social activity (Isaac and Crader 1981), and there is currently no evidence that pre-*Homo* hominids were capable of conducting social hunts.

For Acheulian sites, Isaac (1977) postulated social killing to account for the baboon bones found at Olorgesailie. This was supported by further faunal analysis (Shipman et al. 1981), but challenged by Binford and Todd (1982). The interpretation of this site remains unresolved. The purported social kills of elephants in Spain at Torralba and Ambrona have received severe criticism from Binford (1987). He has shown that there is a poor association between stone tools and elephant bones, and that there is good evidence that many elephant bones were water-rolled and probably water-sorted. Villa's recent analysis of the mid-Pleistocene Aridos elephant/artifact sites in central Spain suggests that elephant carcasses were scavenged for meat, and the humans seem to have competed successfully against carnivore scavengers. However, there is no artifactual evidence that the elephants were killed by humans, nor were the carcasses in a context which could be described as a trap (Villa 1990:301). Gamble (1987) has also pointed out the potential for scavenging carcasses of megafauna in Middle Pleistocene Europe as an alternative to organized hunting.

For the early Middle Paleolithic, the only site that might fit the criteria for social killing is La Cotte de St. Brélade, Jersey (Scott 1980, 1986). At this site, remains of mammoth and rhinoceros were recovered from a partially roofed vertical-sided gully at the end of a headland on what is now an island, and would have been a steep-sided plateau on a coastal plain at the time the site was occupied. Scott argues that the parts represented (especially mammoth skulls) were unlikely to have been dragged uphill to the gully by carnivores, and argues that they represent remains of animals which were driven into the gully from above. That some human activity is responsible for the two bone concentrations seems likely. There is evidence that mammoth scapulae were stacked, and one mammoth skull appears to have had a portion of rib driven through it. There are also over 1000 associated lithic artifacts. Carnivore activity seems to have been minimal. However, there are other human activities which could have resulted in such a concentration of bones. The element frequencies for mammoth, especially in layer 3, are very unusual because the assemblage is dominated by crania, tusks, mandibles, scapulae, and innominates. There are hardly any limb bones or vertebrae. Scott interprets this as evidence that other parts of the skeleton were transported away from the kill site at the bottom of the gully to a processing area elsewhere.

Recently reported data on elephant kills by Efe and Lese people in the Ituri forest provide some modern comparative data (Fisher 1992, 1993). Based on a sample of three kills, Fisher suggests that certain elements—cranium, mandibles, scapulae, and innominate—are always left at the kill site (Fisher 1992:71), and the feet and upper limbs are commonly removed. However, there appears to be considerable variation in whether other areas of the skeleton remain at the kill or are transported elsewhere for processing. It is therefore possible that the La Cotte mammoth remains are the remnants of an efficiently exploited multiple kill in which all but the most unwieldy skeletal elements were removed.

An alternative explanation, which Scott dismisses (1986:181), is that the unusual element frequencies are the result of transporting selected bones to the gully, rather than away from it. The preponderance of bones from the head and the girdles is reminiscent of later Paleolithic practice at sites on the Russian steppes where mammoth bones were collected to build structures. Soffer (1985:278) reports that few systematic inventories of mammoth bone have been made, and suggests that all parts of the mammoth were present at such sites. While it is true that most parts of the body are represented, examination of the element frequencies from Mezhirich (Dnepr River) shows that different parts of the body are differentially represented. Using minimum number of bones as a measure of element frequency, 32% of the Mezhirich mammoth elements (excluding loose teeth but including tusks) are from the head and girdles (data from Soffer 1985:table 5.14). At La Cotte layer 3, head and girdles account for 37 out of 44 identified bone fragments (84%), and in layer 6, for 44 out of 64 fragments (69%). The La Cotte figures are therefore even more heavily biased towards certain body parts than the Mezhirich data. One reason for this may be that the Mezhirich data refer to all mammoth bone, rather than the bone found solely as part of structures. Many mammoth bone structures seem to display higher frequencies for head and girdle than the Mezhirich data would suggest (see, for example, figs. 2.45, 2.53 in Soffer 1985).

The case for the La Cotte mammoth bones representing a social drive over a cliff edge should be evaluated against the hypothesis that the bones were part of a shelter. Both hypotheses are supported by the strong selectivity for certain elements. On the other hand, there would have been plenty of stone for building purposes at La Cotte de St. Brélade, and Middle Paleolithic stone structures are known from other sites (Hayden 1993:132–137). One would have to explain the advantage of bringing mammoth bone to the site for building material. The social hunting hypothesis also has flaws. If the bones represent the elements abandoned after other parts of the body were removed, one must ask why it was necessary to take parts of the carcass away, and why one would move large quantities of bone out of a sheltered locale. The Efe and Lese remove elephant bones from kills to processing camps in order to chop up bones with metal axes and boil them for marrow and grease extraction (Fisher 1993). It is debatable whether bone boiling was practiced in early Middle Paleolithic times.

In later Middle Paleolithic times there is somewhat more convincing evidence from Western Europe for organized social killing, although one must still be wary in accepting interpretations of such events without adequate consideration of alternative hypotheses. Mellars (1989) suggests that in France both La Quina and Mauran provide evidence for social hunts. At La Quina there is a dense accumulation of a variety of ungulates, including reindeer, horse, and bovids, at the base of a cliff with associated Mousterian artifacts (Jelinek et al. 1989). At Mauran there are thousands of bovid bones at the base of a steep escarpment (Farizy and David 1989). Chase (1986, 1989) reviews Middle Paleolithic hunting in much of Europe and Asia. He notes that during the Mousterian one finds sites in which there appears to have been specialization on a particular species, as well as sites with a more generalized hunting economy. In addition to Mauran, he cites a number of other examples of possible social hunting. These include Starosel'e (Crimea), with over 98% ass, and Volgograd and Il'skaya (western Caucasus), with heavy use of bison. Although he rejects most Alpine cave bear sites as having a human component, he accepts Erd as a site where social hunting of migrating cave bear occurred (Chase 1986:111–125), echoing a prevalent view of a number of archaeologists (e.g., Bouchud 1976:693) which has been disputed by others (e.g., Gamble 1986:318). Although Chase concludes that hunting of large herds was "a common feature" of Middle Paleolithic Europe (1986:333), the evidence he uses to support this view often consists of the presence of large numbers of animals at a site or within a layer. Because the length of time involved in the deposition of these assemblages is unclear, this is rather a poor criterion.

Gaudzinski (1995) has shown that taphonomic analysis of apparently diverse faunal assemblages may reveal that only a single species was hunted by hominids. She suggests that the faunal assemblages at Wallertheim (Germany) are the result of selective predation on bison, and that other large mammals represent a "background" natural faunal accumulation. Gaudzinski reports ten Middle Paleolithic sites at which there appears to have been specialized hunting of bovids, although many of these lack complete analysis of fauna. Interestingly, taphonomic analysis suggests that multiple predation may not have been responsible for the accumulation of numerous individual bison at Wallertheim (Gaudzinski 1995:62). Differential abrasion and heavy bone processing suggest that individuals or small groups of bison were killed in separate incidents, rather than a single herd. This pattern may characterize other Middle Paleolithic bovid sites (Gaudzinski 1995:64).

Stiner's (1990; Stiner and Kuhn 1992) analysis of Middle Paleolithic sites in Italy suggests that prior to about

55,000 B.P. human hunters either hunted or scavenged in a way which resembles modern non-human carnivores. This resulted in assemblages with high proportions of very old animals. In later Middle Paleolithic and Upper Paleolithic sites a higher frequency of prime adults occurs. Stiner suggests that this is the result of cooperative ambush hunting.

Evins (1982) discusses wild goat exploitation at Shanidar (Iran) during Mousterian times. Population structure is assessed using crown heights; and juveniles are found to be under-represented in a population dominated by prime adults. This is interpreted as evidence for catastrophic mortality, with juvenile frequencies reduced by poor preservation. The problems of assessing such mortality data have been discussed above. The low frequency of juveniles allows other hunting practices, including the type of cooperative hunting described by Stiner, to be inferred.

Klein (1982) provides a stronger case from mortality profiles for social hunting of eland in Middle Stone Age sites in southern Africa. Juvenile animals are reasonably well represented, and the eland mortality profiles can be contrasted with attritional profiles of more solitary and more dangerous species which would be less amenable to driving.

In conclusion, there is some evidence for social hunting in the Middle Paleolithic. Probably the best evidence in Europe comes from site location rather than faunal asemblages. Both La Quina and Mauran appear to be possible drive sites, and the Mousterian deposits at Solutré (Olsen 1989) may also be associated with social killing. Age structures do not provide convincing evidence for social hunting, except in southern Africa, where Klein's case for the eland seems well documented. On the other hand, assemblages with prime adults may indicate the development of social hunting systems within the Middle Paleolithic.

There is somewhat more evidence for social hunting during the Upper Paleolithic of Europe. Looking first at locational data, a number of sites appear to be good candidates for identification as social kill sites. The classic example must remain Le Solutré. Olsen's recent review (1989) clearly spells out the evidence for this as a site of repeated mass kills: dense bone beds, articulated body units, relatively light butchery (suggesting an abundance of meat), and little evidence for transportation of bones away from the site. The locational data support the idea that horses were driven upslope, possibly into an artificial enclosure against a steep slope.

Although the Perigord region contains numerous Upper Paleolithic sites, no definite kill sites have been excavated (White 1985:21), although most prehistorians have assumed that social hunting was common. White (1985) provides a review of locational data on Magdalenian sites in the Périgord. There is a noticeable regularity in the location of Upper Paleolithic sites (especially Solutrean and Magdalenian) at fords, and White (1985:129–131) suggests these were sited to take advantage of caribou crossing the major rivers. He also notes that large Magdalenian sites tend to be located near fords, probably because large herds of reindeer could support temporary aggregations of people. Two Solutrean sites provide further evidence of social hunting in the Périgord. At Laugerie Haute there is evidence for a reindeer kill between the rock shelter and the river, while at Badegoule the presence of very large numbers of reindeer (including articulated limb segments) suggests the possibility that they were driven over the cliff above the site (White 1985:150–151).

Straus (1987) has provided a general review of Upper Paleolithic hunting in western Europe, and suggests that systematic social hunting began about 20,000 B.P. In addition to the sites discussed above, he presents a variety of other cases where locational data support social hunting scenarios. At Petersfels (southern Germany), reindeer may have been driven somewhere in the steep-sided valley in front of the cave by Magdalenian hunters. Good representation of skeletal parts supports the idea of a nearby kill. "Les Trappes" in the Vézère Valley may be ambush pits or traps for reindeer. As with many other surveys of European Paleolithic hunting, most other evidence discussed by Straus concerns (a) specialization on particular species, and (b) the sheer numbers of bones or MNI within occupations. Neither of these is necessarily good evidence for social hunting.

Other evidence for social hunting can be adduced from studies of age and sex. Levine's (1983) interpretations of horse dentitions have been discussed above, and I do not consider her data as unequivocal evidence for social hunting resulting in catastrophic kills. However, catastrophic death assemblages have been documented from some sites in Spain. Klein et al. (1983) have shown that red deer at the Magdalenian site of El Juyo display high juvenile mortality, and that the overall age structure suggests catastrophic kills of entire herds. Red deer from the Upper Paleolithic (Solutrean, Magdalenian) and Mesolithic (Azilian and Asturian) occupations from La Riera show a similar pattern (Clark and Straus 1983). Pike-Tay's (1991) analysis of red deer from southwest France demonstrates a change from Early to Late Upper Paleolithic. Early sites have a prime-dominated mortality pattern, which Pike-Tay relates to a social hunting strategy operated by people with spears but without spear-throwers. Late sites contain higher frequencies of juveniles, which may result from individual stalking with spear-throwers. Juveniles were more vulnerable to stalking because they were less wary. I am not entirely convinced by Pike-Tay's arguments, especially as sample sizes are quite small. The earlier samples do appear to resemble catastrophic mortality more than the later assemblages, where the percentage of animals less than 4 years old approaches 80% and both prime and senile adults are quite rare. However, it is also possible that people were hunting using the same techniques (e.g., surrounds or drives) in both periods, but that they selected animals for different purposes. For example, in the later sites hunters may have been taking young animals mainly for their hides, rather than for their meat. It is worth noting that red deer were a significant resource in three of the four early Upper Paleolithic sites analyzed, while in the later sites they were dominant in only one assemblage. This might suggest a different economic function for the deer, and hence a different hunting strategy.

Apart from the relatively few instances where location or age structure can be used to suggest social hunting, most authors have used large numbers of animals or concentration on a particular species as evidence that social hunting occurred. For reasons discussed previously, this is not considered good evidence. The evidence from the Upper Paleolithic in Europe appears to suggest that social hunting is best represented in the later part of the period, with reindeer, red deer, horse, and possibly ibex being the major prey species.

Discussion

The model for social hunting presented in the first part of this paper suggests that social hunting of large game should be an important subsistence activity under certain ecological conditions: low diversity of resources; absence of stable, reliable alternatives; pronounced seasonality; and migratory behavior of large game. In addition, human groups must be capable of organizing social hunts, must possess effective hunting weapons to take advantage of the temporarily massed animals, and should have efficient methods for storing meat.

The earliest evidence for social hunting appears in Middle Paleolithic times, but appears to increase in frequency and importance during the later Upper Paleolithic in Europe and possibly parts of Asia. It is possible that the lack of social hunting prior to the Middle Paleolithic is related to poorer organizational abilities of humans. However, non-human predators appear capable of "organizing" social hunts and we should therefore look for ecological factors which relate to the appearance of new strategies. Earlier human occupation may have been in more diverse and less seasonally restrictive environments, and perhaps only when humans regularly occupied less diverse environments did they require new organizational strategies.

Evidence for social hunting in the later part of the Upper Paleolithic (especially in Solutrean and Magdalenian times) may be linked to the development of specific ecological conditions. There seems to be evidence that during and after the late Würm glacial maximum, western European environments experienced reduced faunal diversity, accounting for the widely documented "specialization" on reindeer in France, reindeer and horse in Germany, and red deer and ibex in Spain and Italy. While it is certainly true that not all later Upper Paleolithic sites have evidence for such specialized hunting (White 1985:54–56) and that specialized sites also appear in the Middle Paleolithic (Chase 1989; Gaudzinski 1995), the overall evidence for increased later Upper Paleolithic specialized hunting seems convincing (Altuna 1989; Boyle 1990; Dennell 1983; Freeman 1981; Mellars 1989; Straus 1987). If increased evidence of specialization indicates reduced species diversity, we would expect to see greater effort directed towards social hunting in order to minimize risks inherent in relying on a single species. It is also interesting to note the increasingly sophisticated weapons which appear during the later Upper Paleolithic. These include finely worked stone and antler projectile points, and may include the bow and arrow (Dennell 1983:88).

In spite of the considerable numbers of Upper Paleolithic sites excavated, it is worth asking why more evidence for social hunting has not emerged. One fairly obvious explanation is that sampling methods and site preservation have together rendered evidence for social hunts difficult to detect. A great deal of research has been undertaken on habitation sites of various types (especially caves and rockshelters), and these sites may not preserve good evidence for social kills (Farizy and David 1989). White (1985) has pointed out that most extant rockshelters of the Périgord contain later Upper Paleolithic material, while earlier deposits are often found in collapsed caves and shelters. The considerable geomorphological remodeling of many European landscapes in the last 50,000 years may account for the paucity of kill sites.

Secondly, we may postulate that social hunting was not possible until humans had evolved more efficient means of communication and social organization. I suspect that the appearance of art in Upper Paleolithic sites signals an important change in conceptual and communicative ability, just as the appearance of the spear-thrower and a wide range of projectile points signals increasingly efficient hunting technology. Although these organizational and technical developments were important in the social exploitation of large game, they appear too early in the archaeological record to explain the apparent increase in social hunting in the later part of the Upper Paleolithic.

Thirdly, one could argue that social hunting is poorly represented because human-animal interactions are better described as "game management" than "hunting." This has been argued by a number of Cambridge "palaeoeconomists" (e.g., Sturdy 1975; Bahn 1978) and denounced by White (1989). In spite of White's sweeping condemnation, very few archaeologists have seriously pursued the zooarchaeological distinctions between assemblages produced by hunters and those produced by nomadic pastoralists, or how to identify societies which own some domesticated animals and also hunt. Alternatively, the paleoeconomists have not explored the full range of behaviors implied by the term "hunting." However, in support of White's position, one should note that the location of Magdalenian sites close to ideal killing locations provides strong support for a hunting hypothesis, as do the improvements in weaponry and the age structures of red deer from Spain.

Fourthly, one should consider the possibility that ecological conditions did not make social hunting a frequently used option in Europe prior to 20,000 B.P. Heavy reliance on social hunting is frequently associated with environments in which predation upon one species is critically important for survival (e.g., bison or caribou). When acceptable alternative resources are available, the reliance on social hunting declines. If European environments were less diverse after 20,000 B.P., this would explain the increased evidence for specialization and the increased evidence for social hunting. Under such conditions one would expect social hunting to provide reliable quantities of meat in an environment made more risky by a reduction in alternate subsistence strategies.

It is apparent from archaeological evidence that social hunting does not have a long history when compared with other methods of meat procurement. The idea that a band of primitive hunters could mob a single prey animal may be valid, but the incident would probably leave little distinctive trace in the archaeological record. If by social hunting we mean the organized killing of large numbers of animals, then there is little evidence for this prior to about 50,000 B.P. on a world-wide scale. In Europe, the best evidence for social hunting appears in the later Upper Paleolithic, coinciding with greater specialization on individual species. Although some archaeologists seem to characterize this development as a form of industrialization, it may well represent a period in which restricted availability of animals coupled with a reduced diversity of prey species meant that human groups often had to kill large numbers of animals to survive periods of shortage.

Acknowledgments

I am grateful to Doug Campana for encouraging me to write this paper and for his persistence in producing this volume. Brian Hayden's critical insights and encyclopedic knowledge of hunter-gatherer ecology have improved the paper significantly. Some of the ideas in the paper result from discussions many years ago with Michael Wilson and Phil Duke, whom I thank for their continued stimulus. An anonymous reviewer forced me to critically re-evaluate my concept of communal hunting and brought a significant article to my attention.

References

Altuna, J. 1989. Subsistance d'origine animale pendant le Moustérien dans la région cantabrique (Espagne). In *L'homme de Néandertal*. Vol. 6: *La subsistance*, ed. M. Patou and L. G. Freeman, pp. 31–43. Etudes et Recherches Archéologiques de l'Université de Liège 33. Liège.

Anell, B. 1969. *Running Down and Driving of Game in North America*. Studia Ethnographica Upsaliensis 30. Upsala.

Arkush, B. S. 1986. Aboriginal Exploitation of Pronghorn in the Great Basin. *Journal of Ethnobiology* 6(2):239–255.

Bahn, P. 1978. The "Unacceptable Face" of the Western European Upper Palaeolithic. *Antiquity* 52:183–192.

Barth, E. K. 1983. Trapping Reindeer in South Norway. *Antiquity* 57:109–115.

Bedord, J. N. 1974. Morphological Variation in Bison Metacarpals and Metatarsals. In *The Casper Site: A Hell Gap Bison Kill on the High Plains*, ed. G. C. Frison, pp. 199–240. Academic Press, New York.

Binford, L. R. 1978. *Nunamiut Ethnoarchaeology*. Academic Press, New York.

―――― 1981. *Bones. Ancient Men and Modern Myths*. Academic Press, New York.

―――― 1985. Human Ancestors: Changing Views of Their Behavior. *Journal of Anthropological Archaeology* 4:292–327.

―――― 1987. Were There Elephant Hunters at Torralba? In *The Evolution of Human Hunting*, ed. M. H. Nitecki and D. V. Nitecki, pp. 47–105. Plenum, New York.

Binford, L. R., and L. Todd. 1982. On Arguments for the "Butchering" of Giant Geladas. *Current Anthropology* 23:108–110.

Blehr, O. 1990. Communal Hunting as a Prerequisite for Caribou (Wild Reindeer) as a Human Resource. In *Hunters of the Recent Past*, ed. L. B. Davis and B. O. K. Reeves, pp. 304–326. Unwin Hyman, London.

Borrero, L. A. 1990. Fuego-Patagonian Bone Assemblages and the Problem of Communal Guanaco Hunting. In *Hunters of the Recent Past*, ed. L. B. Davis and B. O. K. Reeves, pp. 373–399. Unwin Hyman, London.

Bouchud, J. 1976. La chasse. In *La préhistoire française, Tome 1*, ed. H. de Lumley, pp. 688–698. Centre Nationale de la Recherche Scientifique, Paris.

Boyle, K. V. 1990. *Upper Palaeolithic Faunas from South-west France: A Zoogeographic Perspective*. BAR International Series 557. British Archaeological Reports, Oxford.

Brain, C. K. 1981. *The Hunters or the Hunted?* Chicago University Press, Chicago.

Brink, J. W., and M. Rollans. 1990. Thoughts on the Structure and Function of Drive Lane Systems at Communal Buffalo Jumps. In *Hunters of the Recent Past*, ed. L. B. Davis and B. O. K. Reeves, pp. 152–167. Unwin Hyman, London.

Chase, P. G. 1986. *The Hunters of Combe Grenal*. BAR International Series 286. British Archaeological Reports, Oxford.

———— 1989 How Different was Middle Palaeolithic Subsistence?: A Zooarchaeological Perspective on the Middle to Upper Palaeolithic Transition. In *The Human Revolution*, ed. P. Mellars and C. Stringer, pp. 321–337. Edinburgh University Press, Edinburgh.

Clark, G. A., and L. G. Straus. 1983. Late Pleistocene Hunter-Gatherer Adaptations in Cantabrian Spain. In *Hunter-Gatherer Economy in Prehistory*, ed. G. Bailey, pp. 131–148. Cambridge University Press, London.

Conkey, M. 1980. The Identification of Prehistoric Hunter-Gatherer Aggregation Sites: The Case of Altimira. *Current Anthropology* 21:609–630.

Davis, L. B., and B. O. K. Reeves. 1990. *Hunters of the Recent Past.* Unwin Hyman, London.

Dennell, R. 1983. *European Economic Prehistory.* Academic Press, New York.

Driver, J. C. 1983. Bison Death Assemblages and Communal Hunting. In *Carnivores, Human Scavengers and Predators: A Question of Bone Technology*, ed. G. M. LeMoine and A. S. MacEachern, pp. 141–155. Archaeological Association, University of Calgary, Calgary.

———— 1985. *Zooarchaeology of Six Prehistoric Sites in the Sierra Blanca Region, New Mexico.* Museum of Anthropology, University of Michigan Technical Report 17. Ann Arbor.

———— 1990a. Meat in Due Season: The Timing of Communal Hunts. In *Hunters of the Recent Past*, ed. L. B. Davis and B. O. K. Reeves, pp. 11–33. Unwin Hyman, London.

———— 1990b. Bison Assemblages from the Sierra Blanca Region, Southeastern New Mexico. *Kiva* 55:245–263.

Evins, M. A. 1982. The Fauna from Shanidar Cave: Mousterian Wild Goat Exploitation in Northeastern Iraq. *Paléorient* 8(1):37–58.

Farizy, C., and F. David. 1989. Chasse et alimentation carnée au Paléolithique moyen, l'apport des gisements de plein air. In *L'homme de Néandertal*. Vol. 6: *La subsistance*, ed. M. Patou and L. G. Freeman, pp. 59–62. Etudes et Recherches Archéologiques de l'Université de Liège 33. Liège.

Fisher, J. W., Jr. 1992. Observations on the Late Pleistocene Bone Assemblage from the Lamb Spring Site, Colorado. In *Ice Age Hunters of the Rockies*, ed. D. J. Stanford and J. S. Day, pp. 51–81. University Press of Colorado, Niwot.

———— 1993. Foragers and Farmers: Material Expressions of Interaction at Elephant Processing Sites in the Ituri Forest, Zaire. In *From Bones to Behavior: Ethnoarchaeological and Experimental Contributions to the Interpretation of Faunal Remains,* ed. J. Hudson, pp. 247–262. Center for Archaeological Investigations, Southern Illinois University at Carbondale Occasional Paper 21.

Forbis, R. G. 1978. Some Facets of Communal Hunting. In *Bison Procurement and Utilization: A Symposium*, ed. L. B. Davis and M. Wilson, pp. 3–8. Plains Anthropologist Memoir 14.

Freeman, L. G. 1981. The Fat of the Land: Notes on Palaeolithic Diet in Iberia. In *Omnivorous Primates*, ed. R. S. O. Harding and G. Teleki, pp. 104–165. Columbia University Press, New York.

Frison, G. C. 1973. *The Wardell Buffalo Trap 48 SU 301: Communal Procurement in the Upper Green River Basin, Wyoming*. Museum of Anthropology, University of Michigan Anthropological Paper 48. Ann Arbor.

———— 1974. *The Casper Site: A Hell Gap Bison Kill on the High Plains*. Academic Press, New York.

———— 1978. *Prehistoric Hunters of the High Plains*. Academic Press, New York.

———— 1987. Prehistoric, Plains-Mountain, Large-Mammal, Communal Hunting Strategies. In *The Evolution of Human Hunting*, ed. M. H. Nitecki and D. V. Nitecki, pp. 177–223. Plenum, New York.

———— 1991. Hunting Strategies, Prey Behavior and Mortality Data. In *Human Predators and Prey Mortality*, ed. M. C. Stiner, pp. 15–30. Westview Press, Boulder, CO.

Frison, G. C., C. A. Reher, and D. N. Walker. 1990. Prehistoric Mountain Sheep Hunting in the Central Rocky Mountains of North America. In *Hunters of the Recent Past*, ed. L. B. Davis and B. O. K. Reeves, pp. 208–240. Unwin Hyman, London.

Frison, G. C., M. Wilson, and D. J. Wilson. 1976. Fossil Bison and Artifacts from an Early Altithermal Period Arroyo Trap in Wyoming. *American Antiquity* 41:28–57.

Gamble, C. 1986. *The Palaeolithic Settlement of Europe*. Cambridge University Press, London.

———— 1987. Man the Shoveler. Alternative Models for Middle Pleistocene Colonization and Occupation in Northern Latitudes. In *The Pleistocene Old World: Regional Perspectives*, ed. O. Soffer, pp. 81–98. Plenum, New York.

Gaudzinski, S. 1995. Wallertheim Revisited: A Reanalysis of the Fauna from the Middle Palaeolithic Site of Wallertheim (Rheinhessen/Germany). *Journal*

of Archaeological Science 22:51–66.
Gordon, B. 1990. World *Rangifer* Communal Hunting. In *Hunters of the Recent Past*, ed. L. B. Davis and B. O. K. Reeves, pp. 277–303. Unwin Hyman, London.
Hayden, B. 1981. Subsistence and Ecological Adaptations of Modern Hunter/Gatherers. In *Omnivorous Primates*, ed. R. S. O. Harding and G. Teleki, pp. 344–421. Columbia University Press, New York.
―――― 1993. The Cultural Capacities of Neandertals: A Review and Re-evaluation. *Journal of Human Evolution* 24:113–146.
Isaac, G. Ll. 1977. *Olorgesailie: Archaeological Studies of a Middle Pleistocene Lake Basin in Kenya*. University of Chicago Press, Chicago.
Isaac, G. Ll., and D. C. Crader. 1981. To What Extent Were Early Hominids Carnivores? An Archaeological Perspective. In *Omnivorous Primates*, ed. R. S. O. Harding and G. Teleki, pp. 37–103. Columbia University Press, New York.
Jelinek, A. J., A. Debenath, and H. L. Dibble. 1989. A Preliminary Report on Evidence Related to the Interpretation of Economic and Social Activities of Neandertals at the Site of La Quina (Charente), France. In *L'homme de Néandertal*. Vol. 6: *La subsistance*, ed. M. Patou and L. G. Freeman, pp. 99–103. Etudes et Recherches Archéologiques de l'Université de Liège 33. Liège.
Johnson, D. L., P. Kawano, and E. Ekker. 1980. Clovis Strategies of Hunting Mammoth (*Mammuthus columbi*). *Canadian Journal of Anthropology* 1(1):107–114.
Klein, R. G. 1973. *Ice-Age Hunters of the Ukraine*. Chicago University Press, Chicago.
―――― 1982. Age (Mortality) Profiles as a Means of Distinguishing Hunted Species from Scavenged Ones in Stone Age Archaeological Sites. *Paleobiology* 8(2):151–158.
Klein, R. G., K. Allwarden, and C. Wolf. 1983. The Calculation and Interpretation of Ungulate Age Profiles from Dental Crown Heights. In *Hunter-Gatherer Economy in Prehistory*, ed. G. Bailey, pp. 47–57. Cambridge University Press, London.
Landals, A. 1990. The Maple Leaf Site: Implications of the Analysis of Small-scale Bison Kills. In *Hunters of the Recent Past*, ed. L. B. Davis and B. O. K. Reeves, pp. 122–151. Unwin Hyman, London.
Lee, R. B. 1968. What Hunters do for a Living, or, How to Make Out on Scarce Resources. In *Man the Hunter*, ed. R. B. Lee and I. DeVore, pp. 30–48. Aldine Press, Chicago.
Levine, M. A. 1983. Mortality Models and the Interpretation of Horse Population Structure. In *Hunter-Gatherer Economy in Prehistory*, ed. G. Bailey, pp. 23–46. Cambridge University Press, London.

Lyman, R. L. 1994. *Vertebrate Taphonomy*. Cambridge University Press, Cambridge.
Marean, C. W. 1989. Sabretooth Cats and their Relevance for Early Hominid Diet and Evolution. *Journal of Human Evolution* 18:559–582.
Mellars, P. 1989. Major Issues in the Emergence of Modern Humans. *Current Anthropology* 30(3):349–385.
Morris, E. A. 1990. Prehistoric Game Drive Systems in the Rocky Mountains and High Plains Areas of Colorado. In *Hunters of the Recent Past*, ed. L. B. Davis and B. O. K. Reeves, pp. 195–207. Unwin Hyman, London.
Nelson, R. K. 1973. *Hunters of the Northern Forest*. Chicago University Press, Chicago.
Olsen, S. L. 1989. Solutré: A Theoretical Approach to the Reconstruction of Upper Palaeolithic Hunting Strategies. *Journal of Human Evolution* 18:295–327.
Packer, C., and L. Rutton. 1988. The Evolution of Cooperative Hunting. *The American Naturalist* 132(2):159–198.
Pike-Tay, A. 1991. *Red Deer Hunting in the Upper Paleolithic of South-West France: A Study in Seasonality*. BAR International Series 569. British Archaeological Reports, Oxford.
Price, T. D., and J. A. Brown (eds.). 1985. *Prehistoric Hunter-Gatherers: The Emergence of Cultural Complexity*. Academic Press, Orlando.
Reeves, B. O. K. 1990. Communal Bison Hunters of the Northern Plains. In *Hunters of the Recent Past*, ed. L. B. Davis and B. O. K. Reeves, pp. 168–194. Unwin Hyman, London.
Reher, C. A. 1973. The Wardell *Bison bison* Sample: Population Dynamics and Archaeological Interpretation. In *The Wardell Buffalo Trap 48 SU 301: Communal Procurement in the Upper Green River Basin, Wyoming*, by G. C. Frison, pp. 89–105. Museum of Anthropology, University of Michigan Anthropological Paper 48. Ann Arbor.
Reher, C. A., and G. C. Frison. 1980. *The Vore Site, 48CK302, a Stratified Buffalo Jump in the Wyoming Black Hills*. Plains Anthropologist Memoir 16.
Scott, K. 1980. Two Hunting Episodes of Middle Palaeolithic Age at La Cotte de Saint-Brélade, Jersey (Channel Islands). *World Archaeology* 12(2):137–152.
―――― 1986. The Bone Assemblages of Layers 3 and 6. In *La Cotte de St. Brélade 1961–1978*, ed. P. Callow and J. M. Cornford, pp. 159–183. Geo Books, Norwich.
Shipman, P., W. Bosler, and K. L. Davis. 1981. Butchering of Giant Geladas at an Acheulian Site. *Current Anthropology* 22:257–268.
Soffer, O. 1985. *The Upper Paleolithic of the Central*

Russian Plain. Academic Press, Orlando.

——— 1989. Storage, Sedentism and the Eurasian Palaeolithic Record. *Antiquity* 63:719–732.

Speth, J. D. 1983. *Bison Kills and Bone Counts*. University of Chicago Press, Chicago.

Speth, J. D., and K. A. Spielmann. 1983. Energy Source, Protein Metabolism, and Hunter-Gatherer Subsistence Strategies. *Journal of Anthropological Archaeology* 2:1–31.

Spiess, A. E. 1979. *Reindeer and Caribou Hunters*. Academic Press, New York.

Stanford, D. 1978. The Jones-Miller Site: An Example of Hell Gap Bison Procurement Strategy. In *Bison Procurement and Utilization: A Symposium*, ed. L. B. Davis and M. Wilson, pp. 90–97. Plains Anthropologist Memoir 14.

Steele, D. G., and B. W. Baker. 1993. Multiple Predation: A Definitive Human Hunting Strategy. In *From Bones to Behavior: Ethnoarchaeological and Experimental Contributions to the Interpretation of Faunal Remains*, ed. J. Hudson, pp. 9–37. Center for Archaeological Investigations, Southern Illinois University at Carbondale Occasional Paper 21.

Stiner, M. C. 1990. The Use of Mortality Patterns in Archaeological Studies of Hominid Predatory Adaptations. *Journal of Anthropological Archaeology* 9(4):305–351.

——— 1991. An Interspecific Perspective on the Emergence of the Modern Human Predatory Niche. In *Human Predators and Prey Mortality*, ed. M. C. Stiner, pp. 149–185. Westview Press, Boulder, CO.

Stiner, M. C., and S. L. Kuhn. 1992. Subsistence, Technology and Adaptive Variation in Middle Palaeolithic Italy. *American Anthropologist* 94(2):306–339.

Straus, L. G. 1987. Hunting in Late Upper Paleolithic Western Europe. In *The Evolution of Human Hunting*, ed. M. H. Nitecki and D. V. Nitecki, pp. 147–175. Plenum, New York.

Sturdy, D. A. 1975. Some Reindeer Economies in Prehistoric Europe. In *Palaeoeconomy*, ed. E. S. Higgs and M. R. Jarman, pp. 55–95. Cambridge University Press, London.

Todd, L. C. 1987. Analysis of Kill-Butchery Bonebeds and Interpretation of Paleoindian Hunting. In *The Evolution of Human Hunting*, ed. M. H. Nitecki and D. V. Nitecki, pp. 225–266. Plenum, New York.

Verbicky-Todd, E. 1984. *Communal Buffalo Hunting Among the Plains Indians*. Archaeological Survey of Alberta Occasional Paper 24. Edmonton.

Vereshchagin, N. K. 1967. Primitive Hunters and Pleistocene Extinction in the Soviet Union. In *Pleistocene Extinctions: The Search for a Cause*, ed. P. S. Martin and H. E. Wright, Jr., pp. 365–398. Yale University Press, New Haven.

Villa, P. 1990. Torralba and Aridos: Elephant Exploitation in Middle Pleistocene Spain. *Journal of Human Evolution* 19: 299–309.

Vivian, B. C., and D. Hanna. 1993. Seeking Simplicity in 'Complex' Communal Hunting. Paper presented at the 26th Chacmool Conference, Calgary, November.

Wheat, J. B. 1972. *The Olsen-Chubbock Site: A Paleo-Indian Bison Kill*. Society for American Archaeology Memoir 26.

White, R. 1985. *Upper Paleolithic Land Use in the Périgord*. BAR International Series 253. British Archaeological Reports, Oxford.

——— 1989. Husbandry and Herd Control in the Upper Palaeolithic. *Current Anthropology* 30:609–632.

Wilkinson, P. F. 1972. Current Experimental Domestication and its Relevance to Prehistory. In *Papers in Economic Prehistory*, ed. E. S. Higgs, pp. 107–118. Cambridge University Press, London.

Wilson, M. C. 1980. Population Dynamics of the Garnsey Site Bison. In *Late Prehistoric Bison Procurement in Southeastern New Mexico: The 1978 Season at the Garnsey Site (LA-18399)*, ed. J. D. Speth and W. J. Parry, pp. 88–129. Museum of Anthropology, University of Michigan Technical Report 12. Ann Arbor.

——— 1983. Canid Scavengers and Butchering Patterns: Evidence from a 3600-year-old Bison Bone Bed in Alberta. In *Carnivores, Human Scavengers and Predators: A Question of Bone Technology*, ed. G. M. LeMoine and A. S. MacEachern, pp. 141–155. Archaeological Association, University of Calgary, Calgary.

ENVIRONMENTAL AND SOCIOECONOMIC BACKGROUND TO DOMESTICATION IN THE SOUTHERN LEVANT

Eitan Tchernov

Department of Evolution, Systematics and Ecology, The Hebrew University of Jerusalem, Jerusalem 91904 Israel

Introduction

If bioarchaeology is perceived as a multidisciplinary approach concerned with the interplay between humans and environment, such essentially biological relationships may legitimately be considered an integrative system in which all the interacting components produce the forces of change. The aim of the zooarchaeologist therefore is to provide the concepts and the methods needed to define and understand the rules that drove the ever greater changes in the exploitation of animals as humans evolved. Over time, human interference in biological systems eventually reversed the successional development of biological systems to an earlier stage of complexity, or a less mature status, with lower energetic flow or higher thermodynamic equilibrium. Thus, victims of their own energy-absorbing mechanism, in ascending the ladder of social/cultural complexity humans shifted to ever more diversified modes of subsistence: from early loosely organized groups hunting and scavenging mainly large game to organized groups depending on a wide variety of comprehensively collected plants and animals; and eventually to self-dependent food production. Humans moved from nomadism and mobility to sedentism, from cultural control of wild populations, cultivation, domestication, and industrialization to manipulation of the genetic code. Consequently humans enlarged their domain of influence over all four biosphere categories: first the flora and the fauna, then the abiotic substrate, and finally the climate. Indeed, through increased social complexity, the adoption of novelties in technology and subsistence, and increasing pressure on the habitat, the anthropogenic factor became the unique cause and mechanism promoting environmental changes that far exceeded the limits that would have occurred naturally had humans not been present. Can this fundamental phenomenon of increasing complexity in humans be explained strictly by sociological, anthropological, or economical interpretations?

Until very recently in the history of science, anthropological studies have generally been rigorously framed by historians, archaeologists, and humanists in terms of "man against nature," in contrast to natural scientists, who pursue such studies in terms of "man as part of nature." For example, two contradictory dogmas have existed to explain the constant irreversible increase in human technology, exploitation of resources, interactions with the biotic and abiotic environment, social complexity, and consciousness. The earlier stages of our development were usually understood as being the consequence of biological laws, while the later stages were regarded as propelled by inner and innate human forces and laws utterly detached from natural phenomena. Yet no one attempted to demarcate the shift from one set of laws to the other. Due to this bifurcated conceptual tradition of the place and role of humans in nature, the study of humans became something of a chimera. However, during recent decades it has become clear that the basic universal 'super rules' also include the behavioral pattern of humans and their interrelationship with the environment. Indeed, so long as we explained phenomena of social complexes as in a class apart from physical laws, science could not be used to explain human phenomena. But the concept of man as part of the the organic world and with an explicable (and refutable) status within the hierarchical (or biological) open system enables us to explain this process dialectically, and no longer rely on entelechy or vitalism. Culture does not begin only where nature, and the science of nature, ends. It is beyond the scope of this paper to revive the old question of whether life can be reduced to physics, or to confront again Democritus' atomism versus Aristotle's holistic teleology. Yet we do intend to show that explaining phenomena in human socioecological evolution requires much more than sociological, socioanthropological, or even biological rules. Therefore it is the task of the natural scientists to explain bioanthropological (including cultural) phenomena, using biological as well as physical rules. Reunification of biology and anthropology is hence the first imperative step to a better definition of our role in nature.

At the end of the Pleistocene, small groups of Epipaleolithic hunters and gatherers gave rise to larger, functionally interdependent groups, hierarchically organized along economic, social, and political lines, yet still primarily dependent on hunting and gathering techniques. This transformation was fully realized during the later part of the Epipaleolithic (the Natufian period) of the southern Levant. Most scholars will agree that humans in no way shifted directly from nomadism to any of the earliest forms of agriculture. Not only did a relatively long time (at least 2,000 years) elapse between the earliest emergence of sedentism and the incipient management of domesticated animals, but (as it is our aim in this essay to show) the phenomenon of sedentism was the main cause that must have led human populations into an utterly different economic domain. Before a shift to practical agriculture could take place, there had to be a period characterized by increased socialization, mental capacity (Cauvin 1989), self-consciousness, and development of better means for the accumulation of traditional knowledge.

The spontaneous reorganization of the entire population within a given area from bands of hunter-gatherers to relatively large societies of sedentary foragers is one of the best examples of an abrupt increase in human socioeconomic complexity. Belfer-Cohen (1991) argues that the shift to sedentism in the Levantine took place in such a short time that archaeologists have great difficulty in identifying the transition phase between the Geometric Kebaran complex and the Early Natufian. Was there a transitional phase?

While nomadism, or mobility, was the rule in human settlement behavior throughout most of human history, analogous vagility among other mammals seems to be an uncommon behavioral pattern. High mobility in mammals is normally found among species that are either a dominant component within the ecosystem, like elephants, rhinoceroses, or top carnivores; or among species living in large herds, in which case the whole colony behaves as a dominant ecological component, such as a large herd of herbivores (Bertram 1974; Damuth 1981). It is hence surprising that humans, who became in later prehistoric times such a dominant factor in the ecosystem, should show, at one particular time and place, a punctuational transformation from an essentially nomadic way of life (with ephemeral occupation of habitats) to sedentism.

The essential strategy of large carnivores is to maximize their prey size and minimize the amount of energy invested in high frequency predation (Harestad and Bunnell 1979; Shipman and Walker 1989). This is obvious, as the act of predation is a high energy–consuming event, and hence should be efficient and infrequent. Yet, to detect large prey, large carnivores have to be able to cover large foraging, or scavaging, areas. The only way for them to decrease mobility, or to reduce their foraging area, and to establish a more sedentary behavioral pattern, is to shift into predation of smaller animals, and to become less specialized or more omnivorous. By analogy, we may expect that reducing mobility in humans should have changed their exploitation behavior to include a broader spectrum of food resources, to become more vegetarian, or in general, to become more omnivorous, assuming their feeding behavior was more carnivorous during most of the history of the genus *Homo* (Binford 1981; Potts 1988; Shipman 1986; Shipman and Walker 1989).

With a sedentary way of life we would also expect to see concomitant ecological effects evidenced in the exploitation and feeding behavior of these human populations. Generally, if more carnivorous species that spend less time on feeding but cover larger home ranges shift into a more restricted exploitation area, they will have to spend more time on feeding and also broaden their food spectrum. We may expect a similar change in the ecological attitude of humans. This is due to the basic ecological rule which states that whenever an organism shifts to a lower stage in the ecological pyramid, or from the stage of a secondary consumer to a primary consumer (or from a less herbivorous to more herbivorous dietary system), it will lose energy (Odum 1971). Hence, any shift of human populations to a less mobile life cycle should have brought about a change in the trophic level; sedentism would have lowered the population on the trophic scale.

A major question is why human beings, in a particular period and within a relatively small geographic region, suddenly 'aggregated' into much larger social entities and changed to a sedentary way of life. If the major cause for changes in the complex interplay between man and animals is directly connected with the biosocial status of humans, then understanding the reasons for such a directional increase in human organizational complexity is essential for comprehensive understanding of the nature of the interactions with the biotic environment, and the logic behind them. What was the tangible impact of sedentism on the immediate environment, and what were the feedback responses of people to those swift changes around them? These are further consequential questions. We will mainly concentrate on the following goals: (1) to discuss in some detail the contention that an increase in human socioeconomic level may be explained by the same basic innate thermodynamic properties and self-organization that extend from DNA molecules, bacteria, protista, multicellular organisms, through biosocialization to cultural transmission and consciousness; (2) to bring forward evidence—mainly biological—to support the argument that sedentism already existed during the Early Natufian in the southern Levant; (3) to explain how the establishment of a sedentary way of life caused a major impact on the environment by virtue of the special habitats that were created around the long-term sites before domestication and farming were regularly practiced; (4) to show that under these special ecological conditions, settling in 'villages' not only forced the sedentary populations to shift to a broader dietary spectrum and rely on a greater proportion of smaller ("lower ranked") animal species, as argued by many archaeologists (like Flannery 1969; Winterhalder 1981; but see also Speth and Scott 1989; Tchernov 1991, 1992 for more references) but also required that the earliest 'villagers' continue to practice intensive hunting of large game. Yet, contrary to the situation in earlier periods, humans gradually focused their hunting experience exclusively on specific species, among which *Gazella gazella* (Bar-Yosef and Belfer-Cohen 1989; Cope 1992; Davis 1983; Henry 1985, 1989; Horwitz et al. 1990; Legge 1972) took a primary place.

A sedentary society characterized by a completely altered habitat from which the food resources are still exploited through hunting and gathering (by more sophisticated techniques), with a population capable of manipulating wild populations of gazelles using highly selective culling, may not be too far from the next step: actual domestication. Those intermediate stages between culling selection and cultural control of wild populations and categorical domestication are not yet well understood. However, there should be a cultural continuum from the Natufian tradition to Neolithic populations that began to practice management of domestic plants and animals.

Climatic changes during the Epipaleolithic and Early Neolithic in the Southern Levant

It is now widely accepted that climatic fluctuations in the temperate zone were relatively mild, but they were of a remarkable magnitude along the Mediterranean-Eremian suture lines (Tchernov 1982, 1988). The southern Palearctic desert belt shifted northward and southward over large regions, due to global and local climatic changes alternately enriching and impoverishing those marginal areas. Palynological studies of van Zeist and Bottema (1991) provide a general paleoecological picture of Southwest Asia. They argue that the general correlation between the well-dated Hula basin (northern Jordan Valley, Israel) and the eastern Mediterranean deep-sea cores may indicate the following climatic fluctuations:

1. Ca. 20,000–14,500 B.P. Warm and dry over the entire region. The forests along the coastal ranges in Syria, Lebanon, and Israel became more open in the south. Lakes (such as Lake Lisan; Begin et al. 1985) were reduced in size (Fig. 1). Only a narrow strip of open forest or a parkland stretched along the Transjordanian plateau. The steppic belt was reduced and the Saharo-Arabian belt expanded westward in Syria and Jordan and northward in the Sinai and Negev region.
2. Ca. 14,500–13,000 B.P. Marked by an increase in precipitation, expansion of forests into the hilly regions and of steppic vegetation into the deserts, the appearance of temporary small lakes, and restored size of larger lakes. The last recognizable paleosol was formed during this period.
3. Ca. 13,000–10,000 B.P. A brief warm spell followed by a warm and still somewhat wet period, which finally became dry and cold (ca. 10,800–10,000 B.P., known in Europe as the Younger Dryas). Sometime around 10,000 B.P. conditions became wet and warm.

Indeed, it is now generally accepted that during the Late Glacial Maximum (LGM: 24 to 14,000 B.P.) the climate of the eastern Mediterranean was significantly colder and drier than today. The increase in precipitation of the whole region during the post-LGM period (14 to 11,000 B.P.) was followed by an abrupt decrease in rainfall (from ca. 11 to 10,000 B.P.), and may be correlated with the Younger Dryas. The return of wetter (pluvial) conditions around 10 to 8,000 B.P. never reached its previous peak, as is recorded in pollen cores of the southern Levant (Baruch and Bottema 1991). There is also enough evidence to show that the Indian Ocean monsoonal system penetrated the southern and eastern portions of the eastern Mediterranean during the period from 12 to 9,000 B.P. The terminal date approximates 8,300 to 8,000 radiocarbon years, and marks the end of the PPNB. This period could have still enjoyed a significant amount of summer rainfall, as all the PPNB faunal assemblages show.

The warming and drying trend of the post-PPNB caused an environmental degradation. It became much more severe when extensive wood-cutting and grazing were commonly experienced in the whole area (Rollefson and Köhler-Rollefson 1989; Simmons et al. 1988; Tchernov and Horwitz 1990).

The Hula region

After recent coring in the Hula Valley (Fig. 1), Baruch and Bottema (1991) were able to suggest the general climatic sequence of the Levant from about 15 to 8,000 B.P., derived from their intensively sampled pollen cores. The recent palynological profile from the Hula basin, as yet dated by only two readings, correlates well with the earlier palynological graph from another borehole in the Hula Valley done by H. Tsukada, which is dated by 16 radiocarbon samples (van Zeist and Bottema 1991). According to Baruch and Bottema (1991), in the earlier part of the Epipaleolithic (ca. 17 to 15,000 B.P.) the forest cover in the Hula area must have been rather limited, whereas the cover of steppe and desert plants must have been quite extensive (Table 1). Climate was dry, and since this time-span coincides with the Pleniglacial maximum, it may be assumed that it was also rather cold. From about 15,000 B.P.

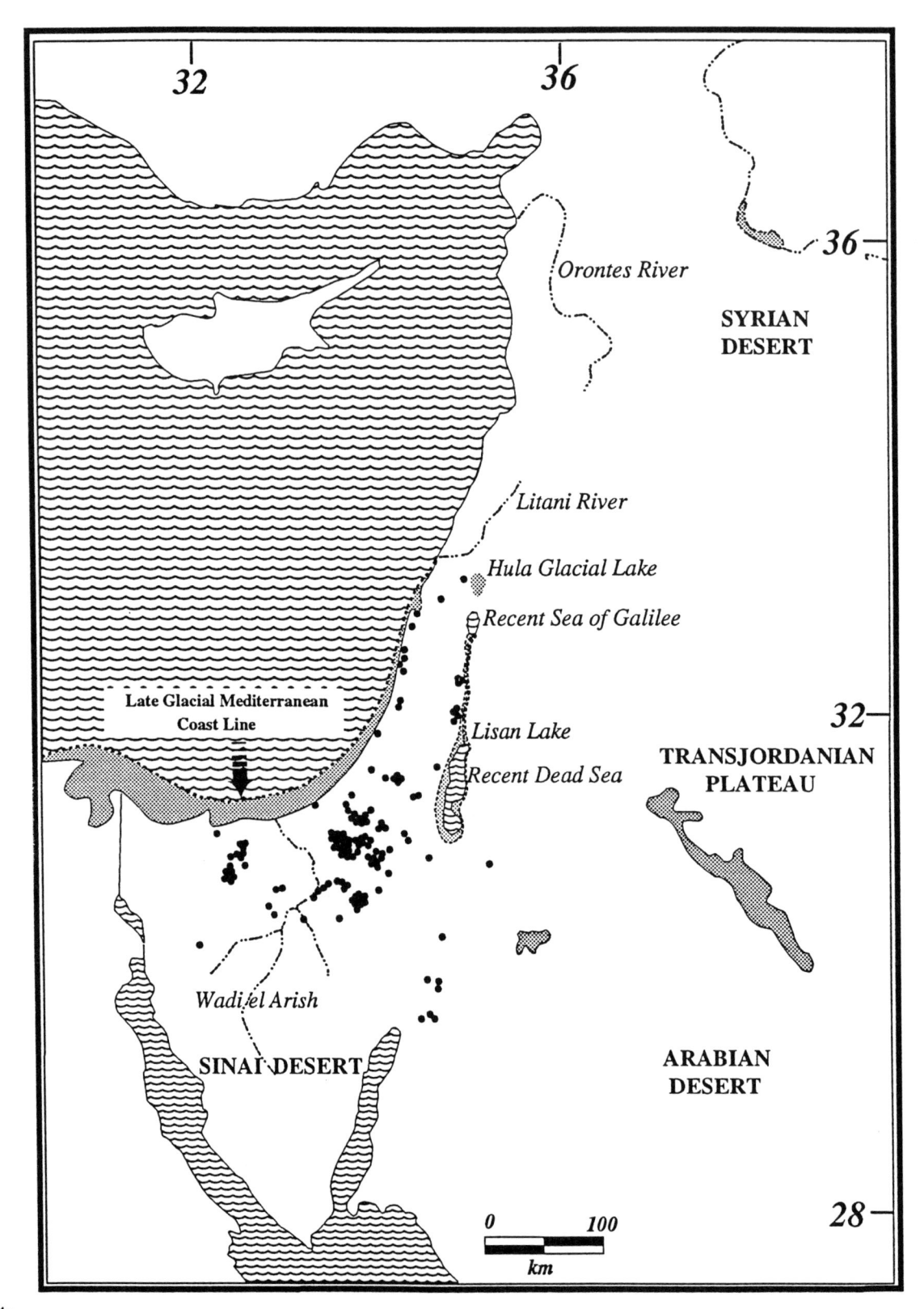

Fig. 1:
The general pattern of Geometric Kebaran settlements in the southern Levant, surrounded by the Syro-Arabian desert belt. The late Glacial Mediterranean coast line and Lisan Lake within the Dead Sea Transform are reconstructed mainly after Horowitz (1992).

Table 1. The sequence of environmental changes from the early Kebaran period to the latest PPNB in the southern Levant.

Period (B.P.)	Culture	Geographic Locality	Site	Climate	Flora (and Soil)	Fauna	Reference
19,000	Early Kebaran	Southeast of Dead Sea	Wadi Hama	Wet	*Quercus* sp., *Pistacia* sp., *Amygdalus* sp. Moist ground paleosol.		(1)
19,000–14,500	Kebaran	North of Dead Sea	Fazael VII	Wet	*Olea* sp., *Ulnus* sp., *Equisetum* sp., *Quercus calliprinos*, *Quercus ithaburenesis*, *Alnus* sp., *Nympheacaea*		(2)
19,000–14,500	Kebaran	Western Galilee	Hayonim Cave	Somewhat drier		Increase in % of *Microtus guentheri* and *Meriones tristrami*; appearance of *Acomys russatus* and *Gerbillus dasyurus* (Arabian rock dwellers); decrease in % arboreal rodents	(3)
14,500–12,500	Geometric Kebaran	Lower Jordan Valley	Fazael VIII Salibiya IX	Drier	Less arboreal pollen. *Alnus* sp., *Quercus calliprinos*, *Quercus ithaburenesis*, *Olea* sp., *Fraxinus* sp., *Fontanesia* sp., *Pinus halepensis*. Calcic horizon of soil in Negev.	Cervidae	(2)
12,500–11,000	Early Natufian	South Jordan, Arava Valley	Wadi Hama Wadi Judayid	Wet	High frequency of arboreal pollen, high grass. *Ficus* (cf. *carica*), *Alnus* sp., *Quercus* sp.	*Ovis* sp., *Bos* sp.	(2)
12,500–11,000	Early Natufian	Lower Jordan Valley	Salibiya XII Fazael VI	Wet	*Quercus calliprinos*, *Olea* sp., *Fraxinus* sp., *Pinus halepensis*	*Bos primigenius*, *Sus scrofa*, Cervidae	(2) (4)
12,500–11,000	Early Natufian	Western Galilee	Hayonim Cave	Wet	Substantial increase in arboreal pollen	Increase in % of arboreal rodents (*Apodemus* spp., *Sciurus anomalus*)	(3) (4)
11,000–10,500	Late Natufian	Lower Jordan Valley	Fazael IV Salibiya I	Progressively drier	Substantial increase in Chenopodiacae. *Quercus calliprinos* and *ithaburenesis*, *Olea* sp., *Fraxinus* sp., *Pinus halepensis*, *Ceratonia siliqua*.		(2)
11,000–10,000	Late Natufian	Western Galilee	Hayonim Terrace	Progressively drier	*Quercus calliprinos* and *ithaburenesis*, *Pinus halepensis*, *Pistacia* sp., *Phyllyrea* sp.	Decrease in % of *Sciurus* and *Apodemus*; increase in *Microtus* and *Meriones*	(2) (3) (4)
10,500–9,500	PPNA	Lower Jordan Valley	Netiv Hagdud Gilgal	Wet	Substantial increase in arboreal pollen	Dominance of waterfowl; 100% of Mediterranean reptiles, dominance of Mediterranean rodents, Cervidae	(2) (5) (6)
10,500–9,500	PPNA	Southern Sinai	Abu Madi I	Wet		*Spalax ehrenbergi*, significant % of waterfowl	(4)
9,100–8,200	PPNB	Negev	Nahal Hemar	Wet	*Quercus ithaburenesis*, *Alnus* sp., *Myrtus* sp., *Fraxinus* sp., *Olea* sp., *Prunus* sp.	*Bos primigenius*	(2) (7)
9,000–8,000	PPNB	Southern Sinai	Wadi Tbeik Ujrat el-Mehed	Wet		*Bos primigenius*, *P. porphyrio* (Aves), *Clarias* (Teleostei), *G. gazella*	(8) (9)
9,200–8,000	PPNB	Jordan highlands	'Ain Ghazal	Wet		*Sciurus anomalus*, *R. rattus*, *Spalax ehrenbergi*, *Sus scrofa*, *Bos primigenius*, *Ophisaurus apodus*, and *Testudo graeca* (Reptilia)	(10)
8,000–7,500	"PPNC"	Jordan highlands	'Ain Ghazal	Progressively drier		Significant decrease in species diversity	(10)

(1) Henry 1985; (2) Darmon 1984, 1987, 1988; Leroi-Gourhan and Darmon 1987; (3) Tchernov 1981, 1982; (4) Tchernov, unpublished data; (5) Bar-Yosef et al. 1991; (6) Noy et al. 1980; (7) Davis 1988; (8) Tchernov and Bar-Yosef 1982; (9) Dayan et al. 1986; (10) Simmons et al. 1988; Köhler-Rollefson and Rollefson 1990.

on, more humid conditions must have gradually developed in the Hula region, resulting in a gradual expansion of the forest. More specifically, an increase in precipitation between roughly 14 and 13,000 B.P. (Geometric Kebaran) has been demonstrated. This resulted in an expansion of continuous evergreen oak forests into the hilly regions between the coastal plain and the Jordan Valley and along the margin of the Transjordanian plateau. It also led to an expansion of the steppic Irano-Turanian vegetational belt both southwards and eastwards into formerly desertic areas (Baruch and Bottema 1991; Henry 1987; Rognon 1987). This is reflected by the wider distribution of Geometric Kebaran sites, which are not only found in the core Mediterranean region of the southern Levant, but also in more marginal areas such as the Negev, Sinai, and the Transjordanian Plateau (Bar-Yosef 1981). From about 13,000 B.P., this process accelerated, with humidity attaining its maximum value, and the forest its maximum extent, at about 11,500 B.P. (Table 1).

The later slight decrease in arboreal pollen in the Hula basin possibly represents the Younger Dryas and a slight increase in arboreal pollen marks the onset of the wetter early Holocene conditions probably around 10,000 B.P. The pollen evidence indicates that the early Holocene was wetter than the mid- and late Holocene. This general climatic interpretation is also supported through the faunal analyses of large samples retrieved from Kebaran, Natufian, and Neolithic sites (Bar-Yosef et al. 1991; Tchernov 1975, 1981).

The arid zone

Following the dry period of the last glacial maximum at ca.18,000 B.P. (Gat and Magaritz 1980), a wet period is recorded at various localities. The widespread development of a soil profile during the period of ca. 15 to 11,000 B.P. is indicated by radiocarbon-dating of the top calcic horizon in the northern Negev (Magaritz 1986) and in the coastal plain of Israel (Magaritz et al. 1981), and by an archaeologically dated calcic horizon in northern Sinai (Goldberg 1977), where a freshwater lake occupied a large region at Gebel Moghara. An increase in the number of human occupation sites in the present-day desert of the Negev and Sinai was documented by Goldberg and Bar-Yosef (1982) and reinforced the suggestion of relatively moist conditions (Table 1).

The climatic conditions during the Kebaran complex were cold and dry and human occupation was limited to the Mediterranean vegetation belt and margins of the steppic Irano-Turanian belt. The subsequent climate amelioration that brought increased temperature and precipitation enabled the later Geometric Kebaran groups to inhabit many of the formerly arid areas.

Magaritz and Heller (1980) have shown that snail shells from archaeological sites provide evidence of shifts of the desert boundary. They argue for arid conditions at ca. 11 to 10,500 B.P. (Late Natufian) in a now moist area of Israel, citing the enrichment of the shell carbonate and the smaller size of the shells. Analysis of pollen from a Late Natufian site in the semi-arid region of Syria also indicates relatively dry conditions from 10,500–10,200 B.P., with a slight increase in moisture between 10,200 to 10,000 B.P. (Leroi-Gourhan 1982) (Table 1).

Pollen spectra for the PPNB and the Late Natufian settlements in the central Negev highlands (Horowitz 1976, 1977, 1992) show considerably higher percentages of arboreal components as compared with the present day, including oak, cypress, olive, pistachio, and almond trees. The Chalcolithic settlements in the central Negev show similar tendencies (Horowitz 1979), but with somewhat lower arboreal pollen shares (compared to none at present). Horowitz (1979, 1992) stressed that the wealth of sites varies with climatic fluctuations, testifying to the intimate connection between environment and human dispersal and settlements during the Pleistocene and early Holocene in the arid regions.

The data from both southern Sinai PPNB sites (Wadi-Tbeik and Ujrat el-Mehed: Dayan et al. 1986; Tchernov and Bar-Yosef 1982) imply a significantly wet climate during the earliest Holocene that could have supported typical Palearctic elements. The freshwater elements recovered from Wadi-Tbeik (*Porphyrio porphyrio* and *Clarias anguillaris*) (Table 1), the remains of *Gazella gazella* and *Bos primigenius* from both sites, and *Lepus capensis* and *Alectoris chukar* are among the northern species that characterized the fauna in southern Sinai during the PPNB.

The Lower Jordan Valley

According to Horowitz (1992) the present day values for arboreal pollen north of the Dead Sea, within continental sediments, are around 1–2%. These compare with the values for arboreal pollen obtained from Kebaran sediments at the same locality, 18 to 14,500 B.P., which are in the range 5-12%. The Geometric Kebaran, 14 to 12,500 B.P., yielded values in excess of 10%, while the Early Natufian (12 to 11,000 B.P.) had values between 8 and 10%. The Late Natufian (11 to 10,750 B.P.) values were 2–4%; while during the Terminal Natufian (ca. 10,500 B.P.) the values of arboreal pollen spectra dropped down to zero. Following the PPNA (10 to 9,200 B.P.), when arboreal pollen had values of 10–15%, an increase of up to 20% during the PPNB (9,200 to 8,000 B.P.; Darmon 1988) was shown.

In summary, according to Horowitz (1992), Kebaran cultures seem to have enjoyed environments that were only slightly more humid than in the present day (Table 1, Fig. 2). Humidity increased during the following Geometric Kebaran, until approximately 12,500 B.P. The Natufian is characterized by gradual desiccation, reaching an extreme

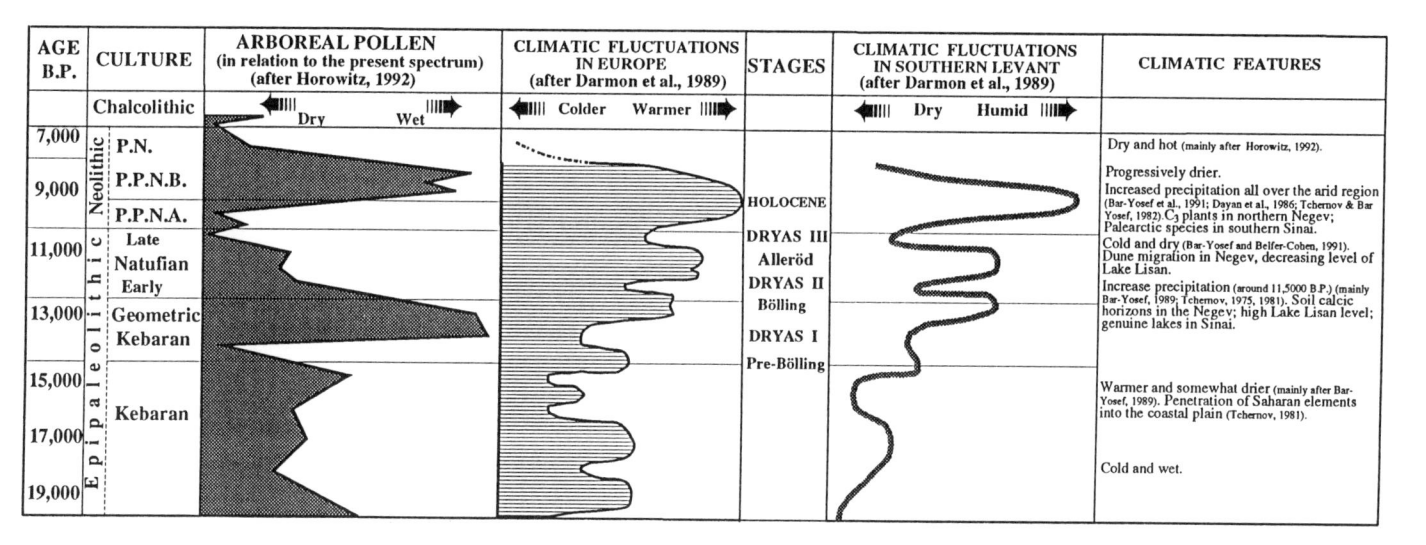

Fig. 2:
Climatic fluctuations in the southern Levant during the Epipaleolithic and Neolithic periods, correlated with the general European curve.

during the Terminal Natufian, corresponding to Oxygen Isotope Stage 1, in which arboreal pollen is entirely absent from the sites' deposits. During the beginning of the Neolithic, humidity increased, and in concert with Darmon's (1988) results, a similar trend was observed at the beginning of the European Holocene.

The faunal assemblages of the PPNA sites within the Lower Jordan Valley (Gilgal, Salibiya, and the PPNA level of Jericho) reveal the existence of an ecosystem that is completely different (Fig. 2) from the present one (Bar-Yosef et al. 1991). The only way to understand the remarkable composition of the faunal assemblages of these sites is to assume that entirely different climate and environmental conditions prevailed during this period. Animals like *Lacerta trilineata*, *Chameleo chameleon*, *Ophisaurus apodus*, *Testudo graeca* of the reptiles; *Corvus corone*, *Pica pica*, *Serinus serinus*, *Turdus merula* (song birds); a plethora of anatidae and other waterfowl; as well as *Arvicola terrestris*, *Microtus guentheri* (rodents); *Erinaceus europaeus* (Insectivora); *Capreolus capreolus*, and *Dama mesopotamica* (Cervidae)—all of which do not exist in these regions at present—clearly indicate a dramatic faunal break toward the end of the PPNB caused by a conspicuous climatic shift to arid conditions.

The swift shift of the Mediterranean region during the PPNA into the Eremian belt of the Levant is supported by other evidence. Palynological analyses of Salibiya IX (Darmon 1988; Darmon et al. 1989; Leroi-Gourhan and Darmon 1987) have shown a marked development of trees around 8,000 B.P., suggesting relatively forested conditions during Netiv Hagdud's occupation until 9,840 B.P. (Fig. 2). In Salibiya IX Leroi-Gourhan and Darmon (1987) identified the following trees: *Quercus calliprinos*, *Fontanesia* (Oleaceae), *Ceratonia*, as well as representatives of aquatic Nympheaceae. *Ficus carica* was also identified from Salibiya IX and Netiv Hagdud (Bar-Yosef 1989; Bar-Yosef et al. 1991) where the arboreal pollen amounts to 21% (Darmon 1988; Darmon et al. 1989; Leroi-Gourhan and Darmon 1987). As is the case with the vertebrate remains, all the plant species belong to the Mediterranean flora, with Oleaceae being dominant, while aquatic plants (Nympheaceae) distinctively increased. Darmon (1988) also argued that in general the pollen analyses from the area have shown that the somewhat drier Late Natufian was followed by a wet period, marked by a significant increase of trees and water plants, and a decrease in steppic species in the Lower Jordan Valley. The palynological spectrum hence stays in full concert with the faunal record.

The sharp and brief biotic changes that took place after the PPNA–PPNB (Fig. 2, Table 1) were mainly expressed by a considerable attenuation of the local communities. The evacuated niches were rapidly occupied by Eremian species (mainly Arabian, Tchernov 1988), but the total diversity greatly declined.

Archaeological and biological evidence for sedentism

Sedentism seems to be a very late phenomenon in human evolution, and its earliest appearance is recorded from the Natufian, 12 to 10,000 B.P. (Bar-Yosef 1983; Braidwood 1975; Perrot 1966; Valla 1987). It is also relatively restricted to a limited area in the Southern Levant: from the Euphrates in the north (Moore 1989) to the Negev highlands in the south and the Jordanian plateau in the east (Bar-Yosef and Belfer-Cohen 1989; Henry 1985, 1989). Most of the Early and Middle Natufian sites (Valla 1987) are found within the Mediterranean and Irano-Turanian phytogeographic belt (Henry 1989), and

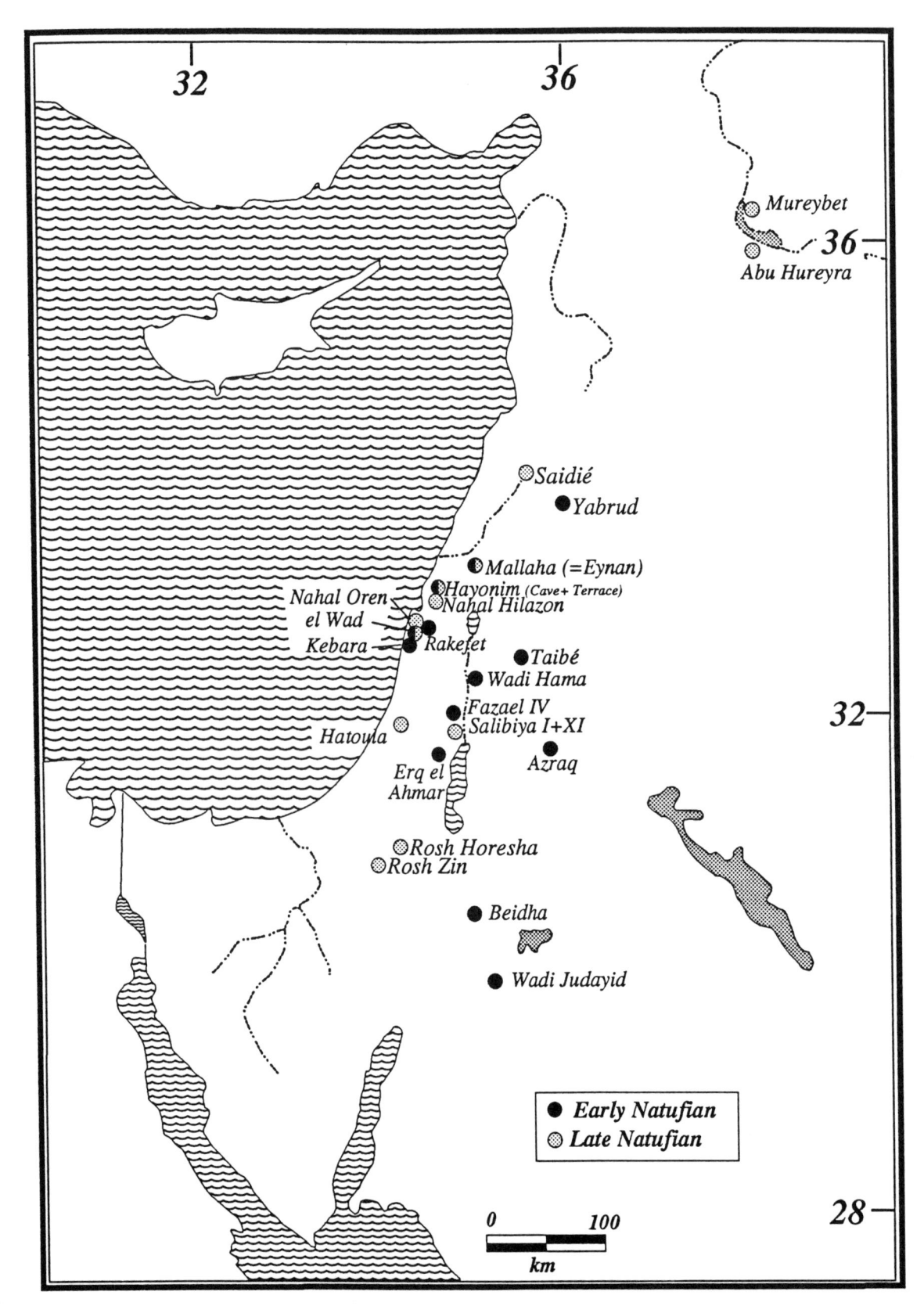

Fig. 3:
The main Early and Late Natufian sites in the southern Levant.

the core area is mainly along the pistacia-oak belt (Contenson and van Liere 1964) (Fig. 3). According to Valla (1987, 1988), radiocarbon dates show that the most ancient period of the Natufian dates from 12,500 B.P. to 11,000 B.P.; the recent phase lasts to about 10,500 B.P., followed by the final phase to about 10,200 B.P. It seems that the Natufian territory increased in time, so that later Natufian sites are known from more marginal areas, and even from within the desert belt (Henry 1985, 1989). Yet these peripheral sites were much smaller in size (Bar-Yosef and Belfer-Cohen 1989), and were probably inhabited by populations with higher mobility.

The Epipaleolithic entities preceding the Natufian are generally viewed as continuing the Upper Paleolithic way of life, namely that of small groups occupying small camps in which general activities took place (Gilead 1984; Hovers et al. 1988). A number of archaeological indicators corroborate the hypothesis that Kebaran hunter-gatherers were essentially transhumant between higher elevations in the spring and summer and lower elevations in the fall and winter (Lieberman 1993a, b). With the exception of a few highly dispersed sites, such as Kfar Darom 8 (Bar-Yosef 1970) and Wadi Kharaneh IV (Garrard et al. 1988; Muhesein 1985) that probably result from multiple occupations and erosion, most Kebaran and Geometric Kebaran sites are very small in size (between 15-25 m^2 and 400 m^2) and ephemeral in nature (Bar-Yosef 1989) (Fig. 1).

The sedentary settlements and agricultural communities of the southern Levant developed out of the Epipaleolithic hunter-gatherers' way of life (Hovers 1989; Hovers et al. 1988). Bar-Yosef and Belfer-Cohen (1989) agree that the irreversible transformation of several families, extended families, or even small bands into more complex social organization required new properties, such as division of labor, formation of task groups, and/or intergroup identification. Social and economic changes from the foraging mode of subsistence are clearly visible with the appearance of the Natufian entity, when sedentism, harvesting of wild cereals, and some storage took place (Bar-Yosef 1981, 1983; Henry 1989). The theory that the Natufian is characterized by sedentism was first proposed by Garrod (1932, 1957) and Neuville (1934, 1951), who defined the Natufian on the basis of its lithic industry which is dominated by lunates. They assumed, therefore, that the Natufians were the first agriculturalists. Subsequent researchers, influenced by Childe's (1951) theories concerning the origins of agriculture, furthered the assumption that the Natufians were sedentary. Binford (1968), Braidwood (1973), Flannery (1972), Cauvin (1977, 1987, 1989), and Perrot (1966) all argued that Natufian sites were continuously occupied villages, on the basis of permanent architecture uncovered in a wide variety of sites from different regions in the southern Levant. The multidisciplinary evidence collected by the extensive excavations of Bar-Yosef (1970, 1975, 1981, 1983), Henry (1985, 1989), and Valla (1975, 1987, 1988) has also been interpreted as substantial evidence for a system of relatively permanent base-camps with outlying logistical sites. Bar-Yosef and Belfer-Cohen (1989) and Henry (1989) have argued that Natufian sedentism was a necessary precondition for the subsequent development of agriculture. The issue of Natufian sedentism was categorically raised by Perrot (1966, 1989) when he suggested that the site of Mallaha (= Eynan) in the northern Jordan Valley can be actually considered a small village. This idea was accepted by Cauvin (1987, 1989) and Bar-Yosef (1983).

Lieberman (1993a, b) defined sedentism as a condition in which a site is continuously occupied on a relatively permanent basis for at least one year. Sedentism, however, is a more profound change in human lifeways, an event that irreversibly brought about completely new eco-social strategies. The impact of sedentism was so profound (evolution of commensalism, sex and age culling; see later discussion) that it must have taken place over many years. Hence we prefer a modification of the definition as follows: Sedentism is a state in which a site is occupied over a long-enough period that the following changes in human relationships with the environment result: (1) alteration of the ecological belts around the site (Tchernov 1991, 1992); (2) attraction of obligatory and facultative commensal species; and (3) significant change in the strategies of foraging exploitation of the resources. Among other attributes, sedentism also involves intensive and prolonged building activities; larger proportions (compared with the earlier Kebaran phases) of sickle blades, mortars, and pestles, which may indicate intensification of cereal gathering; increase in number and methods of burials (Arensburg 1985); exploitation of avifauna throughout the year (Pichon 1987, 1989); and the presence of human commensalism (Tchernov 1991, 1992).

Strong evidence in the form of burials, ground stone, and permanent architecture suggests that Natufian base camps were permanent village sites with occupation areas averaging 700 m^2; 500 m^2 larger than the Upper Paleolithic average (Bar-Yosef 1970; Henry 1973). The larger site size implies a larger population that may have relied more heavily on vegetal foods than in preceding periods. Intensive exploitation of wild grain stands would have allowed Natufians the luxury of stored surpluses, permanent residence, and large population size (Henry 1973). These factors might have led to a profound change in hunting strategies.

In the case of human sedentism, when a new habitat was created within and around the primeval villages, confrontation between humans and other species became a reality. At that moment we contemplate a severe competition among the species with similar or (partly) overlapping niches. Sedentary people and those highly hierarchical competitors, which are basically omnivorous and catholic (mice, rats, wolves, sparrows, etc.), found themselves co-occurring broadly in and around the anthropogenic sites, developing commensal relationships.

Lieberman (1993a, b) has clearly proved that cementum bands in artiodactyls (based mainly on gazelle teeth) are primarily caused by changes in diet hardness that alter the orientation of collagen fibers in cementum and by changes in nutrient intake that affect the mineral density of different bands. He has elegantly shown that the analysis of cementum increments of animals from archaeological sites can enable archaeologists to determine the season of death of animals killed or eaten by early hunter-gatherers. Such data are invaluable for providing estimates of the season of occupation of archaeological sites. His analyses on cementum increments of artiodactyl teeth from many Epipaleolithic sites confirm that many thousands of years later, Natufian hunter-gatherers adopted a strategy of reduced mobility in some of the same sites that were occupied on a multi-seasonal basis by archaic humans during the height of the Pleistocene. Natufian sedentism, however, differed from the pattern of radiating mobility of archaic humans in a number of important ways. The Natufians reduced their mobility, and reacted to the increased energetic costs of reduced mobility through cultural elaboration and intensification. Ultimately, the adoption of a less mobile subsistence strategy by Natufians, coupled with the environmental consequences of their solutions, set in motion an irreversible dynamic that led to increasing reliance on different food resources.

Self-organization, increase in complexity, and socialization

Explanations for increased complexity

In a certain place and at a certain period, a spontaneous increase in the organizational level of human communities was followed by a swift augmentation in communication, techniques of exploitation, and subsistence. Wenke (1981), seeking the reason for the sudden "unexplainable" appearance of cultural complexities, argues that with the appearance of complex cultures, we encounter kinds of group interaction, methods of transmitting cultural characteristics, forms of social control, and many other elements that contrast with those of the Pleistocene, and that cannot be explained to any great degree by existing ecological principles.

Various arguments try to simulate the impact of climatic changes on the Levantine environment and various models are offered as explanation for the cultural transitions that led to the establishment of farming communities by about 10,000 B.P. According to Bar-Yosef (1989), it was the onset of wetter conditions around 10,000 B.P. that enabled the well-established Natufian settlements within the Mediterranean phytogeographic belt to expand their knowledge as intensive users of wild cereals and to successfully practice cultivation (Figs. 2 and 3). Such an abrupt climatic change together with a period of social stress is suggested as a logical explanation for the "decision" made by Geometric Kebarans to become sedentary, or considerably less mobile, than their predecessors. Bar-Yosef and Belfer-Cohen (1989, 1991) suggest that before shifting to sedentary life, hunter-gatherers should have maintained their population size below the level of mean carrying capacity of the region. It has frequently been shown (Hassan 1981; Yellen 1977) that a direct functional relationship exists between the size of the site and the size of the group. On this basis Bar-Yosef (1987) and Bar-Yosef and Belfer-Cohen (1991) hypothesize that the rapid and instantaneous population growth of the Natufians was an event that took place within a relatively restricted geographical area, and that this growth led to a higher socioeconomic level. For Bar-Yosef and Meadow (in press) the abrupt "emergence of the Natufian from a population of hunter-gatherers was a 'threshold event' that took place in the 'Levantine homeland' to be followed by another threshold event, namely, the establishment of early farming communities." They argue that such swift cultural changes could have been triggered by climatic shifts. As for the sudden appearance of sedentary societies in the Natufian period, their "combined model" is based on other interrelated phenomena, such as abundance and predictability of plants, seeds, and animal resources and heavy demographic pressure, all of which lead to the necessity for territorial rearrangements with clear demarcation between the different groups. Bar-Yosef and Meadow (in press) claim that "rapid environmental changes resulting from abrupt climatic shifts are seen as the triggers for cultural changes." They argue that "behavior of the common local game (e.g., the 'sedentism' of *Gazella dorcas*) and the predictability of vegetal resources within small territories of the coastal Levant encouraged greater sedentism, i.e., smaller exploitation territories and sites occupied for longer periods of time each year." They claim also that "'demographic pressure' being a relative measure can be invoked by noting that from ca. 14,500 B.P., people occupied every ecozone within the Near East. Under conditions of subsistence stress, territorial rearrangements and shifts in settlement pattern were necessary." For Bar-Yosef and Meadow (in press), therefore, the emergence of farming communities is seen as a socioeconomic response to the forcing effects of the "Younger Dryas" on the Late Natufian in the Levantine corridor. They postulate that "the cold and dry 'Younger Dryas' caused yields of natural cereal stands to decrease and, under the existing territorial restrictions, created the motivation for intentional cultivation to increase."

Hayden (1990) argues that in contrast to earlier hunter/gatherers, highly competitive individuals with accumulative personality emerged in the new resource-rich communities, and they used the competitive feast as a means of developing, extending and consolidating their power. It is in the context of these "accumulators" and the feasting complex that the first domesticates generally appear. In the reality of the southern Levant, domesticates appear a long time—about 2,000 years—after the earliest sedentism during the Natufian period. Hayden emphasizes, however, the fluctuating resource base as a principle well established in ecological anthropology. When resource stress occurs, hunter/gatherers move out of stricken areas. Yet during the late Kebaran (Bar-Yosef and Belfer-Cohen 1989; Byrd 1989) there was no avenue for expansion, dispersal, or immigration, as the number of settlements and the distribution density of occupational sites were too high for any population movement. Any attempt to overcome resource shortages by migration would be doomed to failure, as territoriality and competition of all the surrounding communities would have prevented any violation of their territorial range and hence any dispersal effort. This idea is raised by Kelly (1983), who argues that one of the factors leading to more complex societies was the limited movement of populations, due either to natural conditions or to social causes, such as the presence of neighboring groups. Territorial behavior practices by various groups is inferred from the spatial distribution of the sites and the stylistic differences in their lithic assemblages (Hovers et al. 1988). We do not have any evidence that the abrupt sedentism of the Natufians and the punctuational increase in their socioeconomic status was indeed the outcome of agglomerations of small settlements into larger ones, or through extinction of many small settlements and an in situ growth of a few small settlements into much larger societies.

As far as cultural developments are concerned, it may be inferred from the Hula diagram (Baruch and Bottema 1991) that the origins of the Natufian cultural complex in the region referred to as its "core area" occurred under the most favorable Mediterranean climatic conditions prevailing throughout the final Pleistocene–early Holocene timespan. This calls for revision of models suggesting that the emergence of the Natufian culture may have resulted from environmental stress (Bar-Yosef 1987; Bar-Yosef and Vogel 1987; Goring-Morris 1987, 1988). Rather, it seems that the success of the Natufian subsistence strategies, largely based on sedentism, at least in the Mediterranean territory, was underlined by the improved climatic conditions.

It seems logical that if the climate began to deteriorate at the end of the Geometric Kebaran period, ca. 13,000 B.P. (Fig. 2 and Table 1), then one response of the groups would be to contract their home ranges and return to their original homeland, the Mediterranean phytogeographic belt of the southern Levant. On the other hand, if there was no climatic deterioration at the end of the Geometric Kebaran period, then it is more likely that a "cultural" explanation obtains for the nucleation of settlements within this environmental heartland. Climatic shifts, as harsh as they were, will not explain a major punctuational change from one level of organization to a more complex one. Throughout the history of humanity we do not observe direct, or indeed any, correlations between climatic fluctuations and increases in the socioeconomic level of humans. Climatic fluctuations may mainly affect dispersal and migration of populations associated with gradual adaptation to changing environment. As shown in the preceding section the rapid shift from high mobility to some form of sedentism in the transition to the Early Natufian cannot be linked or related (Lieberman 1993a, b) to abiotic factors. Lieberman also argues that the interpretation of the appearance of wild cereals in the beginning of the Holocene as a motivation for sedentism is without foundation. While it is possible that the distribution of cereals may have increased at the beginning of the Holocene, cereals were definitely present in significant quantities in the southern Levant and gathered by hunter-gatherers before the Natufian (Bar-Yosef and Belfer-Cohen 1989; Nadel and Hershkovitz 1991; Tsukada in van Zeist and Bottema 1991).

How can we explain in different terms this unique increase in human socialization during the transition from Geometric Kebaran to the Natufian periods?

The role of energy in increased complexity

The concept of 'hierarchy' in natural and human systems is not a new one. Ecologists have long recognized 'levels of organization' in biological systems: organism–population–community–ecosystem–biome–biosphere. Analogously, in the context of eco-sociology, we can identify a hierarchy from an individual to a state, which is essentially an organizational hierarchy. The increase of complexity in living beings is multifaceted and is expressed by increase in multicellularity, number of cell types, diversity of species, longevity and gestation time, care for offspring, shifting from r- to K-selection strategies, increasing in genic and non-genic DNA load, social integration, increase in body size, and other traits (Fig. 4). Human socioeconomic and ecological systems clearly distinguish, within a hierarchical framework, between different orthogenetic developmental levels: from scavengers-hunters-gatherers of food, through producers of food, up to urban societies. These categories may parallel sociopolitical organizations: band, tribe, chiefdom, kingdom, state, etc. These stages along a linear scale of complexity have an interdependent relationship with the amount of energy expenditure of each level, or the amount of energy incorporated by a social unit (Shawcross 1972; Sherratt 1972) (Fig. 5).

The concept that new and higher ordering can be derived from a fluctuation in a system was originally

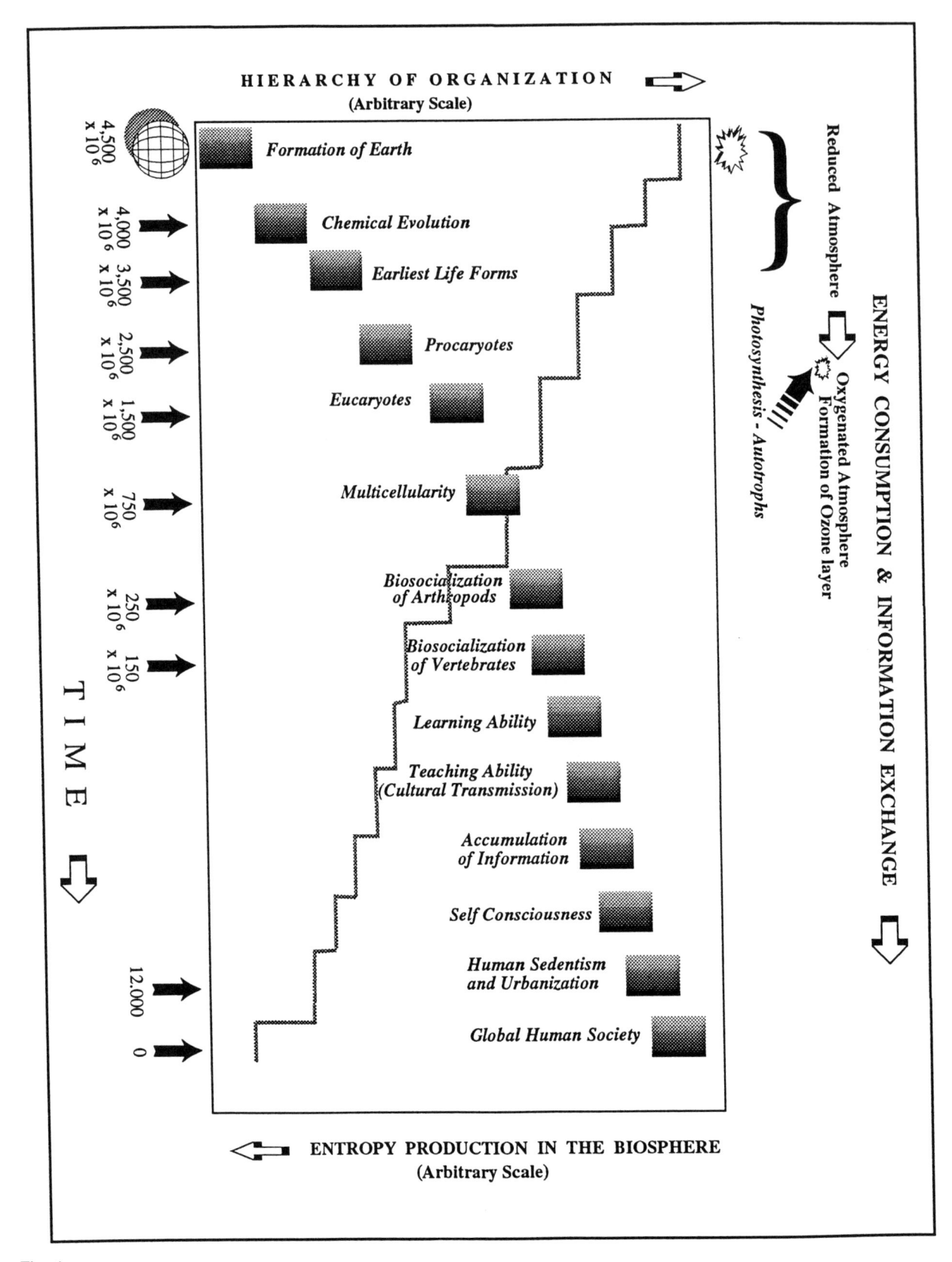

Fig. 4:
The unidirectional increase in complexity of open systems with time on earth, followed by a decrease in entropy production in the biosphere.

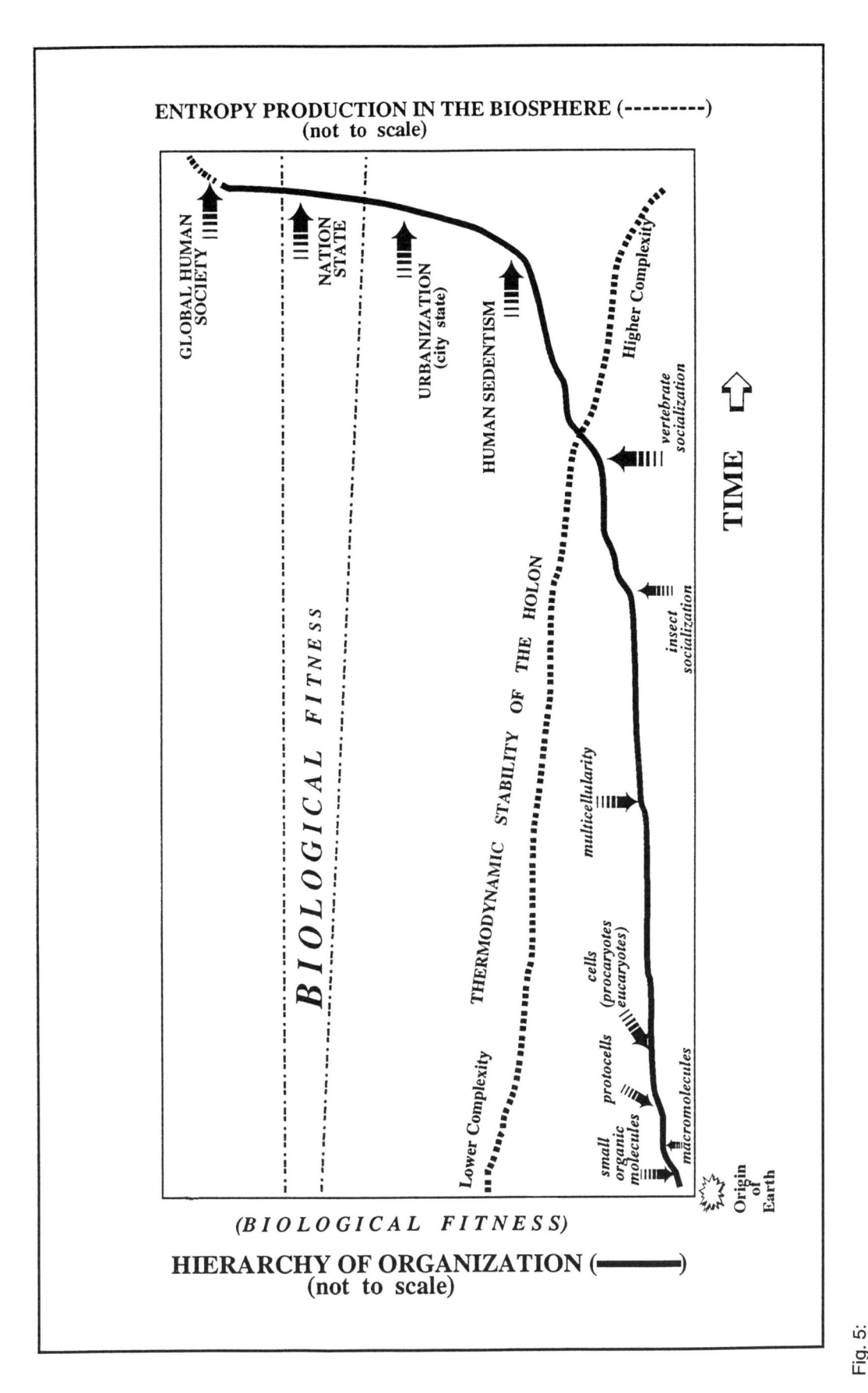

Fig. 5:
The increase of complexity in living beings is expressed by increase in multicellularity, number of cell types, diversity of species, longevity and gestation time, care for offspring, shifting from r- to K-selection strategies, social integration, increase in body size; and (within higher vertebrates), by increase in learning abilities, teaching abilities, accumulation and transmission of information, and (lastly) the development of self-consciousness. All these processes connote irreversible unidirectional events over time, yet with no regard to the speed with which they happen: a true "time's arrow" phenomenon. However, it seems that there is no change in the performance (the fitness) of any organism regardless of its level of complexity. The unidirectional successional development of ecosystems with time, much as the increase in biosocial organization, is caused by the higher stability gained with the increase in the maturity of the system (= complexity).

introduced by Nicolis and Prigogine (1977), Prigogine (1961, 1978), Prigogine et al. (1972), and Prigogine and Stengers (1984). From their definition we understand that self-organization will not occur if the concerned system is in a stationary state. Thus, the system should be in another state of order to be organized autonomously. Prigogine (1961, 1978) has called it "dissipative structure," which is defined as the macrostructure that appears in a non-equilibrium open system. As this definition indicates, the dissipation structure of open systems was originally devised in the field of thermodynamics. Therefore living systems, by extracting energy from their environment, and thus counteracting entropy, display typical dissipative structures, a concept which at present has been applied in such fields as chemical reactions (Nicolis and Prigogine 1977), ecosystems (Allen 1976), urban development (Allen et al. 1978; Dyke 1988), and economics (Silverberg 1984). Morowitz (1968) already stressed that since organisms are open themodynamic systems, there are no particular energy constraints on increasing biological complexity and organization. While all physical systems are transformational as long as they are not in thermodynamic equilibrium, dissipative structures, or individualized open systems, use energy flow to maintain themselves in a dynamic, non-equilibrium state. Living beings are open in terms of energy, thus transformational and cyclic, but essentially closed in terms of information (Wiley 1983) and cohesion, such as observed in ontogenetic and phylogenetic processes. In other words, while organisms require a continuous exchange of matter/energy with the environment to maintain a steady state, they do not require a continuous exchange of instructional information with the environment to maintain a steady state. Yet in this case human beings became an exceptional case during evolution. As Collier (1986) has characterized it, instructional information comprises a physical array whose informational properties depend only on the properties internal to the system in question. The properties of this instructional information depend on the properties intrinsic to DNA molecules, not on the surroundings or environment. The environment does not "mold" DNA molecules. In other words, organisms carry their blueprints inside and constantly refer to them. Humans have reached a stage when they may circumvent their innate information and make use of (exchange) outside information for manifestation of their lifeways and adaptations, in opposition to the main biological dogma that states that the environment cannot provide instructional information to an organism. Biological systems have a particular advantage over other dissipative structures because genetic information not only ensures proper functioning, but also encodes the history of the system into the macromolecules in a way not available to other hierarchical systems (Fig. 4). Thus, if we grant that biological systems are constrained by the same physical laws that made their emergence possible, we can expect that such systems will evolve toward greater complexity (in accord with Dollo's Law). On this basis Dyke (1988:358) argues that if human institutions and systems are indeed dissipative structures "we have to identify structures and relate their ability to sustain, maintain and reproduce themselves according to the resources (material and energy) available to them," resources that flow by and through the system (Fig. 5). He further suggests that "from an economic point of view, families, villages, cities, regions, provinces, states, etc., all the way up to nations seem to be prospective candidates for investigation as dissipative structures" (Dyke 1988:358).

From organism to ecosystem we find dissipative structures that use energy from outside systems to subsidize their highly ordered states of life (Schrödinger 1944; Morowitz 1968). And because dissipative systems select stable states with the largest possible stored energy, more highly organized systems, or more complex eco-social societies, will always have a higher expenditure of energy budget per component, or per individual. Hence the origin and evolution of ecological associations can be understood as nonequilibrium entropic phenomena, and as such we would expect them to be energy-processing systems and to exhibit self-organizing capabilities. The universal application of the principle of energy flow has shown that all biosystems are selected for a continual increase in throughput of energy (Margalef 1963; Odum 1969).

A fluctuation in a societal complex that will bring it far from thermodynamic equilibrium and, following Prigogine's theorem (1961; and Prigogine et al. 1972), from minimum entropy production, will reach a point beyond a critical threshold where more stable choices are available. Any choice that a social system shifts into will be more stable than the former stage; and hence the system will stay there. The situation that can arise when societal equilibrium becomes unstable enough to bring the system to the bifurcation point of higher stability can be simply expressed by an increase in the number of individuals, as well as the input/output of energy. I may agree with Cohen's (1977) statement that, historically, human populations have in fact tended to grow almost continuously, and that this growth has forced them more or less constantly to define new adaptive equilibria with their environment. Yet cultural and biological adaptation to new environments—or selection for higher fitness, in both its biological and its cultural meaning—constantly happens as a gradual process and always within a certain level of organization. But a transitional event to a higher level of organization (biosocialization) is not an outcome of Darwinian selection forces, and it does not take place through adaptive equilibria within a given level of organization, but through a punctuational self-organizational process.

Hamilton (1977) puts forward clearly the notion that the theory of evolution is unable to explain the origin of life, the appearance of multicellularity, or the organization of social systems, because the theory of biological evolution is innately only able to cope with evolutionary processes and mechanisms within organizational levels, but not between them. Indeed, for our discussion it is imperative to understand that there is nothing in Darwinism or Neo-Darwinism which enables us to predict a long unidirectional increase in complexity, because increased complexity may not, by itself, confer greater fitness on the organism (Maynard-Smith 1969). Is there any advantage in biological complexity? Is there any connection between "survival of the fittest" and increasing complexity? Was the increase in complexity the outcome of evolutionary process that demands an ever increasing complex system for survival, or is it innate within the basic physical law that drives biological systems to higher energetic levels in spite of fitness? There is no change in the performance (the fitness) of any organism regardless its level of complexity (Fig. 5). What is the biological benefit the individual will gain by relating to a socialized group? Was his fitness so low before? Will the group's inclusive fitness become higher? Higher energy consuming systems do not necessarily increase the inclusive fitness of their individuals; they may even lower it down. Were the last and highest levels of organization gained by humans achieved consciously for better fitness, or were they natural consequences of physical laws? Fisher (1930) predicted an increase in "mean fitness" with increasing complexity. Nitecki (1988:15) argues that "the theory of evolution does not predict an increase in anything," and has shown that it would be a mistake to think that there is any quantity that necessarily increases, as entropy increases in a closed physical system (but see also Maynard-Smith 1969, 1983). Moreover, he emphasizes that natural selection does not lead to continuing change, still less to anything that could be recognized as increase in complexity or progressive adaptation (Ayala 1988; Gould 1988).

The shift to a higher organizational level brings about a genetically heterogenous entity in which its components are obliged to interact, but the transmission of the genetic code is carried out by only part of the individuals, as is known in many insect complex societies. In highly complex societies where decision making is extremely centralized (Dunnell 1988), it is difficult to see exactly when natural selection works, yet it is certainly not always on the individual level. Hence, given this inevitability of the physical laws of self-organization when, as Thomas Hood might have said, "there is nowhere to go but up," I argue that the increase in the complexity of human systems, and consequently the proximal need for ever more elaborated technologies and devices, to allow more efficient exploitation of the resources, was not driven by intrinsic human traits, nor by climatic changes, nor even by biological rules (and apparently operated beyond "conscious decisions" made by people), but by higher natural laws. All one can say is that all that happened ever since the first living being appeared must have been in the direction of increasing complexity. "Nowhere to go but up" has nothing innate in the biological principles that will explain why integration occurs at all, or why the average level of complexity continues to rise.

The goal of any elaboration of subsistence behavior is the thrust for more energy, or some function of energy return per unit of expenditure (Margalef 1963; Morowitz 1968; Odum 1969; Zotin and Zotina 1967). The energy expenditure within a social unit is indeed higher in a more complex social organization. Although it is rarely quantified, this rule seems to be universally correct for all organisms: the higher the social organization, the higher the energy incorporation of the individual within its social system. Indeed, many anthropologists and sociologists today recognize sociocultural systems as group entities at their own ontological stage of organization with emergent features. Several interesting experiments have been carried out that examine socioeconomic phenomena using the concept of energy. They are, as a rule, based on the close relationship between the exploitation of a resource and the expenditure of energy necessary for the exploitation. Shawcross (1972), for instance, calculated the energy units incorporated in a certain settlement according to the ability of the people to supply themselves with food, by computing the energy value of the amount of food, and hence the size and duration of the society at the site. More recently Miyata and Yamagusho (1990) have examined the improvement of the interregional imbalance of population distribution in Hokkaido prefecture by employing dynamic self-organization theory.

As society evolves toward greater complexity, the cost to each individual within that society substantially increases. At a certain point, however, the costs may exceed the benefits derived. When this occurs economists refer to the "law of diminishing marginal utility." Lamberg-Karlovsky (1989:xii) describes a collapsed situation as a

> decline in the level of socio-political complexity and the severing of ties to their regional polities (Sumerian and proto-elamite).... The costs of administration, ... logistics of transport, communication, ... made the costs inordinately high while the benefits were increasingly marginal. The upward spiralling competitive costs and downward marginal returns saw a common ... response: collapse!

In other words, if the biological selection operates negatively on individuals due to a decrease in their inclusive fitness within their social organization, and, as mentioned before, results in a fundamental incompatibility between the level of organization and its building stones, a collapse of the system may well happen. As complexity grows, so does the "effort" needed by its components to adapt themselves to the new order.

Hence another way to explain the punctuational shift to a higher level of organization, or the aggregation of a group of components to a higher (social) structure, which emerged with completely new properties, is through a swift fluctuation in the energy absorption of the late Geometric Kebaran people, which demanded, rather than impoverishment, an improvement of the environment.

The impact of sedentism on the economy of humans: Natufian subsistence

The shift from ephemeral and/or seasonal occupation to prolonged habitation of relatively large communities had a far-reaching and profound impact on the proximate biotic environment. Such effects could have happened only in the course of a long period of intensive occupation of a place, and not through a recurrent usage of a site:

1. Due to the necessity for a sedentary community to exploit its resources within a geographically limited area, its subsistence became ever more restricted, forcing the people to become more specialized in exploitation of the environment, resulting in a broad array of animal remains, including small-sized mammals, birds, reptiles, fishes, as well as large pulmonates ("broad spectrum exploitation," Flannery 1969, 1972).
2. Cultural control of wild populations of gazelles, expressed by the highly selective culling of males, resulted in phenotypic deformation of body proportion and sizes, mainly toward a drastic disproportional allometric size diminution, and a highly skewed curve of the population structure (Cope 1992; Horwitz et al. 1990).
3. Commensal animals appeared around and within Natufian habitations (Tchernov 1984, 1991, 1992).

The prolonged occupation of a site by a group of people is an enormous drain on the vicinity areas, which ultimately turn into a barren land. Intensive exploitation of the resources, killing off the game, and more time spent just to maintain a constant level of food intake within the limited area available for the people will utterly alter the natural habitats around the sites (Tchernov 1992). A centripetal ecological gradient will be created by the intensive anthropogenic activities around the site. It is expected that the nearest belt to the occupational site will be constantly and extensively used by the inhabitants. Ecologically, it will be completely stripped of plants and animals. The peripheral belts around the core of the site will show gradual relaxation in the exploitation of the resources, but the width of these ecological belts will fluctuate with the seasonal changes in the carrying capacity of the area. It is obvious that in certain seasons (under Mediterranean climatic conditions), such as during the autumn, the biological resources around the site will be extremely exhausted or non-supportive. Habitats will gradually revert to more natural conditions in the outer belts, so that hunting can be undertaken only at a certain distance from the site. It is important to emphasize that the constant depletion of biological resources from and around early human settlements created a unique and isolated mini-ecosystem that was virtually devoid of most plants and animals, but opened new niches and opportunities for preadapted colonizers.

Broad spectrum economy

Widening the array of food resources is one of the ultimate consequences of Natufian sedentism (Tchernov 1992). Very few quantitative studies have been undertaken that show precisely and in detail the use of a significantly larger variety of species, and the rapid increase of efforts to procure certain animal species. Many of the Natufian sites have not yet been fully and thoroughly studied, qualitatively and quantitatively.

The principal Natufian sites from which most of our information is garnered are as follows (Fig. 3):

Hayonim Cave and *Hayonim Terrace* (western Galilee, northern Israel). These are two parts of the same site. The first was excavated in the late 1960s and 1970s by O. Bar-Yosef, E. Tchernov, and B. Arensburg. Most of the lithics, the bone and stone tools (Bar-Yosef and Goren 1973), have been studied recently by Belfer-Cohen (1989, 1991) and Bar-Yosef and Belfer-Cohen (1989), who present detailed results concerning the typological and technological dynamics through the Natufian sequence, as well as studies of the incised limestone slabs.

Valla (1987) has recently finished long-term excavations at Hayonim Terrace. He has published extremely detailed analyses of the remains of houses, identifying hearths, burials, and dumping zones. A large sample of animal remains was uncovered from the Terrace of Hayonim.

El Wad. A re-examination of the deposits at el Wad (Mt. Carmel) (Valla et al. 1986) was carried out in 1980–1981. Layers B.2 (Early Natufian) and B.1 (Late Natufian) were found to be closely similar to Garrod's (1932; and 1957) original description.

Mallaha (= *Eynan*). Located in the Hula basin (northern Israel), this is one of the largest and most important sites (ca. 2,000 m^2) (Perrot 1966; Valla 1991).

Hatoula (Layers 4–5). The site is located on the western flanks of the Judean hills, at present well within the Mediterranean vegetational belt. The site contains levels of Late Natufian and "transition" to the PPNA (Khiamian) (Ronen and Lechevallier 1985, 1992).

Salibiya I. This is a Late Natufian site located in the Lower Jordan Valley, 230 m below sea level and about 17 km north of Jericho (Crabtree et al. 1992; Schuldenrein and Goldberg 1981).

The ultimate consequence of the primeval sedentism was correctly phrased by Simmons et al. (1988:39) for the

Neolithic site of Ain 'Ghazal (Jordan): "Sedentary populations will consume themselves out of the rich environment." Yet we know that during the Neolithic the strategic solution for continuing and surviving in a deteriorating and exhausted habitat is to rely more strongly on animal husbandry and early farming. But during the Early Natufian, economical solutions should have been sorted out in other directions, and the ultimate ones should have followed behavioral patterns of other vagile animals that shift into low mobility, as mentioned in the introduction; i.e., exploiting a wider ecological niche ("broader spectrum" exploitation of the local resources, Flannery 1969, 1972). With a close similarity to other large mammals with restricted mobility, the ultimate outcome of human sedentism triggered a larger scale and much more intimate biological interaction with coexisting (sympatric and syntopic) species. The early sedentary populations not only shifted to a broader dietary spectrum, and relied on a greater proportion of smaller ("lower ranked") animal species, as argued by many archaeologists (like Winterhalder 1981, but see also Speth and Scott 1989 for more references), but also specialized on specific species.

A significant increase in the species diversity of terrestrial mollusks, birds, and reptiles is observed (Tchernov 1992) throughout the sequence of Hayonim Cave, from the Aurignacian through the Kebaran to the Natufian. The great majority of the species were used for food, but "broad spectrum" exploitation also comprises other functions in addition to food. Although most of the species were not edible due to their minute sizes, they represent the high motivation of these people for collecting 'objects'. Along with many other species that were either rarely, or not at all used before the Natufian (many species of birds [Pichon 1984, 1987]), different species of reptiles (*Ophisaurus apodus*, chameleons, snakes), *Alectoris chukar* (Phasianidae, Aves), and *Lepus capensis* (Lagomorpha) became an integrative part of the food resource in the Natufian period (Table 2 and Fig. 6). Fishes were never much in the favor of the eastern Mediterranean human populations; however, there is an obvious increase in the amount of marine fish brought to Natufian sites, where it reached a relatively significant level (Tchernov 1992). There is, however, a decrease in the representation of carnivores in all the Natufian deposits, which are highly dominated by a few commensal or semi-commensal species, like foxes and dogs.

The best-recorded Late Natufian floral assemblages come from Abu Hureyra (Hillman et al. 1989), where 150 species of edible seeds and fruits were identified. Evidence from late Kebaran sites is rare. From this site there is no positive evidence that indicates that wild einkorn wheat or wild rye were cultivated, nor did histological studies reveal any characteristics of domesticated grains.

It is not only the almost revolutionary broadening of the range of exploited animal species that characterizes the Natufians, but the specialization on hunting certain small species (like *Lepus* and *Alectoris*) (Fig. 6 and Table 2) in extremely high proportions and throughout the year (Pichon 1989; Tchernov 1991). Henry (1989) has noted that small animal species are much better represented in Natufian deposits than before, but the absolute numbers of small game, fish, turtle, fowl, and invertebrate remains indicate that they could not have made a significant contribution to the overall diet. Yet, insignificant as it was, the Natufians were forced to consume whatever was available in the over-exploited area around their sites.

Exploitation of gazelles

The earliest 'villagers' continued to practice intensive and specialized hunting of large game. But contrary to earlier periods, they gradually focused their hunting strategy on a single species, which in the southern Levant was almost exclusively *G. gazella* (Table 3) (Bar-Yosef and Belfer-Cohen 1989; Cope 1992; Davis 1983; Henry 1985, 1989; Horwitz et al. 1990; Legge 1972; Tchernov 1992). Much work has been done in the last two decades on the reconstruction of Natufian gazelle exploitative systems

Table 2. The relative representation of hares (*Lepus capensis*) and partridges (*Alectoris chukar*), and the total number of bird species at various sites from Mousterian to early Neolithic periods.

Culture	Site	Locality	Lepus capensis % of all rodents	Lepus capensis % of all ungulates	Alectoris chukar % of all non-passeriforms	Number of bird species
PPNA	Netiv Hagdud	Lower Jordan Valley	45	57	24	–
Natufian	Hayonim Cave	Western Galilee	55	12.5	30	94
Kebaran	Hayonim Cave	Western Galilee	1	0.5	18	42
Upper Paleolithic	Kebara Cave	Mt. Carmel	2.4	1.8	11.2	36
Upper Paleolithic	Hayonim Cave	Western Galilee	2.2	0.05	14	32
Upper Mousterian	Kebara Cave	Mt. Carmel	0.8	0.03	5.8	37
Mousterian	Hayonim Cave	Western Galilee	0.16	0.1	7	–

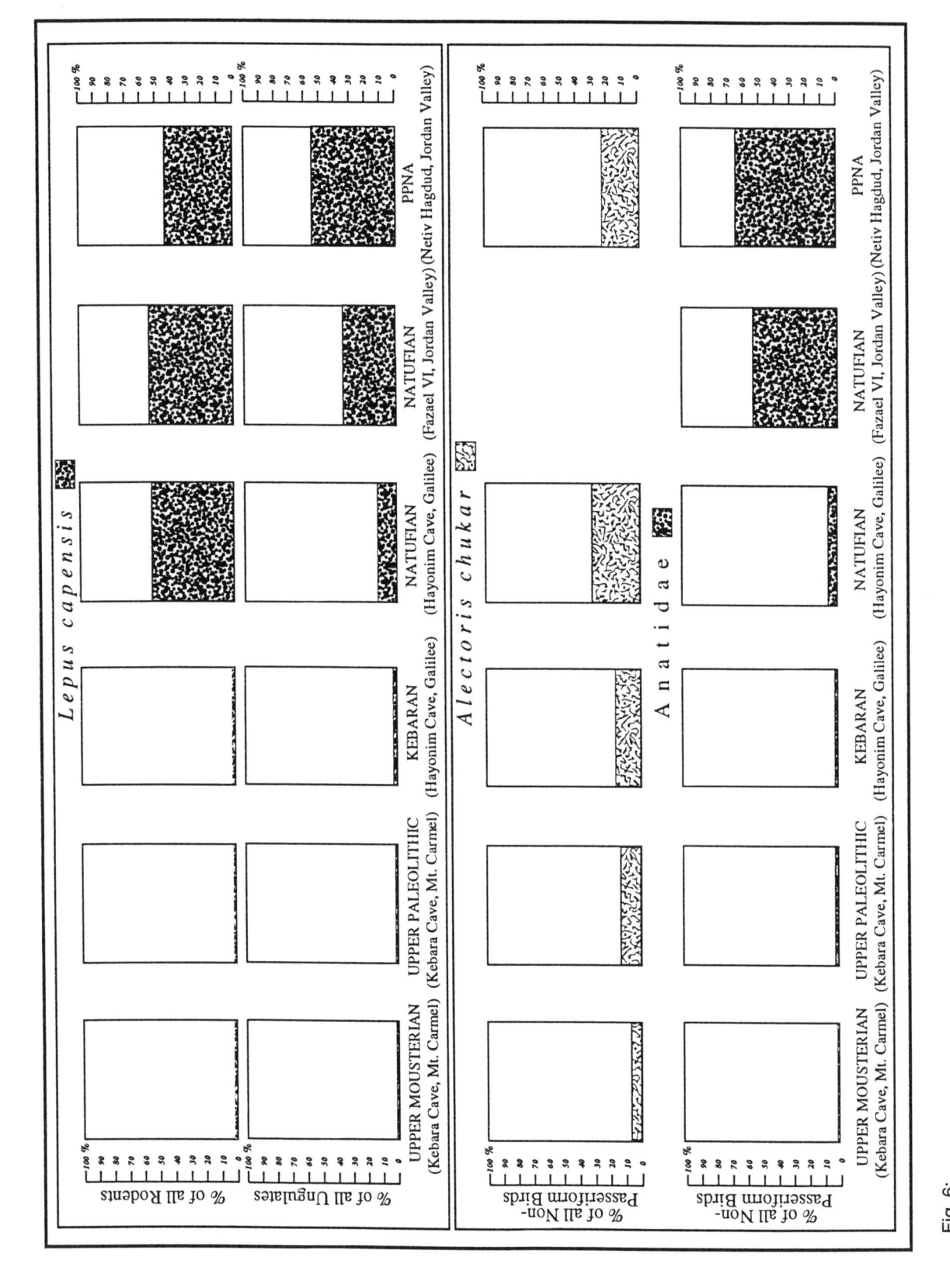

Fig. 6:
The relative representation of hares (*Lepus capensis*), partridges (*Alectoris chukar*), and waterfowl (Anatidae) from Mousterian to early Neolithic periods. Hares and partridges obviously became the favorite species for the Natufian and early Neolithic people.

Table 3. A comparison of the relative frequencies of ungulates from all the available Kebaran, Natufian, PPNA, PPNB, and PN sites. The mean frequency (X) for each period was calculated (in %) from the available information on bone remains.

Period SPECIES	Kebaran Total Range	X (%)	Natufian Total Range	X (%)	PPNA Total Range	X (%)	PPNB Total Range	X (%)	PN Total Range	X (%)
Capra aegagros/ibex (Ovicaprids)	0–16	3.2	0.2–6.0	2.3	0–7.5	3.0	13.9–98.0	59.0	69.4–85.0	75.4
Gazella spp.	46–79	65.3	58.4–97.6	73.0	49.5–95.0	70.2	6.7–76.4	16.5	5.0–22.0	11.2
Bos primigenius	1–5	4.7	0–6.0	3.0	0–9.5	5.5	0–42.7	11.0	6.2–9.3	7.4
Sus scrofa	1–75	10.5	0.6–13.2	4.5	0.7–14.5	7.5	0.3–27.4	8.9	1.5–11.0	4.7
Equus spp.	0–0.5	0.2	0–1.2	0.9	0–4.0	2.0	0–3.6	1.7	0.3–1.7	1.1
Cervidae	10–34	15.1	0–25.7	15.4	0–23.0	9.8	0–12.1	2.9	0.6	0.6
Alcelaphus buselaphus	1	1	0–1.5	0.9	0–11.0	2.0	–	–	–	–

(Cope 1992; Davis 1978; Henry 1989; Henry et al. 1981; Legge 1972). Legge was the first to suggest that the Natufians practiced sophisticated manipulative techniques in gazelle exploitation. Based on age profiles, Legge suggested that this species may have been domesticated (Legge 1972). Davis (1974) refuted this theory, pointing out that the natural behavior of the gazelle makes it extremely unlikely that it was ever herded as a domesticate. Analyzed Natufian faunal assemblages are, however, striking in their pronounced bias toward gazelle in ungulate relative frequencies (Cope 1992; Henry 1989; Henry et al. 1981; Horwitz et al. 1990; Legge 1972). It is apparent that there was a definite preference for this species in the Natufian and PPNA periods, as gazelle bones consistently predominate over those of other ungulates regardless of the local environment. As it appears unlikely that gazelles underwent actual domestication, their high relative frequencies in Natufian deposits must be the result of preferential hunting practices, more intensive than in the Kebaran period (Cope 1992).

Cope (1992) and Horwitz et al. (1990) have clearly shown that all sampled Natufian sites exhibit a pronounced bias toward *Gazella gazella* in ungulate relative frequencies (Fig. 7 and Table 3). At Hayonim Cave, gazelles make up 58.4% of the megafaunal collection; at Hayonim Terrace, 64% of all economically important species; at Mallaha, 56.7%. Seventy percent of the Late Natufian collection at Hatoula is gazelle, and in the overlying Khiamian (Hatoula, layers 3–4) the percentage amounts to 75%! Most sampled Natufian sites have also been found to have a strong bias in favor of mature versus immature individuals, as well as in favor of males (Campana and Crabtree 1991a, b; Cope 1992; Horwitz et al. 1990; summarized in Tchernov 1993) (Fig. 7). At Hayonim Cave 36% of the gazelles were immature; at Hayonim Terrace about 37%; and at Mallaha, 36%. Sixty percent of the gazelles of the Late Natufian of Hatoula were immature individuals. Six species of ungulate were present in layers 3–4 (Khiamian) of Hatoula of which *G. gazella* constitutes a unique economic importance in terms of relative frequencies (71% of the megafaunal collection). Cope (1992) argued that 65.5% of gazelles were under one year of age at the time of death.

Every sampled Natufian site has shown at least some degree of a bias toward males in the gazelle samples (Fig. 7). The samples of all other ungulate species are characterized by a 1:1 sex ratio. During the Early Natufian, as represented in layer B of Hayonim Cave, 80% of the gazelles are male. This represents the highest figure for the period. The bias seems to decrease throughout the period to a mere 60% as recorded in the Terminal Natufian of layers 4–5 of Hatoula. The male-biased sex ratios that seem apparent for Natufian sites are all the more surprising, considering that female-biased sex ratios are common in modern herds of *Gazella gazella* in Israel (Baharav 1983a). The bias towards males has completely disappeared by the Khiamian (Fig. 7).

The result of this long period of human interference in gazelle mating systems was pronounced diminution and allometric changes in the population. Certain elements such as astragali and metapodia seem most affected by diminution, while more proximal elements like humeri are least affected. Allometric changes of this type are similar to those usually seen in domestic ungulates (Clutton-Brock 1979). The probable cause of such effects may be reproductive isolation inflicted on a breeding population. In the case of Natufian gazelles the mechanism involved may have been selective hunting of males, reducing a normal degree of female choice. This artificial intervention in the natural selection of the gazelle populations also caused an abnormal range of variability and hence very high v (variance) values. As was the case with the primeval dogs (Davis and Valla 1978), the gazelles underwent significant size diminution counter to the general trend of the prominent Bergmannian size increase that we witness in many

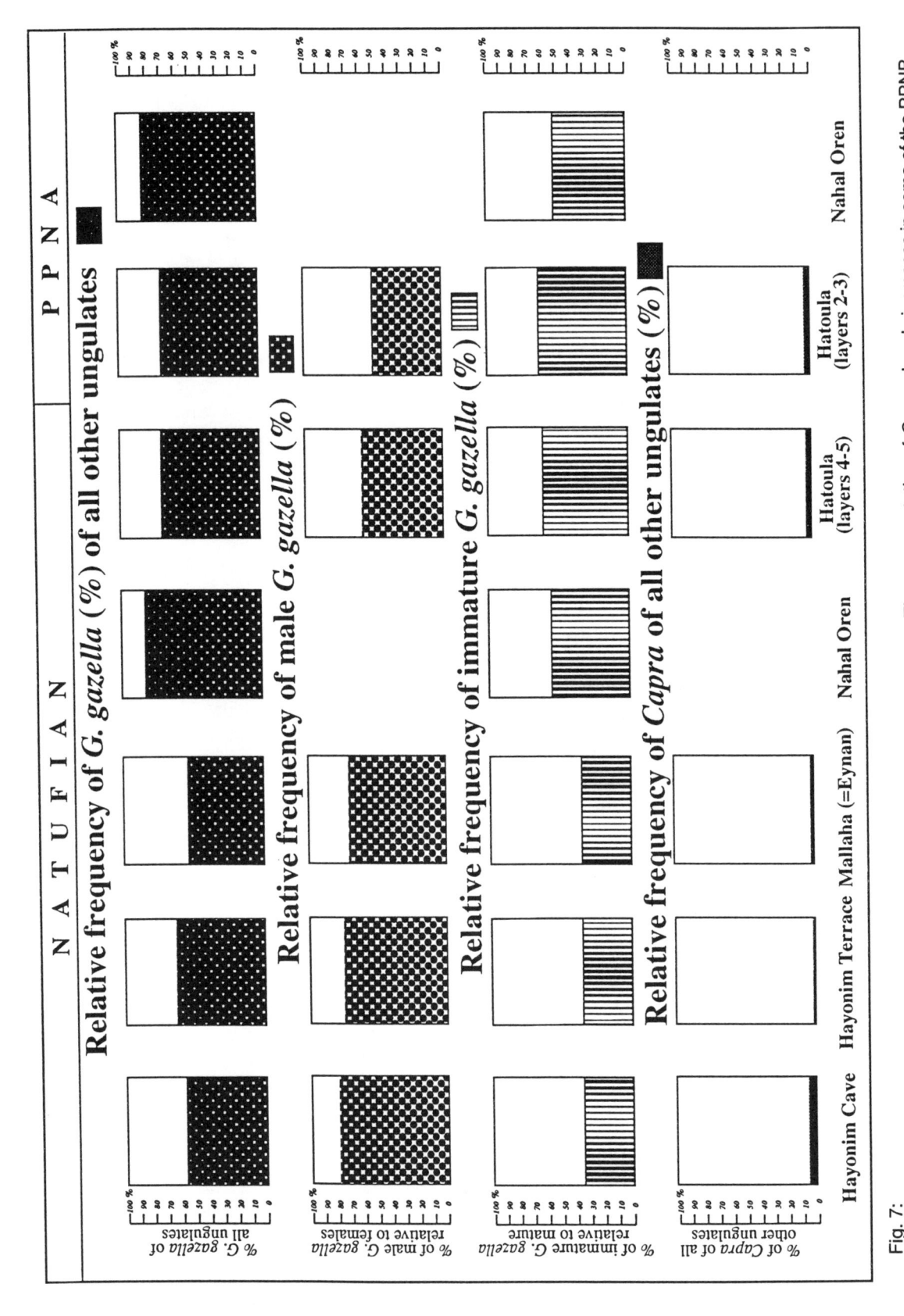

Fig. 7:
The relative frequency of *Gazella* and *Capra* in relation to all other ungulates. The representation of *Capra* sharply increases in some of the PPNB sites, mainly along the Jordan Valley corridor. The relative frequency of immature versus mature and male versus female gazelles is shown in several Natufian and PPNA sites. The predominance of males is universal in all Natufian sites. The data are mainly based on Bouchud (1987), Cope (1992), Legge (1972), Noy et al. (1973), and personal observations.

other birds and mammal species during this period (Davis 1981; Dayan et al. 1989a, b; Klein 1986; Kurtén 1965; Tchernov 1981; Tchernov and Horwitz 1991). This intentional selection differs from actual domestication in the degree of control that humans have over the mating system. While intentional selection strongly inhibits natural selection by restricting female choice, actual domestication reduces it drastically (Cope 1992, Horwitz et al. 1990). The increase in diminution of individuals in the Natufian produced highly abnormal ranges of variation throughout the period. For protected domesticates such potentially allometric damage can be tolerable. However for populations of wild *G. gazella*, whose only protection is flight, it is unlikely such a trait would be retained under normal conditions of natural selection. These types of allometric changes resemble those seen for populations of ungulates under insular isolation.

Cope (1992) suggests that the genetic consequences of extensive culling of males is far-reaching intra-population inbreeding due to the drastic decrease in the number of males available for the females in a panmyctic population. If fewer males copulate with more females, homozygosis will consequently increase. As *G. gazella* males are territorial and their mobility is relatively limited (Baharav 1983b), gene flow between the affected population and the 'natural' populations should be greatly restricted, augmenting the effect of genetic drift and explaining the abrupt morphogenetic changes that the local gazelle populations underwent during this period.

As shown by Cope (1992), there is no evidence, however, for male bias in *Dama* and *Capreolus*. Sex ratios for *Dama* are close to 1:1. Its relative frequency amounts to 5.9% at Hayonim Cave, but increases to 18% in Hayonim Terrace. The percentage of immature individuals of *Dama* is similar for both sites: 38% for Hayonim Cave and 40% for Hayonim Terrace. Relative frequencies were not calculated for *Dama* at Mallaha (= Eynan), but in the Late Natufian of Hatoula (layers 3–4) this species has become rare (4% of the ungulate assemblage), and by the PPNA it is absent from the assemblage. *Capreolus* is common at Hayonim Cave (19.8%) but drops to 9% at the somewhat later period of Hayonim Terrace. At Hatoula roe deer constitute 8.5% of the assemblage.

Cope (1992) suggests that the Natufian strategy for gazelle exploitation was to keep the animals in a semi-wild state, perhaps with some degree of predator protection, and then in communal hunting and drives to cull the young males of the bachelor herds, allowing females to live and produce the important meat staple. A stable supply of grain was the catalyst leading to the necessity for more control over the gazelle. This control over the sex ratio of a species that is not suitable for actual domestication may have created a cultural climate conducive to the acceptance of imported domestics in the succeeding period. Such a strategy would have the advantage of preserving the population's ability to increase, while allowing hunters to harvest individuals at will. The females could have been perceived as a stable reproductive base (Cope 1992). This pattern of gazelle procurement faded toward the end of the period, but appeared again during the PPNA, as demonstrated at Netiv Hagdud (Bar-Yosef et al. 1991). The reason for such a relaxation in sexual and age culling of gazelles towards the end of the Natufian could have been the consequence of a shift into intensive communal hunting, as argued by Campana and Crabtree (1991a, b). Their argument is based on the kill pattern found at the site of Salibiya I which produced approximately 50% immature gazelles, hence closely resembling Baharav's (1974) age profile for modern *G. gazella* (= 47%; but see Edwards 1991 for an opposing opinion). The overkill structure of Salibiya I can be explained also as a catastrophic mortality due to a "communal drive" hunting strategy (Klein and Cruz-Uribe 1984). Campana and Crabtree's (1991a, b) results for the gazelle age profile are not in line with all other Natufian and PPNA sites.

An anomaly in the relative frequencies of *Capra ibex* reminiscent of those for Natufian gazelles was found in the PPNB of Wadi Tbeik (southern Sinai) (Tchernov and Bar-Yosef 1982). The remains of mature males were twice as frequent as those of females. The result is all the more surprising when viewed in light of the wider range and solitary habits of the *C. ibex* male. The fact that adult males greatly outnumber mature females at Wadi Tbeik, in spite of the fact that the latter are harder to obtain, points to a degree of cultural control or rational cropping of this species. It has been suggested that the idea of cultural control as an exploitation technique was widespread all over the Levant, and that other large ungulates such as *Bos primigenius* or *Gazella gazella* may have been treated similarly (Tchernov and Bar-Yosef 1982). Cultural control of *Gazella gazella* does seem to have been a common element of Natufian culture, a tradition that could have shifted northward toward the end of the Natufian. In the arid region, as seen in the southern Sinai, male-biased cultural controls seem to have lingered until well into the Neolithic (late PPNB).

Commensalism

A long-term occupation of a site will cause a drastic decrease in the species diversity around the site, and in particular, the elimination of most of the elements that occupy the higher trophic levels within the ecosystem, causing it to undergo reversed successional processes, leading to an immature unstable ecological status. One of the most interesting phenomena that followed the long-term occupation of the Natufian sites is the abrupt appearance of commensals around human habitations (Tchernov 1984, 1991, 1992). When new habitats were created by the

Natufians within and around the primeval villages, they attracted special colonizers, basically omnivorous and catholic vertebrates (mice, rats, wolves, sparrows, etc.), which found themselves co-occurring broadly in and around the anthropogenic sites. The result, during a relatively short period (on an evolutionary scale), was the development of indirect commensal relationships by the newly created subspecies or species.

These species are able to benefit by using the human habitats and consequently might shut down their gene exchanges with the outside populations. With the more constant availability of food and/or shelter, the habitat could have attracted fostered (commensal) populations of certain species which would consequently gain an advantage over non-commensal ('wild') populations. Such one-sided symbiosis may increase the survivorship rate, especially of juveniles, of the active commensal partner due to:
1. A constant supply of food, in kitchen middens within and around the sites;
2. A habitation protected from predators; in particular, an increase in the availability of well-sheltered nest and birth sites;
3. The deterrence of most of the other coexisting species due to the proximity of intensive human activities. As a consequence, low species diversity in the close vicinity of the sites will decrease inter-specific competition, but increase intra-specific competition, and hence high selection, genetic drift, and consequently biological changes.

The most abundant commensals in the Middle East are *Mus domesticus, Rattus rattus, Rattus norvegicus* (late colonization), and *Acomys cahirinus* (restricted to semi-arid and arid regions) which belong to the Muridae, Rodentia; *Passer domesticus* (Ploceidae, Passeriformes); and *Columba livia* (Columbiformes). Carnivores like the jackal (*Canis aureus*) and the fox (*Vulpes vulpes*) may show accidental to more permanent associations with humans in rural regions (a stage intermediate to plesiobiosis and early commensalism). The domestication of the wolf (*Canis lupus*) could have been the consequence of an earlier commensal relationship between wolves and humans, which ever since has played an important role in human behavior.

In my view the development of several commensal species, some of which (*Passer domesticus, Mus musculus*) underwent full speciation, is the best indication for a long-term occupation of those Natufian sites where commensals appear.

Subsistence of the PPNA

The emergence of the Levantine PPNA has been explained as a rapid response to changing climatic conditions, like the Younger Dryas, during the Late Natufian. In such a model of cultural "punctuated equilibrium," Natufian lifeways were established following a major socioeconomic crisis and continued in a state close to homeostasis until they went through another major crisis that forced the establishment of the earliest phase of the Neolithic.

The onset of the early Neolithic may be placed in the southern Levant (based on dated wood, mainly *Tamarix*) around 10-10,200 B.P. The radiocarbon readings in phase BI and II in Muryebet are around 10-10,500 B.P. Hence, there is no evidence for synchroneity for the onset of the Neolithic between the northern and southern Levant (Bar-Yosef 1989). The large early Neolithic communities (Bar-Yosef 1989; Cauvin 1987) were already associated at their inception with either cultivated or intensively collected wild barley. Exploitation of vegetal resources seems to have greatly increased (various legumes, oats, acorns, pistachio nuts, and figs [Kislev and Bar-Yosef 1988; Kislev et al. 1986]), while the exploitation of animal resources seems to continue the Natufian tradition (specialized hunting of diverse vertebrates, among which many small species of mammals, birds, and reptiles are represented).

Most authorities indeed agree that early Neolithic communities subsisted on cereals, legumes, and wild seeds and fruits, as well as on a very broad spectral array of vertebrates, obtained through hunting, trapping, and fishing (Bar-Yosef and Belfer-Cohen 1991; Clutton-Brock 1978, 1979; Davis 1983; Helmer 1989; Hillman et al. 1989; Hillman and Davies 1992; Miller 1992; Moore 1985). Intentional cultivation seems to have marked the most significant departure in subsistence strategy from the Epipaleolithic. A large array of seeds and fruit remains has been recovered from PPNA sites (Bar-Yosef et al. 1991; Hillman et al. 1989; Hillman and Davies 1992; Kislev 1989; Miller 1992; van Zeist and Bakker-Heeres 1985; Zohary and Hopf 1988).

The most poorly known phase is the earliest Neolithic, ca. 10,500-9,500 B.P. (Bar-Yosef et al. 1991), mainly because of the rarity of excavated sites. The few archaeological deposits known from this period are the lower layers in Jericho, originally named "Pre-Pottery Neolithic A" (PPNA) by Kenyon (1957); the lower levels in the Tell of Mureybet on the middle Euphrates River (Cauvin 1977); and possibly the lowermost levels in Tell Aswad in the Damascus basin (Contenson 1983). In the southern Levant three additional sites were discovered during the last decade, two in the Jordan Valley: Gilgal (Noy et al. 1980) and Gesher (Garfinkel 1990) and Hatoula, in the western foothills of the Judean Hills (Lechevallier and Ronen 1985). Bioarchaeological data about human activities in the PPNA of the southern Levant are still limited to the following sites (Fig. 8):

Netiv Hagdud. The site lies at about -190/-200 m below sea level at the outlet of Wadi Kakar, 14 km north of Jericho (Bar-Yosef et al. 1991).

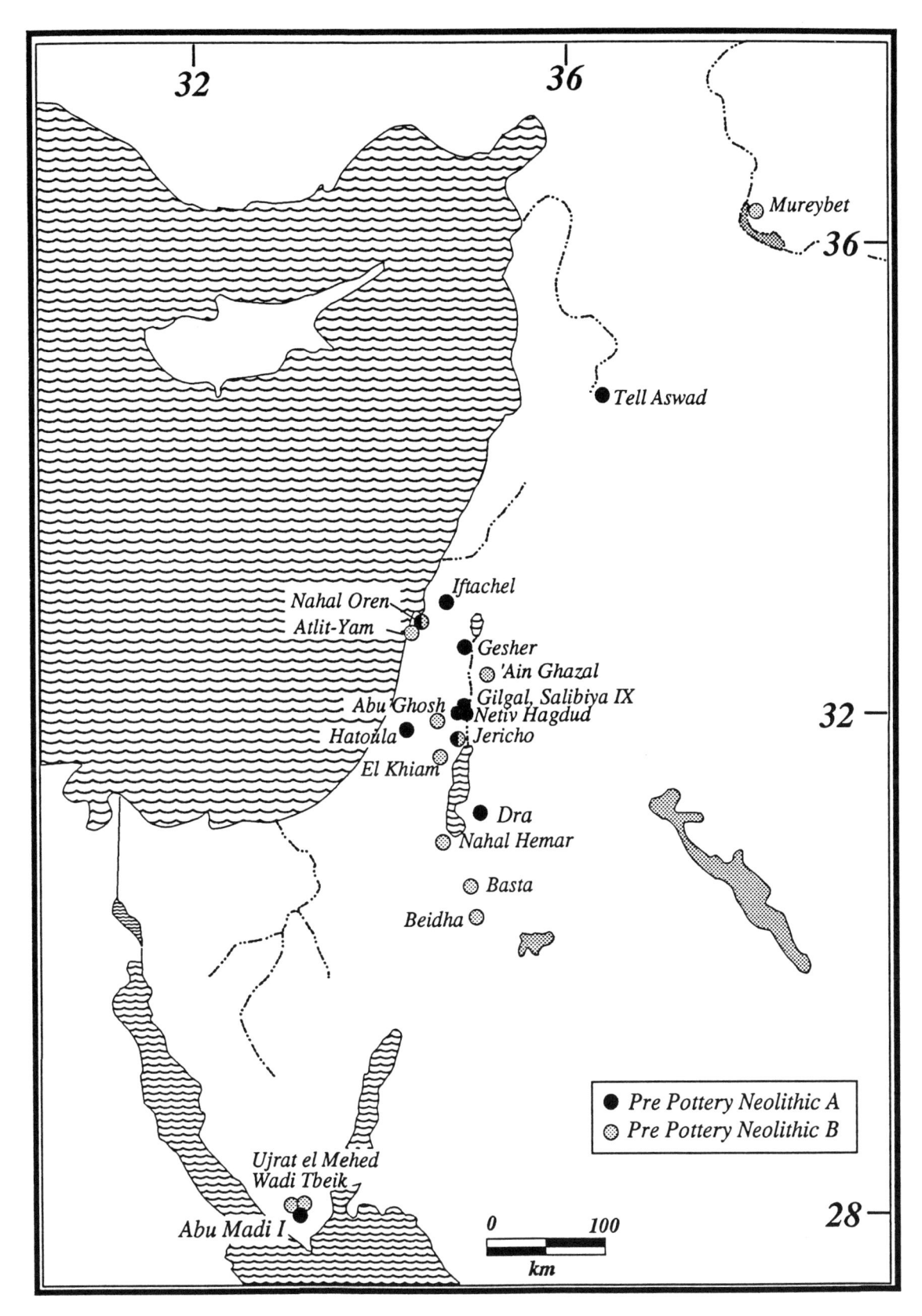

Fig. 8:
The main Pre-Pottery Neolithic A and Pre-Pottery Neolithic B sites in the southern Levant.

Jericho. The detailed results of the excavations here were mainly published by Crowfoot-Payne (1983), Marshall (1982), Kenyon (1981), and Kenyon and Holland (1983).

Gilgal. Situated on an elongated ridge, the site is located near Netiv Hagdud, surrounded by the same habitats and exposed to much the same environmental conditions (Noy et al. 1980; Bar-Yosef et al. 1991).

Salibiya IX. The site was discovered near Gilgal and Netiv Hagdud and produced a "Khiamian" lithic assemblage.

Gesher. Located in the Central Jordan Valley, the site was found to be a small village (Garfinkel 1990; Horwitz and Garfinkel 1991).

Hatoula (Layers 2–3). The site is located in the foothills of Judea and seems to be mostly adapted to the Late Natufian tool-kit, as argued by Ronen and Lechevallier (1985), Lechevallier et al. (1985), and Lechevallier and Ronen (1989).

Specialized hunting and trapping of a large spectrum of animals, but in particular water birds, as well as selective hunting of gazelles and some fishing in a few sites, provided the meat component in the diet of the PPNA villagers. Gazelle was still the main game animal in the Mediterranean belt, while in the arid zone both ibexes and gazelles constituted the main protein resource. Other big game, like *Dama mesopotamica, Bos primigenius, Sus scrofa,* and in a few sites also equids and *Alcelaphus buselaphus*, much as in the Natufian period, comprised a relatively small proportion of the protein resources (Fig. 9). A wide spectral array of smaller vertebrates, particularly water-fowl and hares, continued to comprise a significant portion of their diet.

Although the spectrum of food resources in Netiv Hagdud is extremely broad, in terms of biomass the artiodactyls, and among them the gazelles (and in second place the wild boar) greatly exceed all other groups of animals. However, if taken as a whole, the biomass of birds is very slightly less than that of the artiodactyls (Fig. 9). As in other PPNA sites, in Jericho the gazelle (*G. gazella*) was the predominant species (Clutton-Brock 1971, 1978, 1979, 1983). Clutton-Brock (1979) argues that these gazelles were not controlled by humans as suggested by Legge (1972), but their exploitation by means of drives and surrounds as described by Henry (1975) seems to be feasible. Obvious sex culling of gazelles was demonstrated in Netiv Hagdud. *V. vulpes* was very common in the PPNA assemblage, and, according to Clutton-Brock (1979), was also used for food. As at Netiv Hagdud, large game mammals (*Alcelaphus buselaphus, Dama mesopotamica, Capreolus capreolus, Bos primigenius,* large felids, *Capra ibex, Equus* sp. [*hemionus*]) were not common in the record. Sheep/goat proportion during this period is very low (4.3%), yet the existence of sheep, in particular wild sheep, in these strata should be re-evaluated. The only goat known from this region throughout the late Middle and Upper Pleistocene is *Capra ibex*.

The faunal assemblage of Gilgal is largely similar to that of Netiv Hagdud (Noy et al. 1980). The majority of the species that occupied the area of Gilgal no longer exist in the Lower Jordan Valley; most of them retreated northward, and some do not inhabit the southern Levant region at present. Most of the aquatic dwellers and the woodland and grassland dwellers disappeared from the region; only the rock dwellers, which are *a priori* better adapted to arid conditions, have survived there (*Procavia capensis*). The list of species offers enough evidence, as is also clearly shown in the assemblage of Netiv Hagdud, that the environmental conditions that prevailed there during the PPNA must have been different from those of the barren land of today: an area that can support only a typical desert biota.

The faunal analysis of the site of Hatoula undertaken by Davis (1985) has demonstrated differences between the PPNA and the Natufian faunal assemblages: a relatively higher proportion of birds and fish (and possibly hare too), and larger quantities of larger fish. Davis (1985) stresses as well that there is an increase in the hunting of smaller animals and fishes by more sophisticated techniques. Otherwise the Natufian and Khiamian large mammal assemblages show a striking similarity, which may suggest no significant change in the basic pattern of exploitation of large mammals, and no significant climatic changes.

The faunal assemblage from Gesher is too small for detailed intra-site or inter-site spatial comparisons, yet shows general similarities with the other PPNA sites along the Jordan Valley. *G. gazella* is the predominant large mammal. *Bos primigenius* and *Sus scrofa* are also present. Of the smaller mammals, *Lepus capensis, Vulpes vulpes,* and *Spalax ehrenbergi* were identified by Horwitz and Garfinkel (1991). A few unidentifiable avian and reptilian bones were also recorded, and much like all other PPNA sites along the Jordan Valley, claws of the freshwater crab *Potamon fluviatilis* are very common.

A comparison of the relative frequencies of the ungulate species in PPNA and Natufian sites shows that preferences for gazelles increase in time, from a minimum of 57% in the earlier Natufian of Hayonim Cave to 90% in Netiv Hagdud. Consequently the percentages of all other ungulate species decrease, but in particular that of the cervids. Preference for wild boars (*Sus scrofa*) remains largely the same, however. The frequencies of wild goats and ibexes range from only 2.5% to 6.1%. The steppe and savanna dwellers, like *Equus* sp. and *Alcelaphus buselaphus*, are always low in frequency (Fig. 9).

In most of the PPNA sites of the southern Levant, factors operate to constrain us from undertaking an overall microfaunal comparison for the period: the smaller mammals, as well as the passeriform birds, have not yet been thoroughly studied (Hatoula), or the samples are too small to permit a meaningful study (Gilgal, Salibiya IX), or not enough microfauna were retrieved due to the old archaeo-

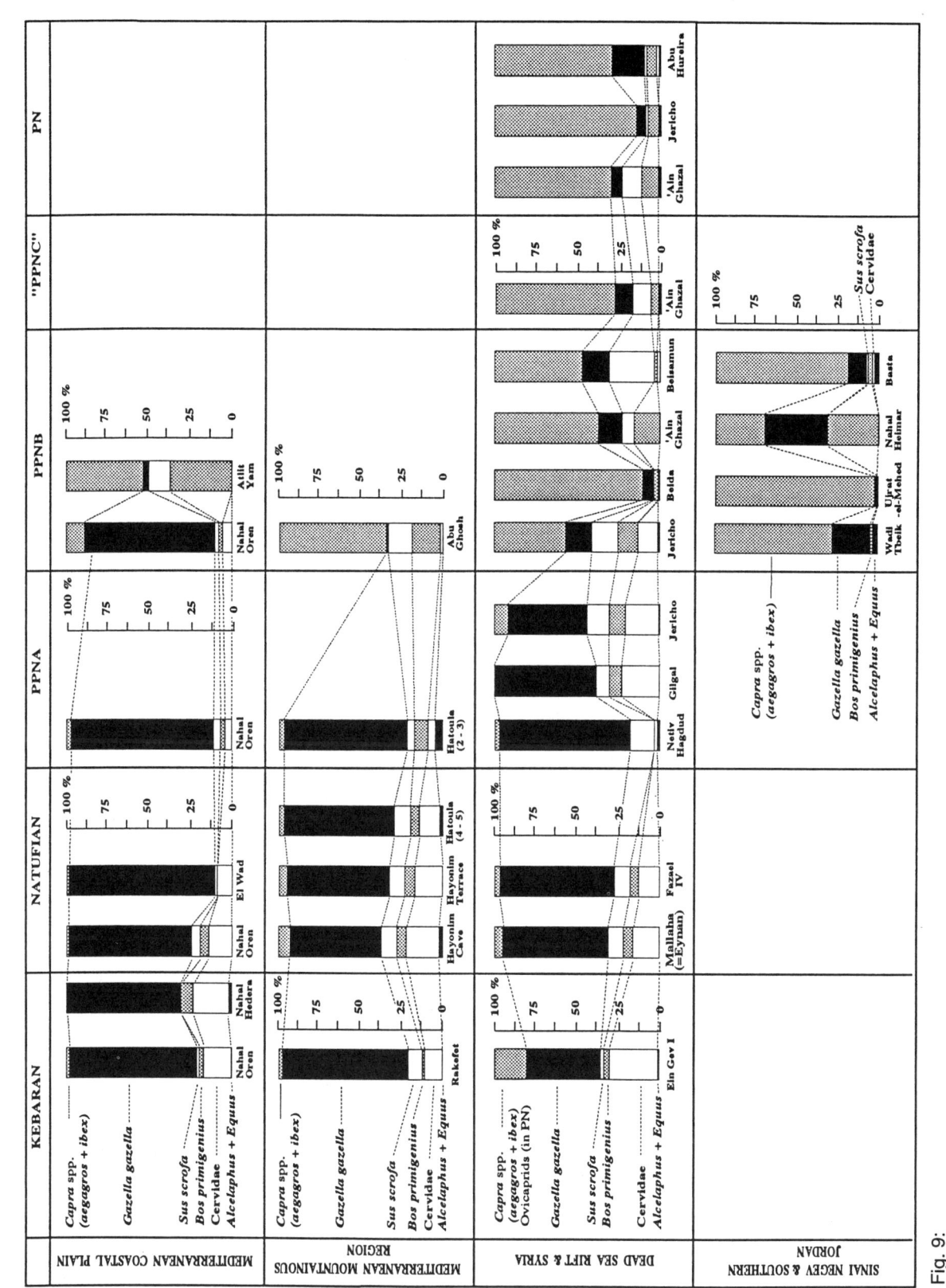

Fig. 9:
The relative abundance of ungulate species in the Kebaran, Natufian, PPNA, PPNB, and PN sites, in different regions of the southern Levant, showing the abrupt change from a universal predominance of gazelles to goats in some of the the PPNB sites.

logical methods by which the site was excavated (Jericho). Overall, it seems that the PPNA assemblages of large and medium-sized mammals and the non-passeriforms are basically similar, in terms of ecological occupation and preferences by their early Neolithic hunters, to those of the Natufian. In a comparison of the PPNA megafaunas of Jericho with those of Netiv Hagdud (sites which are separated by only some 13 km as the crow flies), *Bos primigenius* is absent from Netiv Hagdud, but, although never very common, is found in Jericho (and in all other PPNA sites). *Equus* sp. (probably *Equus hemionus*) and *Capreolus capreolus* are reported from the PPNA of Jericho (Clutton-Brock 1979), but are absent from all other PPNA sites. This disparity in the faunal makeup may be due to the great variability of the assemblages rather than to biological, geographical, or cultural factors.

Subsistence of the PPNB

The main PPNB sites in the southern Levant are as follows (see Fig. 8):

'Ain Ghazal (eastern part of the Jordan Valley, Jordan). A detailed description of the site has been published by Rollefson (1987), Rollefson and Köhler-Rollefson (1989), Rollefson and Simmons (1988), and Simmons et al. (1988), including the wide spectrum of floral and faunal remains recovered. The faunal assemblage alone consists of approximately 500,000 bone fragments, of which some 50,000 have been identified. Most of the material recovered dates to the PPNB component, but tantalizing evidence from the "PPNC" and Yarmoukian layers may shed light on the fate of the site in its latest phases.

Nahal Oren (Mt. Carmel). A very long cultural sequence was exposed here (Stekelis and Yizraeli 1963), based on numerous artifacts that indicated the presence of two phases of the Kebaran, Natufian, and PPNA and PPNB industries. Details on the site, excavations, lithics, and fauna are given in Noy et al. (1973).

Beidha. Located in southern Jordan roughly 165 km south of Jericho and 80 km south of the Dead Sea, and about 5 km north of Petra, it was excavated by Kirkbride over the course of seven seasons from 1958 to 1967 (Kirkbride 1966; Hecker 1975, 1982). It is situated on a terrace 900 m above sea level at the edge of a narrow belt of rugged mountainous terrain. This region marks the westernmost border of the higher and generally flat Arabian plateau (1,200-1,600 m a.s.l.).

Basta. The site is located southeast of Wadi Musa (Jordan), south of the Dead Sea, near Petra, at 1,420–1,460 m a.s.l. with 100–200 mm annual precipitation, within the Irano-Turanian phytogeographic belt (Becker 1991; Gebel 1986; Gebel et al. 1988).

Ujrat el-Mehed. Situated on top of an elongated low hill at the juncture of Wadi ed-Deir and the flat valley known as Sahel er Raha in southern Sinai (Bar-Yosef 1985; Dayan et al. 1986), the site is located about 1,600 m a.s.l. and served as a winter habitation. The technological and typological traits of the flint industry at Ujrat el-Mehed relate it to the second half of the PPNB period.

Wadi Tbeik. Located on the bank of a small gully of a tributary of Wadi Tbeik in southern Sinai (Bar-Yosef 1985; Tchernov and Bar-Yosef 1982), Wadi Tbeik's architecture indicates that the same group of people returned to the site, but its use was most probably for a relatively short period (something on the order of 20–40 years seems most likely). The site is regarded as a winter occupation site, the inhabitants of which occupied summer campsites in higher, more open areas.

Nahal Hemar Cave. A small, dark chamber on the geographic border between the Negev and the Judaean desert, Nahal Hemar, with its wealth of domestic objects and paraphernalia, is best explained as a territorial marker for a social unit that existed during PPNB times (Bar-Yosef and Alon 1988; Bar-Yosef and Schick 1989).

Yiftahel. The site is a huge PPNB village in the foothills of the Lower Galilee (Garfinkel 1987; Garfinkel et al. 1987).

Atlit-Yam. The site is a submerged village in the Mediterranean coast of Mt. Carmel (Galili and Nir 1993; Galili et al. 1993; Horwitz and Tchernov 1987).

A conspicuous increase in complexity in all aspects of the socioeconomy is the hallmark of the PPNB, especially when we examine sites outside the Levantine corridor, mainly on the western side of the intermontane Mediterranean belt where populations continued the tradition of the PPNA by practicing a mixed economy based on cultivation, specialized hunting with heavy reliance on gazelles, and gathering of wild plants and fruits. Cultivation of cereals and pulses was practiced within the Levantine corridor. By the middle of the ninth millennium B.P., goats and sheep, possibly diffused from the Taurus-Zagros region, make their appearance in some of the southern Levantine sites, followed by a significant shift from dependency on *Gazella* (or wild *Capra ibex nubiana* in the arid belt) to an abrupt reliance on (?domesticated) goat (Fig. 9), associated with a sharp reduction in the faunal spectrum. The archaeological remains that date to the end of the time span of the PPNB (9,500-8,000 B.P.) indeed testify to the presence of a highly complex socioeconomic structure in the Mediterranean Levant, demonstrated by long-distance connections and exchange relations within the PPNB area. The literature suggests that most cultural diffusions dispersed from north to south (Bar-Yosef and Belfer-Cohen 1989; Cauvin 1987; Gopher 1989; Kenyon 1957; Mellaart 1975).

According to Bar-Yosef and Meadow (in press), the shift in the pattern of early Neolithic settlement about 10,000 years ago led to a major socioeconomic change due to the pluvial conditions of the PPNA that ensured the survival of farming communities along the Levantine corridor. The success of these communities consequently led to rapid population increase, as revealed by the number of PPNB sites and the spread of the suite of cultivated plants into neighboring areas.

At the same time, the semi-arid and arid belt of the Syro-Arabian and Sinai deserts accommodated the old lifeways based on hunting and gathering. Plant remains (rarely preserved) and animal bones reflect the continuation of gathering and hunting (gazelles, ibexes, microvertebrates like hares, and a very broad spectrum of species of birds). The presence of grinding tools, often similar to those found in the villages, indicates the processing of seeds or grain of wild species. The latter could have been obtained either from local production or through exchange with the farming communities. It has been suggested that animal drives, known as "desert kites," were probably used by the desert groups to obtain large quantities of meat required by farming communities who depleted their nearby hunting grounds (Bar-Yosef 1986; Helms and Betts 1987). Thus the evidence for village sedentism in the PPNB is very strong and so are the indications for anticipated mobility in the desertic region (Bar-Yosef 1984, 1986; Moore 1985). Moreover, archaeological finds testify to various degrees of interaction between the two economic systems.

Many sites collapsed or were abandoned toward the end of the period, constituting a major break in the PPNB settlement pattern. At the site of 'Ain Ghazal, there is sufficient evidence to demonstrate significant cultural change toward the later phases of the PPNB (identified as "PPNC" by Rollefson 1987; Rollefson and Köhler-Rollefson 1989; Rollefson and Simmons 1988). The next cultural change brought about the establishment of what is known as the Yarmukian culture, which already contains ceramics and may be defined as early Pottery Neolithic.

Within the core area of farming communities, raising/hunting goats and sheep was supplemental to the economy. During the Middle PPNB the processes of incipient domestication, sensu Köhler-Rollefson (1987, 1989), Köhler-Rollefson et al. (1988), and Simmons et al. (1988), were well under way; and there is little doubt that goats were fully domesticated by the end of this phase. They argue that domesticated cattle and sheep appeared during the Late PPNB, and pigs and dogs joined the domesticates in the final phases of the PPNB ("PPNC" period: 7,500-8,000 B.P., Köhler-Rollefson 1989). The Late PPNB also witnessed an expanded exploitation of the desert-steppe regions as exemplified by sites in the eastern reaches of Syria and Jordan and in the Negev and Sinai. The pattern of arid lands exploitation intensified in the final phases of the PPNB, perhaps reflecting greater emphasis on pastoralism (Bar-Yosef and Belfer-Cohen 1989; Betts 1989; Garrard et al. 1988) and/or greater interaction between hunter-gatherer steppe dwellers and agriculturally based villagers in more mesic areas of the Levant (Bar-Yosef and Belfer-Cohen 1989). The situation in the coastal region of the southern Levant, even as far inland as Yiftahel (Horwitz, pers. comm.), does not fit the Middle-Late-Final PPNB pattern seen elsewhere in the Levant, for in this area, much as in the arid zone, a reliance on hunting wild game continued, with no evidence of animal husbandry at all. The only abrupt and clear economic break is seen in a very few sites during the late PPNB, when a replacement of gazelles by goats took place.

'Ain Ghazal stands out sharply in this demonstrable shift, showing continuous, or nearly continuous occupation at the same site. Elsewhere in the Levant, a pattern of abandonment and settlement of new sites is the common rule. Even at PPNB sites with a subsequent Pottery Neolithic occupation, such as Jericho, a substantial temporal gap occurs. At 'Ain Ghazal, with the documentation of the "PPNC" phase, a shift from a broad-based economy with a reliance on agriculture to one largely based on the exploitation of a few species of domestic animals can be observed.

Although, with the exception of 'Ain Ghazal, all known PPNB villages in southern Levant were abandoned at the end of the seventh millennium, settlements in the northern regions of the southern Levant (like the Damascus basin and the Mediterranean coast) continued to be occupied. Tentatively, certain economic and ecologic differences between the northern and the southern sites could account for this particular course of events. One of the more obvious economic differences between the two areas is the predominance of sheep in the north and the reliance on goats as the prime domestic animal in the south (Tchernov and Horwitz 1990).

Incipient animal husbandry in the Southern Levant

Harris (1977) emphasized that the origin of agriculture was tied directly to increased sedentism. But for him sedentism developed gradually, and the "broad spectrum" economy triggered an uncontrollable increase in population that consequently created a pressure on ever-shrinking resources. This process inevitably led to increasingly specialized exploitation of agricultural resources.

I argue that sedentism originated abruptly through a punctuational shift not yet to be explained by either biological or anthropological approaches. It is the high level of social organization, the creation of a social hierarchy and economical stratification, the marked division of labor (hunting waterfowl requires utterly different skills than trapping song birds, or partridges, or gathering special kinds of cereals) that mentally prepared and economically led a sedentary society toward food production. It is the new and far more complex and sophisticated pattern of interaction of humans with the environment that enabled the newly emerged sedentary populations to cope more efficiently with the biotic world, as well as with the elements through a new mental insight of the world around them.

For Reed (1983) the origin of agriculture and domestication should be regarded as a part of the evolution of behavior, with emphasis on the increasing use of energy by different living groups of organisms. For him, domesticated animals are an example of cultural symbiosis, with each partner being a secondary energy-trap for the other. Such symbiotic relationships must be developed during a long enough period to allow the development of such (or any) biological interspecific relationships. The "incubation" period from early sedentism to incipient domestication could have allowed the development of this kind of symbiosis. Reed (1983) accepts the idea that sedentism caused increase in population which led to over-hunting, reduction in meat resources, and domestication. Yet he agrees that the behavioral shift from hunting to herding is not clear.

Bar-Yosef and Meadow (in press) conclude that the origins of agriculture must be viewed in the light of a fluctuating climatic regime that broadened and then constricted areas suitable for productive hunting and gathering and later for cultivation and pastoralism.

For Rindos (1984:175) it was the early encouragement of the consumption of low-valued resources; a process that occurred "before domesticates had began to make any substantial contribution to the diet." Yet again it should be emphasized that the first domesticates appeared more than 2,000 years after the abrupt shift to broad spectrum dietary logistics. Rindos (1984), however, agrees that the development of sedentism and agroecology are directly connected with domestication. The question is, why such a long period elapsed between the earliest sedentism of the Natufians that emerged in a limited region of the southern Levant, and the appearance of the earliest domesticates much later in another place (northern Mesopotamia).

Cauvin (1989) pointed out that it is the lengthy sociological and cultural maturation which emerged within the Natufian domain of sedentism that led humans to food production. Neolithization for Cauvin (1989) appears as a progressive and overall transformation, in which the food production is more the consequence of a cultural and mental change than the true cause of other changes. Indeed, the long "incubation" period was mentally, socially, and economically obligatory in order to reach the point of intentional management of wild populations of just the right species, a process that virtually began already in the Early Natufian by selective culling by age and sex of gazelles (unfortunately just the wrong kind of animal to start domestication). Even during the period when domestication was already on its way, the earliest agriculturalists had no preconceived ideas of the end products they wished to get through intentional selection. Rather, morphogenetic changes associated with domestication essentially resulted from unconscious or indirect selection by humans, and appeared as a natural by-product of induced environmental conditions created under domestication (for more details, see Tchernov and Horwitz 1991). Morphogenetic changes observed in primeval domesticates were initially due to spontaneous responses of the animals to the special anthropogenic quasi-isolated habitats.

The idea that the Natufians may have been the earliest farmers was suggested by Garrod in 1932 and, in spite of later criticism, was revived by others and supported by the experimental studies on sickle blades (Unger-Hamilton 1991). Other researchers have also argued that incipient agriculture may have first occurred even as early as the Late Natufian (Cauvin 1977, 1987; Moore 1989). To date there is no substantial evidence for incipient cultivation of cereals during the Natufian, but it must be acknowledged that traces of plant husbandry would be difficult to verify (Hillman et al. 1989). Unger-Hamilton (1989, 1991) has argued that the evidence for harvesting of cereals grown in loose soil suggests that some cultivation of cereals could have been practiced in the Natufian (see, however, Anderson 1991). In any case, the Natufian and PPNA periods can be regarded as an incubation period for the beginning of food production. Systematic cultivation, however, would have rapidly caused the domestication of wheat and barley (Hillman and Davies 1992), and even for the early Neolithic (= PPNA), the state of domestication of cereals is still debated (see below). Therefore intensive and extensive harvesting of wild cereals as part of an anticipated summer mobility pattern of Natufian communities seems to be more plausible.

Archaeologists (Belfer-Cohen et al. 1991) are in general agreement that the appearance of the Neolithic agricultural societies was in response to conditions of stress that prevailed in the preceding Natufian culture (Henry 1989). Smith et al. (1984), however, stress that at least in this region (southern Levant), the initial steps in plant and animal domestication were not associated with environmental stress or deteriorating health status. Moreover, contrary to the view expressed by Sillen (1984; see also Valla 1987), there is no indication of substantial health deterioration from the Early to Late Natufian. The transition from the Natufian way of living (i.e., intensive exploitation of local resources and hunting) to Neolithic farming and hunting was an intensification of a process that actually began in the Early Natufian: "The emergence of the Natufian was a 'point of no return' that became consolidated in the Early Neolithic" (Bar Yosef and Belfer-Cohen 1989:490).

There is no consistent pattern for the existence of domesticated caprovids, or even incipient domestication, during the PPNB of this region, as stressed by Horwitz

(1989), since the only evidence for "domestication" is based on *Capra/Gazella* frequencies. Yet the proportion of *Capra* to *Gazella* is very inconsistent. However, this unclear picture is mainly due to our profound ignorance about the detailed floral and faunal composition of the assemblages, the detailed anatomical structure of the relevant species, and the lack of common zooarchaeological methods to deal quantitatively with such problems. As a working hypothesis, it may be argued that along the "corridor" (Bar-Yosef 1989; Horwitz 1989) the reliance on caprovids was more well developed than within the montane Mediterranean belt, or on the coastal plains (Yiftahel, Munhatta, Abu Ghosh, Nahal Oren, etc.). The large differences in the exploitation of caprovids may have been due to the critical attrition of the gazelle populations along the Jordan Valley, which compelled people to rely on the more difficult hunting of *Capra*, due to the growing scarcity of gazelles. A complete reliance on hunting of wild (small and large) game during the PPNB is well known from the desert areas of southern Sinai like Wadi Tbeik and Ujrat el-Mehed (Dayan et al. 1986; Tchernov and Bar-Yosef 1982). These regions during this period were still much more mesic and allowed intensive hunting.

Many scholars agree that herding of domestic animals was always associated with access to plant cultivation. Others pointed out that animal herding might have come before cultivation, and that sheep and goat herding emerged in northwestern Mesopotamia in the context of seasonal camps (see, in particular, Hole 1984, 1989). Even if all the evidence pinpoints the time and place of these events, sedentism took place about 2,000 years earlier than animal domestication, dispersing northward and eastward as far as the eastern parts of the Fertile Crescent, transporting not only a plethora of new knowledge and ideas, but new insight of communal life under utterly different socioeconomic rules, and the knowledge of how to manipulate wild populations. Post-sedentism new cultural and technical traditions can be transmitted and applied to everyday life even by quite small groups of people.

One of the problems raised is the traditional "diffusion" vs. "autochthonous" argument concerning the beginning of domestication in the southern Levant. Horwitz (1989) argues that, to date, there are no solid data to support the claim that domestic sheep and goat were introduced into the southern Levant from northern domains. Bar-Yosef and Belfer-Cohen (1989) and Clutton-Brock (1983) prefer, however, the diffusion explanation for the earliest appearance of animal domesticates in this region.

Clear evidence for a shift to early domestic forms (i.e., sheep, goat, cattle, pig) indicates that this change took place during the thousand-year period from 9,500 to 8,500 (i.e., during the PPNB). While sheep were probably domesticated in the plains and the hilly flanks of the Taurus-Zagros region, there is as yet no clear core area for the beginning of domestication of the goat. For Bar-Yosef and Meadow (in press) the reason for domesticating these species is embedded in the impoverishment of the wild life around those sites due to the growing human population, increased sedentism, and over-exploitation of the resources around those long-term sites. Their speculation that the population of game animals, especially ungulates, would have declined both regionally (e.g., in the central and southern Levant) and locally (i.e., immediately around settled communities, wherever located) is in concert with my arguments (Tchernov 1993).

The spread of cultivation and the domestication of caprovines and, later, cattle and pigs took place during the PPNB. This is a long span of time (around 2,000 years). Hence subdividing this period is essential because referring to a site as of "PPNB period" is uninformative. The Natufian period was the formative period of the PPNB. Sometime during the 2,000 years of the PPNB period active food production emerged. In addition, the seed was planted for the appearance of social, religious, and economic complexity that we can already observe toward the end of the PPNB. This is why it is of the utmost importance to subdivide the PPNB into socioeconomic cultural levels, mainly based on existence or non-existence of domesticated animals.

The increase in the relative frequency of *Capra* vs. *Gazella* during the PPNB is obvious. Yet there is no convincing anatomical evidence that these goats were already domesticated anywhere in the southern Levant during the PPNB. On the contrary, it seems that they were mostly wild. There is no argument that there is an obvious shift during the PPNB, particularly along the Jordan Valley or the "corridor," from extensive gazelle hunting to what is sometimes an exclusive reliance on goat. The reason for this phenomenological shift from preferring one species to another could also have been a direct consequence of an "overkill" of gazelles during the PPNA due to prolonged sedentism.

For Köhler-Rollefson et al. (1988) and Köhler-Rollefson and Rollefson (1990), domestication of goat, of all potential animals, might have seemed like an ideal answer to the growing scarcity of faunal resources, and their availability undoubtedly contributed to human population growth. Their rising numbers exerted strains on the environment which at first were imperceptible but steadily gained momentum: they prevented the replenishment of arboreal resources, and instead of articulating with cultivation they competed with it spatially. Their pasture requirements not only increased in proportion to their numbers, but it was necessary to compensate for the gradual decline of the carrying capacity due to year-round grazing. Thus in order to maintain the accustomed supply of game, hunters would need to go farther afield, or more heavily exploit populations of smaller and less rewarding animals such as hares, birds, and reptiles. *Sensu* Bar-Yosef and Meadow (in press), another response would have been "to keep captured animals alive in settlements in order to have them available particularly for critical social functions. Once such animals began to reproduce in captivity, the domestication process had begun."

No less problematic is the issue of the presence of wild sheep during the later Pleistocene–early Holocene in the southern Levant. In spite of the isolated find of Davis et al. (1982) of wild sheep in the Negev of Israel, no other solid evidence for the occurrence of wild sheep in this region is known (but see Uerpmann 1987, 1989). The in situ domestication of sheep in the southern Levant is even less clearly established.

The following arguments support the diffusion scenario: while wild goats occur in the faunal collections of Epipaleolithic and PPNA sites, although in very small percentages, wild sheep are essentially absent from the original wild fauna of the southern Levant south of the Lebanese mountains (but see Davis et al. 1982 and Uerpmann 1987, 1989). However, goat and sheep made up the bulk of the hunted game in the Lebanon region and in the Taurus and Zagros mountains since Mousterian times. There is ample evidence to indicate that the domestication of these herd mammals took place during the early Neolithic period in the Zagros region and perhaps in the eastern Taurus. The exchange networks which enabled the incorporation of domesticated cereals into the Zagros economy were probably responsible for the introduction of goat and sheep into the Levant. Thus, the shift in the faunal spectra is reflected in the PPNB sites which in the southern Levant are located within the "corridor."

One more phenomenon should be discussed here as it may have a direct connection with the issue of in situ domestication. Intentional manipulation of wild populations in the PPNB was shown in several southern Levantine sites within the Arabian desert belt: in Beidha (Hecker 1975, 1982), in Ujrat el-Mehed (Dayan et al. 1986), and in Wadi Tbeik (Tchernov and Bar-Yosef 1982). In all these cases human intervention in the population structure (mainly through selective culling by sex) was executed on *Capra*. Differential culling was already practiced by the Natufians, and hence could have been transmitted traditionally through the local PPNA populations. Our difficulty rests in the unfortunate situation that there are too few PPNA sites with large enough samples of ungulates to allow detailed studies on this period in this region. Even in such rich sites as Netiv Hagdud (Bar-Yosef et al. 1991) the quantity of large mammals is too small for a thorough demographic study of the herbivores. Our present limited knowledge of these periods in the southern Levant allows us only to say that autochthonous domestication is not yet well proven for the region of the Jordan Valley during the PPNB, or even to say that caprovids were morphogenetically indeed domesti-

cated. The inhabitants of the desert regions of the southern Levant do not appear to have either practiced or adapted animal domestication until a much later (Pottery Neolithic, or even Chalcolithic) period.

One of the central disputes concerning these periods is whether there was a cultural continuity from the Natufian to the PPNA. Bar-Yosef and Belfer-Cohen (1989), however, argue that this issue is unjustifiably over-stressed. Despite the undeniable biological persistence of the same indigenous population, both culturally and economically the PPNA marks a major cultural change, but an autochthonous one. This change is evidenced by art objects and technique, the heat treatment of flint tools, the uses of adzes and celts, the long-distance exchange of obsidian, the increase in site size, and building techniques. Yet the basic concepts and technique of animal exploitation may possibly demonstrate an indigenous unilinear continuity from the Natufian tradition (Henry 1989). It does seem plausible that there is a traditional cultural and practical continuum for exploitation of the biotic resources (not necessarily of technology and architecture) which goes all the way from Early Natufian through the PPNB in the southern Levant. With only insignificant changes in animal exploitation during the PPNA, this tradition was still employed by the PPNB populations in those areas where exploitation of caprovids (whether domesticated or not) was still relatively low (Yiftahel, Abu Ghosh, Nahal Oren). Gradualistic approaches deny the abruptness of the emergence of new socioeconomic structures. For example, Perrot (1989) suggests that the Natufian cultural complex gradually became early Neolithic, with oval semi-subterranean dwelling structures, flexed single burials, and the use of lunates being markers of continuity. Bar-Yosef and Meadow (in press), however, emphasize that in the absence of systematic wet or dry sieving one is unlikely to turn up major changes in lithic, faunal, and floral evidence, and hence the role of technological or economic continuity is decidedly problematical. They argue that comparing dwelling forms while ignoring the addition of mud-bricks as building materials, new type of storage facilities, bone tools, and the use of polished celts in the PPNA is meaningless. They also stress that flexed burials already occur in Upper Paleolithic sites.

The observations of Zohary (1989), based on cytogenetic data, conform with our description of successive thresholds in the Neolithic Revolution. It is in the latter phases that domesticated cereals and legumes were moved across the Taurus into Anatolia and to the inter-montane valleys of the Zagros. In conclusion, the role of the direct ancestors of the Natufians, and their social and economic decisions taken around 13,000 B.P., proved to be crucial for the ensuing history of the entire Near East. Plant domestication and incipient animal husbandry constitute the key features of the Near Eastern Neolithic. Although the term "revolution" has become inextricably associated with the events of this period, it is still a matter of dispute whether animal domestication is to be regarded as a punctuational departure from previous types of human-animal relationships or represents the culmination of a long process of increasingly sophisticated exploitation techniques starting with the sedentization of the Natufian populations.

References

Allen, P. M. 1976. Evolution, Population Dynamics, and Stability. *Proceedings of the National Academy of Sciences*, USA. 73:665–668.

Allen, P. M., J. L. Deneubourg, and M. Sanglier. 1978. *Dynamic Urban Growth Models*. Transportation System Center, Cambridge, MA.

Anderson, P. 1991. Harvesting of Wild Cereals During the Natufian as Seen from the Experimental Cultivation and Harvest of Wild Einkorn Wheat and Microwear Analysis of Stone Tools In *The Natufian Culture in the Levant*, ed. O. Bar-Yosef and F. R. Valla, pp. 521–556. International Monographs in Prehistory, Ann Arbor, MI.

Arensburg, B. 1985. A Short Review of Palaeopathology in the Middle East. *Mitekufat Haeven* 21–32.

Ayala, F. J. 1988. Can "Progress" be Defined as a Biological Concept? In *Evolutionary Progress*, ed. M. H. Nitecki, pp. 75–96. The University of Chicago Press, Chicago and London.

Baharav, D. 1974. Notes on the Population Structure and Biomass of the Mountain Gazelle *Gazella gazella gazella*. *Israel Journal of Zoology* 23:39–44.

―――― 1983a. Observation on the Ecology of the Mountain Gazelle in the Upper Galilee, Israel. *Journal of Arid Environments* 4:63–69.

―――― 1983b. Reproductive Strategies in Female Mountain and Dorcas Gazelles (*Gazella gazella gazella* and *Gazella dorcas*). *Journal of Zoology (London)* 200:445–453.

Baruch, U., and S. Bottema. 1991. Palynological Evidence for Climatic Changes in the Levant ca. 17,000–9,000 B.P. In *The Natufian Culture in the Levant*, ed. O. Bar-Yosef and F. R. Valla, pp. 11–20. International Monographs in Prehistory, Ann Arbor, MI.

Bar-Yosef, O. 1970. *The Epi-Palaeolithic Cultures of Palestine*. Ph.D. diss., The Hebrew University of Jerusalem.

―――― 1975. The Epipaleolithic in Palestine and Sinai. In *Problems in Prehistory: North Africa and the Levant*, ed. F. Wendorf. Southern Methodist Press, Dallas.

―――― 1981. The "Pre-Pottery Neolithic" Period in the Southern Levant. In *Préhistoire du Levant*, ed. J. Cauvin and P. Sanlaville, pp. 551–570. Colloques Internationaux du CNRS 598. Paris.

―――― 1983. The Natufian in the Southern Levant. In *The Hilly Flanks. Essays on the Prehistory of Southwestern Asia*, ed. T. C. Young, P. E. L. Smith, and P. Mortenson, pp. 11–37. Studies in Ancient Oriental Civilization No. 36. Oriental Institute of the University of Chicago, Illinois.

―――― 1984. Seasonality among Hunter-gatherers in Southern Sinai. In *Animals and Archaeology*, Vol. 2, ed. J. Clutton-Brock and C. Grigson, pp. 145–160. BAR International Series 202. British Archaeological Reports, Oxford.

―――― 1985. The Stone Age of Sinai. Studi di Paleontologia in Paglisi. *La Sapienza, Roma*, pp. 109–122.

―――― 1986. The Walls of Jericho. *Current Anthropology* 27:157–162.

―――― 1987. Late Pleistocene Adaptations in the Levant. In *The Pleistocene Old World: Regional Perspectives*, ed. O. Soffer, pp. 219–236. Plenum, New York.

―――― 1989. The PPNA in the Levant—An Overview. *Paléorient* 15:57–63.

Bar-Yosef, O., and D. Alon. 1988. The Excavations in Nahal Heimar Cave. *Atiqot* 18:1–30.

Bar-Yosef, O., and A. Belfer-Cohen. 1989. The Origins of Sedentism and Farming Communities in the Levant. *Journal of World Prehistory* 3:445–498.

―――― 1991. From Sedentary Hunter Gatherers to Territorial Farmers in the Levant. In *Between Bands and States*, ed. S. A. Gregg, pp. 181–202. Center for Archaeological Investigations, Occasional Papers 9. Southern Illinois University.

Bar-Yosef, O., A. Gopher, E. Tchernov, and M. E. Kislev. 1991. Netiv Hagdud: An Early Neolithic Village Site in the Jordan Valley. *Journal of Field Archaeology* 18:405–424.

Bar-Yosef, O., and N. Goren. 1973. Natufian Remains in Hayonim Cave. *Paléorient* 1:49–68.

Bar-Yosef, O., and R. Meadow. in press. The Origins of Agriculture in the Near East. In *Last Hunters–First Farmers*, ed. T. D. Price and G. Gebaur. School of American Research, Santa Fe.

Bar-Yosef, O., and T. Schick. 1989. Early Neolithic Organic Remains from Nahal Hemar Cave. *National Geographic Research* 5:176–190.

Bar-Yosef, O., and J. C. Vogel. 1987. Relative and Absolute Chronology of the Epi-Paleolithic in the Southern Levant. In *Chronologies in the Middle East: Relative Chronologies and Absolute Chronology 16,000–4,000 B.P.*, ed. O. Aurenche, F. Hours, and J. Evin, pp. 219–245. BAR International Series 379. British Archaeological Reports, Oxford.

Becker, C. 1991. The Analysis of Mammalian Bones from Basta, a Pre-Pottery Neolithic Site in Jordan: Problems and Potential. *Paléorient* 17:59–75.

Begin, Z. B., W. Broeker, B. Buchbinder, Y. Druckman, A. Kaufman, M. Magaritz, and D. Neev. 1985. Dead Sea and Lake Lisan Levels During the Last 30,000 Years. *Reports of the Geological Survey of Israel* 29:1–17.

Belfer-Cohen, A. 1989. The Definition of the Natufian: A Suggestion. In *Investigations in South Levantine Prehistory*, ed. O. Bar-Yosef and B. Vandermeersch, pp. 297–308. BAR International Series 497. British Archaeological Reports, Oxford.

―――― 1991. The Natufian in the Levant. *Annual Review of Anthropology* 20:167–186.

Belfer-Cohen, A., L. A. Schepartz, and B. Arensburg. 1991. New Biological Data for the Natufian Populations in Israel. In *The Natufian Culture in the Levant*, ed. O. Bar-Yosef and F. R. Valla, pp. 411–424. International Monographs in Prehistory, Ann Arbor, MI.

Bertram, B. C. R. 1974. Serengeti Predators and their Social Systems. In *Serengeti Dynamics of Ecosystem*, ed. A. R. E. Sinclair and M. Norton-Griffiths, pp. 221–248. University of Chicago Press, Chicago.

Betts, A. 1989. The Pre-Pottery Neolithic Period in Eastern Jordan. *Paléorient* 15:147–153.

Binford, S. 1968. Early Upper Pleistocene Adaptations in the Levant. *American Anthropologist* 70:707–717.

―――― 1981. *Bones, Ancient Men and Modern Myths.* Academic Press, San Francisco.

Bouchud, J. 1987. *Les mammifères et la petite faune du gisement Natufien d'Israël.* Mémoires et Travaux du Centre de Recherche Francais de Jerusalem. Association Paléorient, Paris.

Braidwood, R. J. 1973. The Early Village in Southwestern Asia. *Journal of Near Eastern Studies* 32:34–39.

―――― 1975. *Prehistoric Men*, 5th ed. Scott, Freeman, Glenview, IL.

Byrd, B. F. 1989. The Natufians: Settlement Variability and Economic Adaptations in the Levant at the End of the Pleistocene. *Journal of World Prehistory* 3:159–197.

Campana, D. V., and P. J. Crabtree. 1991a. Communal Hunting in the Natufian of the Southern Levant: The Social and Economic Implications. *Journal of Mediterranean Archaeology* 3:223–243.

―――― 1991b. More on Communal Hunting. *Journal of Mediterranean Archaeology* 4:125–128.

Cauvin, J. 1977. Les fouilles de Mureybet (1972–1974) et leur signification pour les origines de sedentarisation au Proche-Orient. *Annual of the American School of Oriental Research* 44:19–48.

―――― 1987. Chronologie relative et chronologie absolue dans le Néolithique du Levant nord et d'Anatolie entre 10.000–8.000 B.P. In *Chronologies in the Middle East: Relative Chronologies and Absolute Chronology 16,000–4,000 B.P.*, ed. O. Aurenche, F. Hours, and J. Evin, pp. 325–342. BAR International Series 379. British Archaeological Reports, Oxford.

―――― 1989. La Néolithisation au Levant et sa première diffusion. In *Néolithisation*, ed. O. Aurenche and J. Cauvin, BAR International Series 379. British Archaeological Reports, Oxford.

Childe, V. G. 1951. *Man Makes Himself.* Mentor Books, New York.

Clutton-Brock, J. 1971. The Primary Food Animals of the Jericho Tell from the Proto-Neolithic to the Byzantine Period. *Levant* 3:41–55.

―――― 1978. Early Domestication and the Ungulate Fauna of the Levant during the Pre-Pottery Neolithic Period. In *The Environmental History of the Near and Middle East since the Ice Age*, ed. W. C. Brice, pp. 29–40. Academic Press, New York.

―――― 1979. The Mammalian Remains from the Jericho Tell. *Proceedings of the Prehistoric Society* 45:135–157.

―――― 1983. The Animal Remains. Appendix I. In *Excavations at Jericho*, Vol. 5, ed. K. M. Kenyon and T. A. Holland, pp. 802–803. British School of Archaeology in Jerusalem, London.

Cohen, M. N. 1977. *The Food Crisis in Prehistory: Overpopulation and the Origins of Agriculture.* Yale University Press, New Haven.

Collier, J. D. 1986. Entropy in Evolution. *Biological Philosophy* 1:5–24.

Contenson, H. de. 1983. Early Agriculture in Western Asia. In *The Hilly Flanks and Beyond: Studies in Ancient Oriental Civilizations*, ed. T. C. Young, P. Smith, and P. Mortensen, pp. 57–65. Series No. 36. University of Chicago Press, Chicago.

Contenson, H. de, and W. van Liere. 1964. Sondage a Tell Ramad en 1963. *Annales Archéologiques Arabs-Syriens* 14:109–124.

Cope, C. 1992. Gazelle Hunting Strategies in the Southern Levant. In *The Natufian Culture in the Levant*, ed. O. Bar-Yosef and F. R. Valla, pp. 341–358. International Monographs in Prehistory, Ann Arbor, MI.

Crabtree, P. J., D. V. Campana, and A. Belfer-Cohen. 1992. First Results of the Excavations at Salibiya I, Lower Jordan Valley. In *The Natufian Culture and the Origins of the Levantine Neolithic*, ed. O. Bar-Yosef and F. R. Valla, pp. 161–172. Archaeological Series 1. International Monographs in Prehistory, Ann Arbor, MI.

Crowfoot-Payne, J. 1983. The Flint Industries of

Jericho. In *Excavations at Jericho*, Vol. 5, ed. K. A. Kenyon and T. A. Holland. British School of Archaeology in Jerusalem, London.

Damuth, J. 1981. Home Range Overlap and Species Energy Use among Herbivorous Mammals. *Biological Journal of the Linnaean Society* 15:185–193.

Darmon, F. 1984. Analyses polliniques de deux sites de la basse vallée Jourdain: Fazael VIII et Salibiya IX. *Paléorient* 10:106–110.

―――― 1987. Analyses polliniques de trois sites Natoufiens (ancien, récent, final) dans la région de Salibiya-Fazael. *Paléorient* 13:121–129.

―――― 1988. Essai de reconstitution climatique de l'Épipaléolithique au début du Néolithique ancien dans la région de Fazaël-Salibiya (basse vallée du Jourdain) d'après la palynologie. *C. R. Academie Scientifique, Paris* 307:677–682.

Darmon, F., A. Emery-Barbier, and A. Leroi-Gourhan. 1989. Examples d'occupation régionale au Proche-Orient en function des variations paléoclimatiques. *Cahiers du Quaternaire* 13:21–38.

Davis, S. J. 1974. Animal Remains from the Kebaran Site of Ein-Gev I: Jordan Valley, Israel. *Paléorient* 2:453–462.

―――― 1978. *The Large Mammals of the Upper Pleistocene-Holocene in Israel*. Ph.D. diss., The Hebrew University of Jerusalem.

―――― 1981. The Effects of Temperature Change and Domestication on the Body Size of Late Pleistocene to Holocene Mammals in Israel. *Paleobiology* 7:101–114.

―――― 1983. The Age Profiles of Gazelles Predated by Ancient Man in Israel. Possible Evidence for a Shift from Seasonality to Sedentism in the Natufian. *Paléorient* 9:55–62.

―――― 1985. A Preliminary Report of the Fauna from Hatoula: A Natufian Khiamian (PPNA) Site near Latrun, Israel. In *Le Site Natufien-Khiamian de Hatoula près de Latrun*, ed. M. Lechevallier and A. Ronen, Appendix B, No. 1, pp. 71–98. Cahiers du Centre de Recherche Francais de Jérusalem, Paris.

―――― 1988. Nahal Hemar Cave. The Larger Mammal Remains. *'Atiqot* 18:68–72.

Davis, S. J., N. Goring-Morris, and A. Gopher. 1982. Sheep Bones from the Negev Palaeolithic. *Paléorient* 8:87–91.

Davis, S. J., and F. R. Valla. 1978. Evidence for Domestication of the Dog 12,000 Years Ago in the Natufian of Israel. *Nature* 276:608–610.

Dayan, T., E. Tchernov, O. Bar-Yosef, and Y. Yom-Tov. 1986. Animal Exploitation in Ujrat-el-Mehed, a Neolithic Site in Southern Sinai. *Paléorient* 12:105–116.

Dayan T., E. Tchernov, Y. Yom-Tov, and D. Simberloff. 1989a. On the Use of Mammalian Size for Inferring Paleoclimatic Changes. In *Environmental Quality and Ecosystem Stability*, Vol. 4B, ed. E. Spanier, E. Y. Steinberger, and M. Luria, pp. 73–80. Environmental Quality ISEEQS Publications, Jerusalem.

―――― 1989b. Ecological Character Displacement in Saharo-Arabian *Vulpes*: Outfoxing Bergmann's Rule. *Oikos* 55:263–272.

Dunnell, R. C. 1988. The Concept of Progress in Cultural Evolution. In *Evolutionary Progress*, ed. M. H. Nitecki, pp. 169–194. University of Chicago Press, Chicago and London.

Dyke, C. 1988. Cities as Dissipative Structures. In *Entropy Information and Evolution*, ed. B. H. Weber and D. J. Smith, pp. 355–367. MIT Press, Cambridge and London.

Edwards, P. C. 1991. More than One, Less than Five Hundred: Comments on Campana and Crabtree, and Communal Hunting. *Journal of Mediterranean Archaeology* 4:109–120.

Fisher, B. A. 1930. *The Genetical Theory of Natural Selection*. Oxford University Press, Oxford.

Flannery, K. V. 1969. Origins and Ecological Effects of Early Domestication in Iran and the Near East. In *The Domestication of Plants and Animals*, ed. P. J. Ucko and T. W. Dimbleby, pp. 73–100. London.

―――― 1972. The Origins of the Village as a Settlement Type in Mesoamerica and the Near East: A Comparative Study. In *Man, Settlement and Urbanism*, ed. R. Tringham, P. J. Ucko, and T. W. Dimbley, pp. 23–53. Duckworth, London.

Galili, E., and Y. Nir. 1993. The Submerged Pre-Pottery Neolithic Water Well of Atlit-Yam, Northern Israel, and its Palaeoenvironmental Implications. *The Holocene* 3:265–270.

Galili, E., M. Weinstein-Evron, I. Hershkovitz, A. Gopher, M. Kislev, O. Lernau, L. Kolska-Horwitz, and H. Lernau. 1993. Atlit-Yam: A Prehistoric Site on the Sea Floor off the Israeli Coast. *Journal of Field Archaeology* 20:133–157.

Garfinkel, Y. 1987. Yiftahel: A Neolithic Village from the Seventh Millennium B.C. in Lower Galilee, Israel. *Journal of Field Archaeology* 14:199–212.

―――― 1990. Gesher, un nouveau site "Néolithique Précéramique A" dans la moyenne vallée du Jourdain, Israël. *L'Anthropologie* 94:903–906.

Garfinkel, Y., I. Carmi, and C. Vogel. 1987. Dating of Horsebean and Lentil Seeds from the Pre-Pottery Neolithic B Village of Yiftah'el. *Israel Exploration Journal* 37:40–42.

Garrard, A. N., A. Betts, B. Byrd, and C. Hunt. 1988. Prehistoric Environments and Settlement in the Azraq Basin: An Interim Report on the 1984 Season.

Levant 18:1–20.

Garrod, D. A. E. 1932. A New Mesolithic Industry: The Natufian of Palestine. *Journal of the Royal Anthropological Society* 62:257–269.

———— 1957. The Natufian Culture: The Life and Economy of a Mesolithic People in the Near East. *Proceedings of the British Academy*, pp. 211–237.

Gat, J. R., and M. Magaritz. 1980. Climatic Variations in the Eastern Mediterranean Sea Area. *Naturwissenschaft* 67:80–87.

Gebel, H. G. 1986. Petra-Region 1983–1985. Untersuchungen zur Siedlungs- und Umweltgeschichte des Fruhneolithikums. *Archiv für Orientforschung* 33:275–382.

Gebel H. G., M. Muhesein, and H. Nissen. 1988. Preliminary Report on the First Season of Excavations at Baska. In *The Prehistory of Jordan, The State of Research in 1986*, ed. A. Garrard and H. G. Gebel, pp. 101–134. BAR International Series 396 (i). British Archaeological Reports, Oxford.

Gilead, I. 1984. Is the Term 'Epi-Palaeolithic' Relevant to the Levantine Prehistory? *Current Anthropology* 25:227–229.

Goldberg, P. 1977. Late Quaternary Stratigraphy of Gebel Maghara. *Qedem* 7:11–31.

Goldberg, P., and O. Bar-Yosef. 1982. Environmental and Archaeological Evidence for Climatic Change in the Southern Levant and Adjacent Areas. *British Archaeological Reports* 133:399–414.

Gopher, A. 1989. Diffusion Processes in Pre-Pottery Neolithic Levant: The Case of the Helwan Point. In *People and Culture in Change*, ed. I. Hershkovitz, pp. 91–106. BAR International Series 508 (i). British Archaeological Reports, Oxford.

Goring-Morris, A. N. 1987. *At the Edge: Terminal Pleistocene Hunter-Gatherers in the Negev and Sinai*. BAR International Series 361. British Archaeological Reports, Oxford.

———— 1988. Trends in the Spatial Organization of Terminal Pleistocene Hunter-gatherer Occupations as Viewed from the Negev and Sinai. *Paléorient* 14:231–244.

Gould, S. J. 1988. On Relating the Idea of Progress with an Operational Notion of Directionality. In *Evolutionary Progress*, ed. M. H. Nitecki, pp. 319–338. University of Chicago Press, Chicago and London.

Hamilton, H. J. 1977. A Thermodynamic Theory of the Origin of Hierarchical Evolution of Living Systems. *Zygon* 12:289–335.

Harestad, A. J., and F. L. Bunnell. 1979. Home Range and Body Weight—A Re-evaluation. *Ecology* 60:389–402.

Harris, D. R. 1977. The Origins of Agriculture: Alternate Pathways toward Agriculture. In *Origins of Agriculture*, ed. C. A. Reed, pp. 173–249. Mouton, The Hague.

Hassan, F. 1981. *Demographic Archaeology*. Academic Press, New York.

Hayden, B. 1990. Nimrods, Piscators, Pluckers, and Planters: The Emergence of Food Production. *Journal of Anthropological Archaeology* 9:31–69.

Hecker, H. M. 1975. *The Faunal Analysis of the Primary Food Animals from Pre-Pottery Neolithic Beidha (Jordan)*. Ph.D. diss., Columbia University.

———— 1982. Domestication Revisited. Its Implications for Faunal Analysis. *Journal of Field Archaeology* 9:217–236.

Helmer, D. 1989. Le dévelopement de la domestication au Proche-Orient de 9500 a 7500 B.P.: Les nouvelles données d'El Kown et de Ras Shamra. *Paléorient* 15:111–121.

Helms, S., and A. Betts. 1987. The Desert "Kites" of Badiyat Esh-Sham and North Arabia. *Paléorient* 13:41–68.

Henry, D. O. 1973. *The Natufian of Palestine: Its Material Culture and Ecology*. Ph.D. diss., Southern Methodist University, Dallas.

———— 1975. Fauna in Near Eastern Archeological Deposits. In *Problems in Prehistory: North Africa and the Levant*, ed. F. Wendorf, pp. 379–385. Southern Methodist University, Dallas.

———— 1985. Preagriculture Sedentism: The Natufian Example. In *Prehistoric Hunter-Gatherers: The Emergence of Complex Societies*, ed. T. D. Price and J. A. Brown, pp. 365–384. Academic Press, New York.

———— 1987. The Prehistory and Paleoenvironments of Jordan: An Overview. *Paléorient* 12:5–26.

———— 1989. *From Foraging to Agriculture: The Levant at the End of the Ice Age*. University of Pennsylvania Press, Philadelphia.

Henry, D. O., A. Leroi-Gourhan, and S. J. Davis. 1981. The Excavation of Hayonim Terrace: An Examination of Terminal Pleistocene Climatic and Adaptive Changes. *Journal of Archaeological Science* 8:33–58.

Hillman, G. C., S. M. Colledge, and D. R. Harris. 1989. Plant-food Economy during the Epipaleolithic Period at Tell Abu Hureyra, Syria: Dietary Diversity, Seasonality, and Modes of Exploitation. In *Foraging and Farming: The Evolution of Plant Exploitation*, ed. D. R. Harris and G. C. Hillman, pp. 240–268. Unwin Hyman, London.

Hillman, G. C., and M. S. Davies. 1992. Domestication Rate in Wild Wheats and Barley under Primitive Cultivation: Preliminary Results and Archaeological Implications of Field Measurements of Selection Coefficient. In *Préhistoire de l'agriculture: Nouvelles approches expérimentales et *ethnographiques*, ed. P. C. Anderson, pp. 113–158. Monographie du CRA no. 6. Editions de CNRS, Paris.

Hole, F. 1984. A Reassessment of the Neolithic Revolution. *Paléorient* 10:49–60.

―――― 1989. A Two-part, Two-stage Model of Domestication. In *The Walking Larder*, ed. J. Clutton-Brook, pp. 97–104. Unwin Hyman, London.

Horowitz, A. 1976. Late Quaternary Palaeoenvironments of Prehistoric Settlements in the Avdat/Agev Area. In *Prehistory and Paleoenvironments in the Central Negev*, ed. A. E. Marks, pp. 57–67. Southern Methodist University Press, Dallas.

―――― 1977. Pollen Spectra from Two Early Holocene Prehistoric Sites in the Har Harif (West Central Negev). In *Prehistory and Paleoenvironments in the Central Negev, Israel*, ed. A. E. Marks, pp. 323–326. Southern Methodist University Press, Dallas.

―――― 1979. *The Quaternary of Israel*. Academic Press, New York.

―――― 1992. *Palynology of Arid Lands*. Elsevier.

Horwitz, L. K. 1989. A Reassessment of Caprovine Domestication in the Levantine Neolithic: Old Question, New Answer. In *People and Culture in Change*, ed. I. Hershkowitz, pp. 153–181. BAR International Series 508 (i). British Archaeological Reports, Oxford.

Horwitz, L. K., C. Cope, and E. Tchernov. 1990. Sexing the Bones of Mountain-gazelle (*Gazella gazella*) from Prehistoric Sites in the Southern Levant. *Paléorient* 16:1–11.

Horwitz, L. K., and Y. Garfinkel. 1991. Animal Remains from the Site of Gesher, Central Jordan Valley. *Mitekufat Haeven* 24:64–76.

Horwitz, L. K., and E. Tchernov. 1987. Faunal Remains from the PPNB of Submerged Site of Atlit. *Mitekufat Haeven* 20:72–78.

Hovers, E. 1989. Settlement and Subsistence Patterns in the Lower Jordan Valley from Epipalaeolithic to Neolithic Times. In *People and Culture in Change*, ed. I. Hershkovitz, pp. 37–52. BAR International Series 508 (i). British Archaeological Reports, Oxford.

Hovers, E., L. K. Horwitz, D. E. Bar-Yosef, and C. Cope-Miyashiru. 1988. The Site of Urkan-E-Rub IIa: A Case Study of Subsistence and Mobility Patterns in the Kebaran Period in the Lower Jordan Valley. *Mitekufat Haeven* 21:20–48.

Kelly, R. L. 1983. Hunter-gatherers Mobility Strategies. *Journal of Anthropological Research* 39:277–306.

Kenyon, K. 1957. *Digging Up Jericho*. Ernest Benn, London.

―――― 1981. *Excavations at Jericho*, Vol. 3. British School of Archaeology in Jerusalem, London.

Kenyon, K. M., and T. A. Holland. 1983. *Excavations at Jericho*, Vol. 5. British School of Archaeology in Jerusalem, London.

Kirkbride, D. 1966. Five Seasons at the Pre-Pottery Neolithic Village of Beidha in Jordan. *Palestine Exploration Quarterly* 98:8–72.

Kislev, M. E. 1989. Pre-Domesticated Cereals in the Pre-Pottery Neolithic A Period. In *People and Culture in Change*, ed. I. Hershkovitz, pp. 147–152. BAR International Series 508 (i). British Archaeological Reports, Oxford.

Kislev, M. E., and O. Bar-Yosef.1988. The Legumes: The Earliest Domesticated Plants in the Near East? *Current Anthropology* 29:175–179.

Kislev, M. E., O. Bar-Yosef, and A. Gopher. 1986. Early Neolithic Domesticated and Wild Cereals from Netiv Hagdud Region in the Jordan Valley. *Israel Journal of Botany* 35:197–201.

Klein, R. G. 1986. Carnivore Size and Quaternary Climatic Change in Southern Africa. *Quaternary Research* 26:153–170.

Klein, R. G., and K. Cruz-Uribe. 1984. *The Analysis of Animal Bones from Archaeological Sites.* University of Chicago Press, Chicago.

Köhler-Rollefson, L. 1989. Changes in Goat Exploitation at 'Ain Ghazal between the Early and Late Neolithic: A Metrical Analysis. *Paléorient* 15:141–146.

Köhler-Rollefson, L., W. Gillespie, and M. Metzger. 1988. The Fauna from Neolithic 'Ain Ghazal. In *The Prehistory of Jordan. The State of Research in 1986*, ed. D. A. Garrard and H. Gebel, pp. 314–396. BAR International Series 396 (ii). British Archaeological Reports, Oxford.

Köhler-Rollefson, L., and G. O. Rollefson. 1990. The Impact of Neolithic Subsistence Strategies on the Environment: The Case of 'Ain Ghazal. In *Man's Role in the Shaping of the Eastern Mediterranean Landscape*, ed. S. Bottema, G. Entjes-Nieborg, and W. van Zeist, pp. 207–215. Balkema, Rotterdam.

Kurtén, B. 1965. The Carnivora of the Palestine Caves. *Acta Zoologica Fennica* 107:1–74.

Lamberg-Karlovsky, C. C. 1989. Introduction. In *The Proto-Elamite Texts from Tepe Yahya*, ed. P. Damerov and R. K. Englund, pp. v–xiv. The American School of Prehistoric Research, Bulletin 39. Peabody Museum of Archaeology and Ethnology, Harvard University Press, Cambridge, MA.

Lechevallier, M., D. Philibert, A. Ronen, and A. Samzun. 1985. Une occupation Khiamienne et Sultanienne à Hatoula (Israël). In *Préhistoire du Levant* II, ed. J. Cauvin and P. Sanlaville. *Paléorient* 15(1):11–18.

Lechevallier, M., and A. Ronen. 1989. L'occupation post-Natoufienne de Hatoula, en Judée occidentale, et sa place dans le cadre régionale. In *Investigations in South Levantine Prehistory*, ed. O. Bar-Yosef and B. Vandermeersch, pp. 309–322. BAR International Series 497. British Archaeological Reports, Oxford.

Legge, T. 1972. Prehistoric Exploration of the Gazelle in Palestine. In *Papers in Economic Prehistory*, ed. E. S.Higgs, pp. 119–124. Cambridge University Press, Cambridge.

Leroi-Gourhan, A. 1982. Palynological Research in Near Eastern Archaeological Sites. In *Palaeoclimates, Palaeoenvironments and Human Communities in the Eastern Mediterranean Region in Later Prehistory*, ed. J. L. Bintliff and W. van Zeist, pp. 353–356. BAR International Series 113. British Archaeological Reports, Oxford.

Leroi-Gourhan, A., and F. Darmon. 1987. Analyses palynologiques de sites archéologiques du Pleistocène final dans la vallée du Jourdain. *Journal of Earth Sciences* 36:65–72.

Lieberman, D. E. 1993a. The Rise and Fall of Seasonal Mobility among Hunter-gatherers. *Current Anthropology* 34:599–631.

——— 1993b. Life History Preserved in Dental Cementum Microstructure. *Science* 261:1162–1164.

Margaritz, M. 1986. Environmental Changes Recorded in the Upper Pleistocene along the Desert Boundary, Southern Israel. *Palaeogeography, Palaeoclimatology, Palaeoecology* 53:213–229.

Magaritz, M., and J. Heller. 1980. A Desert Migration Indicator Oxygen Isotopic Composition of Land Snail Shells. *Palaeogeography, Palaeoclimatology, Palaeoecology* 32:153–162.

Magaritz, M., J. Heller, and M. Volokita. 1981. Land-air Boundary Environment as Recorded by the 18-O/16-O and 13-C/12-C Isotopen Ratios in the Shells of Land Snails. *Earth Planetary Scientific Letters* 52:101–106.

Margalef, B. 1963. On Certain Unifying Principles in Ecology. *American Naturalist* 97:357–374.

Marshall, D. N. 1982. Jericho Bone Tools and Objects. In *Excavations at Jericho*, Vol. 4, ed. K. M. Kenyon and T. A. Holland, pp. 570–622. British School of Archaeology in Jerusalem.

Maynard-Smith, J. 1969. The Status of Neo-Darwinism. In *Toward a Theoretical Biology*, Vol. 2, ed. C. H. Waddington, pp. 82–89. Edinburgh University Press, Edinburgh.

——— 1983. The Genetics of Stasis and Punctuation. *Annual Review of Genetics* 7:11–25.

Mellaart, J. 1975. *The Neolithic of the Near East*. Thames and Hudson, London.

Miller, N. F. 1992. The Origins of Plant Cultivation in the Near East. In *The Origins of Agriculture*, ed. C. W. Cowan and P. J. Watson, pp. 39–58. Smithsonian Institution Press, Washington, DC.

Miyata, Y., and S. Yamagusho. 1990. A Study on Evolution of Regional Population Distribution based on the Dynamic Self-organization Theory. *Environmental Sciences, Hokkaido University* 13:1–33.

Moore, A. 1985. The Development of Neolithic Societies in the Near East. In *Advances in World Archaeology*, Vol. 4, ed. F. Wendorf and A. Close, pp. 1–69. Academic Press, New York.

——— 1989. The Transition from Foraging to Farming in Southwest Asia. In *Foraging and Farming: The Evolution of Plant Exploitation*, ed. D. R. Harris and G. C. Hillman, pp. 620–631. Unwin Hyman, London.

Morowitz, H. 1968. *Energy Flow in Biology*. Academic Press, New York.

Muhesein, S. 1985. L'Epi-Paléolithique dans le gisement de Kharaneh IV. *Paléorient* 11:149–160.

Nadel, D., and I. Hershkovitz. 1991. New Subsistence Data and Human Remains from the Earliest Levantine Epipalaeolithic.*Current Anthropology* 32:631–635.

Neuville, R. 1934. Le préhistoire du Palestine. *Revue Biblique* 43:237–259.

——— 1951. *Le Paléolithique et le Mesolithique du Desert de Judee*. Memoire No. 24. Archives de l'Institut de Paléontologie Humaine, Paris.

Nicolis, G., and I. Prigogine. 1977. *Self-organization in Nonequilibrium Systems*. John Wiley and Sons, New York.

Nitecki, M. H. 1988. Discerning the Criteria for Concepts of Progress. In *Evolutionary Progress*, ed. M. H. Nitecki, pp. 3–24. The University of Chicago Press, Chicago and London.

Noy, T., J. Legge, and E. S. Higgs. 1973. Recent Excavations at Nahal Oren. *Proceedings of the Prehistoric Society* 39:75–99.

Noy, T., J. Schuldenrein, and E. Tchernov. 1980. Gilgal, a Pre-Pottery Neolithic A Site on the Lower Jordan Valley. *Israel Exploration Journal* 30:63–82.

Odum, E. P. 1969. *Fundamentals of Ecology*, 3rd ed. W. B. Saunders Co., Philadelphia, London, and Toronto.

——— 1971. *Environment, Power and Society*. John Wiley and Sons, New York.

Perrot. J. 1966. Le gisement Natoufien de Mallaha (Eynan), Israël. *L'Anthropologie* 70:437–483.

——— 1989. Les variations du mode de sépulture dans le gisement Natoufien de Mallaha (Eynan), Israel. In *Investigations in South Levantine Prehistory*, ed. O. Bar-Yosef and B. Vandermeersch, pp. 287–296. BAR International Series 497. British Archaeological Reports, Oxford.

Pichon, J. 1984. *L'Avifaune Natoufiennne du Levant.*

Systématique, Paléoécologie, Paléoethnozoologie. Thése 3ᵉ Cycle. Université Pierre et Marie Curie, No. 84-58.

———— 1987. L'Avifaune dans l'ouvrage collectif: 'La faune du vilage de Mallaha (Eynan), Israël'. In *La Faune du Gisement Natoufien de Mallaha (Eynan) Israel*, ed. J. Bouchud, pp. 115–150. Mémoires et Travaux du Centre de Recherche Francais de Jerusalem. Association Paleorient, Paris.

———— 1989. L'Enviren du Natoufien en Israël. In *Investigations in South Levantine Prehistory*, ed. O. Bar-Yosef and B. Vandermeersch, pp. 61–74. BAR International Series 497. British Archaeological Reports, Oxford.

Potts, R. 1988. On an Early Hominid Scavenging Niche. *Current Anthropology* 29:153–155.

Prigogine, I. 1961. *Introduction to Thermodynamics of Irreversible Processes.* Wiley-Interscience, New York and London.

———— 1978 Time, Structure and Fluctuations. *Science* 201:777.

Prigogine, I., G. Nicolis, and A. Babloyantz. 1972. Thermodynamics of Evolution. *Physics Today* (November):23–28.

Prigogine, I., and I. Stengers. 1984. *Order Out of Chaos.* Bantam New Age Books, New York.

Reed, C. A. 1983. Archaeozoological Studies in the Near East. A Short History (1960–1980). In *Prehistoric Archaeology along the Zagros Flanks*, ed. L. S. Braidwood, B. Howe, C. A. Reed, and P. J. Watson, pp. 511–536. Oriental Publications 105. The Oriental Institute, Chicago.

Rindos, D. 1984. *The Origins of Agriculture: An Evolutionary Perspective.* Academic Press, San Diego.

Rognon, P. 1987. Relations entre phases climatiques et chronologies au Moyen Orient de 16.000 a 10.000 BP. In *Chronologies in the Middle East: Relative Chronologies and Absolute Chronology 16,000–4,000 B.P.*, ed. O. Aurenche, F. Hours, and J. Evin, pp. 189–206. BAR International Series 379. British Archaeological Reports, Oxford.

Rollefson, G. O. 1987. Local and External Relations in the Levantine PPN Period: 'Ain Ghazal (Jordan) as a Regional Centre. In *Studies in the History and Archaeology of Jordan*, Vol. 3, ed. A. Hadidi, pp. 29–39. Jordan Department of Antiquities, Amman.

Rollefson, G. O., and I. Köhler-Rollefson. 1989. The Collapse of Early Neolithic Settlements in the Southern Levant. In *People and Culture in Change*, ed. I. Hershkovitz, pp. 783–789. BAR International Series 508 (i). British Archaeological Reports, Oxford.

Rollefson, G. O., and A. Simmons. 1988. The Neolithic Settlement at 'Ain Ghazal. In *The Prehistory of Jordan: The State of Research in 1986*, ed. A. N. Garrard and H. G. Gebel, pp. 525–565. BAR International Series 396 (ii). British Archaeological Reports, Oxford.

Ronen, A., and M. Lechevallier. 1985. The Natufian Early-Neolithic Site Hatoula, near Latrun, Israel. *Quartär* 35/36:141–164.

———— 1992. *The Natufian Culture and the Origins of the Levantine Neolithic*, ed. O. Bar-Yosef and F. R. Valla, pp. 149–160. Archaeological Series 1. International Monographs in Prehistory, Ann Arbor, MI.

Schrödinger, E. 1944. *What is Life?* Cambridge University Press, Cambridge.

Schuldenrein, J., and P. Goldberg. 1981. Late Quarternary Paleoenvironments and Prehistoric Site Distributions in the Lower Jordan Valley. *Paléorient* 7:57–71.

Shawcross, W. 1972. Energy and Ecology: Thermodynamic Models in Archaeology. *MODAR*, pp. 477–542.

Sherratt, A. 1972. Socio-economic and Demographic Models for the Neolithic and Bronze Age of Europe. *MODAR*, pp. 477–542.

Shipman, P. 1986. Scavenging or Hunting in Early Hominids. *American Anthropology* 88:27–43.

Shipman, P., and A. Walker. 1989. The Costs of Becoming a Predator. *Journal of Human Evolution* 18:373–392.

Sillen, A. 1984. Dietary Variability in the Epipaleolithic of the Levant: The Sr/Ca Evidence. *Paléorient* 10:79–84.

Silverberg, G. 1984. Embodied Technical Progress in a Dynamic Economic Model. In *The Self-Organization Paradigm, Nonlinear Models of Fluctuating Growth*, ed. R. M. Goodwin, M. Kruger, and M. Vercelli, pp. 192–208. Springer Verlag, Hamburg and Berlin.

Simmons, A. H., I. Köhler-Rollefson, G. O. Rollefson, R. Mandel, and Z. Kafari. 1988. 'Ain-Ghazal: A Major Neolithic Settlement in Central Jordan. *Science* 240:35–39.

Smith, P. O., O. Bar-Yosef, and A. Sillen. 1984. Archeological and Skeletal Evidence for Dietary Change during the Late Pleistocene/Early Holocene in the Levant. In *Paleopathology at the Origins of Agriculture*, ed. M. N. Cohen and G. J. Armelagos, pp. 101–136. Academic Press, New York.

Speth, J. D., and S. L. Scott. 1989. Horticulture and Large-mammal Hunting: The Role of Resource Depletion and the Constraints of Time and Labor. In *Farmers and Hunters*, ed. S. Kent, pp. 71–79. Cambridge University Press, Cambridge.

Stekelis, M., and T. Yizraeli. 1963. Excavations at Nahal Oren: Preliminary Report. *Israel Exploration*

Journal 13:1–12.

Tchernov, E. 1975. Rodent Faunas and Environmental Changes in the Pleistocene of Israel. In *Rodents in Desert Environments*, ed. I. Prakash and D. K. Ghosh, pp. 331–362. Dr. W. Junk Publ., The Hague.

———. 1981. The Impact of the Postglacial on the Fauna of Southwest Asia. In *Contribution to the Environmental History of Southwest Asia*, ed. W. Frey and H.-P. Uerpmann, pp. 197–216. Beihefte zum Tübinger Atlas des Vorderen Orients, Reihe A, Nr. 8. Ludwig Reichert, Tübingen.

———. 1982. Faunal Responses to Environmental Changes in the Middle East during the Last 20,000 Years. In *Palaeoclimates, Palaeoenvironments and Human Commmunities in the Eastern Mediterranean Region in Later Prehistory*, ed. J. L. Bintliff and W. van Zeist, pp. 105–127. (I.N.Q.U.A.). BAR International Series 133. British Archaeological Reports, Oxford.

———. 1984. Commensal Animals and Human Sedentism in the Middle East. In *Animals and Archaeology*, Vol. 2, ed. J. Clutton-Brock and C. Grigson, pp. 91–115. BAR International Series 202. British Archaeological Reports, Oxford.

———. 1988. The Paleobiogeographical History of the Southern Levant. In *The Zoogeography of Israel*, ed. Y. Yom-Tov and E. Tchernov, pp. 159–250. Dr. W. Junk Publ., The Hague.

———. 1991. Of Mice and Men. Biological Markers for Long-term Sedentism: A Reply. *Paléorient* 17:153–160.

———. 1992. Biological Evidences for Human Sedentism in Southwest Asia during the Natufian. In *The Natufian Culture and the Origins of the Levantine Neolithic*, ed. O. Bar-Yosef and F. R. Valla, pp. 315–340. International Monographs in Prehistory, Ann Arbor, MI.

———. 1993. From Sedentism to Domestication—A Preliminary Review of the Southern Levant. In *Skeletons in Her Cupboard*, ed. A. Clason, S. Paine, and H.-P. Uerpmann, pp. 189–234. Oxbow Monographs 34.

Tchernov, E., and O. Bar-Yosef. 1982. Animal Exploitation in the Pre Pottery Neolithic B Period at Wadi Tbeik, Southern Sinai. *Paléorient* 8:17–37.

Tchernov, E., T. Dayan, and Y. Yom-Tov. 1986. The Paleo-geography of *Gazella gazella* and *Gazella dorcas* during the Holocene of the Southern Levant. *Israel Journal of Zoology* 34:51–59.

Tchernov, E., and L. Horwitz. 1990. Herd Management in the Past and its Impact on the Landscape of the Southern Levant. In *Man's Role in the Shaping of the Eastern Mediterranean Landscape*, ed. S. Bottema, G. Entjes-Nieborg, and W. van Zeist, pp. 207–215. Balkema, Rotterdam.

———. 1991. Body Size Diminution under Domestication: Unconscious Selection in Primeval Domesticates. *Journal of Anthropological Archaeology* 10:54–75.

Uerpmann, H.-P. 1987. *The Ancient Distribution of Ungulate Mammals in the Middle East*. Beihefte zum Tübinger Atlas des Vorderen Orients, Reihe A (Naturwissenschaften), Nr. 27. Ludwig Reichert, Tübingen.

———. 1989. *Vorderer Orient. Stammformen der Haustiere und frühe Domestikation.* Tübinger Atlas des Vorderen Orients, 1, Nr. 19. Universität Tübingen. Ludwig Reichert, Wiesbaden.

Ungar-Hamilton, R. 1989. The Epi-palaeolithic Southern Levant and the Origins of Cultivation. *Current Anthropology* 30(1):88–103.

———. 1991. Natufian Plant Husbandry in the Southern Levant and Comparison with that of Neolithic Periods: The Lithic Perspective. In *The Natufian Culture in the Levant*, ed. O. Bar-Yosef and F. R. Valla, pp. 483–520. International Monographs in Prehistory, Ann Arbor, MI.

Valla, F. R. 1975. *Le Natoufien, une culture préhistorique en Palestine.* Cahiérs de la Révue Biblique, Paris.

———. 1987. Chronologie relative et chronologie absolut dans le Natoufien. In *Chronologies in the Middle East: Relative Chronologies and Absolute Chronology 16,000–4,000 B.P.*, ed. O. Aurenche, F. Hours, and J. Evin, pp. 267–294. BAR International Series 379. British Archaeological Reports, Oxford.

———. 1988. Aspects du sol de l'abri 131 de Mallaha (Eynan). *Paléorient* 14:283–297.

———. 1991. Les Natoufiens de Mallaha et l'espace. In *The Natufian Culture and the Origins of the Levantine Neolithic*, ed. O. Bar-Yosef and F. R. Valla, pp. 111–122. Archaeological Series 1. International Monographs in Prehistory, Ann Arbor, MI.

Valla, F. R., O. Bar-Yosef, P. Smith, J. Desse, and E. Tchernov. 1986. Un nouveau sondage sur la terrasse d'El Ouad, Israël (1980–1981). *Paléorient* 12:21–38.

Wenke, R. J. 1981. Explaining the Evolution of Cultural Complexities: A Review. *Advances in Archaeological Methods and Theory* 4:79–127.

Wiley, E. O. 1983. Evolution, Progress and Entropy. In *Evolutionary Progress*, ed. M. H. Nitecki, pp. 275–291. University of Chicago Press, Chicago and London.

Winterhalder, B. 1981. Optimal Foraging Strategies and Hunter-gatherer Research in Anthropology: Theory and Models. In *Hunter-gatherer Foraging Strategies*, ed. B. Winterhalder and A. E. Smith, pp. 13–35. University of Chicago Press, Chicago.

Yellen, J. 1977. *Archaeological Approaches to the Present: Models for Reconstructing the Past.* Academic Press, New York.

Zeist, W. van, and J. A. H. Bakker-Heeres. 1985. Archaeobotanical Studies in the Levant. 1: Neolithic Sites in the Damascus Basin: Aswad, Ghoraifé, Ramad. *Palaeohistorica* 24:165–256.

Zeist, W. van, and S. Bottema. 1991. *Late Quaternary Vegetation of the Near East.* Beihefte zum Tübinger Atlas des Vorderen Orients, Reihe A, Nr. 18. Ludwig Reichert.

Zohary, M. 1973. *Geobotanical Foundations of the Middle East.* Gustav Fischer.

Zohary, D. 1989. Domestication of the Southwest Asian Neolithic Crop Assemblage of Cereals, Pulses, and Flux: The Evidence from Living Plants. In *Foraging and Farming*, ed. D. R. Harris and G. C. Hillman, pp. 358–373. Unwin Hyman, London.

Zohary, D., and M. Hopf. 1988. *Domestication of Plants in the Old World.* Oxford University Press, Oxford.

Zotin, A. I., and R. S. Zotina. 1967. Thermodynamic Aspects of Developmental Biology. *Journal of Theoretical Biology* 17: 57–72.

HUNTING, GATHERING, OR HUSBANDRY? MANAGEMENT OF FOOD RESOURCES BY THE LATE MESOLITHIC COMMUNITIES OF TEMPERATE EUROPE

Marek Zvelebil

Department of Archaeology and Prehistory, University of Sheffield, Sheffield S10 2TN United Kingdom

"Who are you?" asked the little prince, and added, "You are very pretty to look at."
"I am a fox," the fox said.
"Come and play with me," proposed the little prince. "I am so unhappy."
"I cannot play with you," the fox said. "I am not tamed."
"Ah! Please excuse me," said the little prince.
But, after some thought, he added:
"What does that mean—'tame'?"
. . .
"It is an act too often neglected," said the fox. "It means to establish ties."
"'To establish ties'?"
"Just that," said the fox. "To me, you are still nothing more than a little boy who is just like a hundred thousand other little boys. And I have no need of you. And you, on your part have no need of me. To you, I am nothing more than a fox like a hundred thousand other foxes. But if you tame me, then we shall need each other."

(Antoine de Saint-Exupéry, *The Little Prince*, pp. 65–66)

Introduction

The act of taming—and the process of domestication—has been a topic often neglected when discussing the early postglacial hunter-gatherers in Europe. This is partly due to the apparent lack of evidence, partly because Europe lies outside the ambit of the core area for domestication in the Near East. There are other reasons too, however, which are linked to our normative perceptions of the Mesolithic and the Neolithic in Europe.

For at least seventy years the postglacial hunter-gatherers in Europe have been referred to as Mesolithic, yet the meaning of this term has been a subject of debate since its inception (Westropp 1872; Brown 1893; Clark 1936, 1978, 1980; Binford 1968; Mellars 1981; Newell 1984; Zvelebil 1986a, 1996). At present, "Mesolithic" denotes postglacial but pre-Neolithic hunter-gatherer societies in Europe, whose social and economic structure is often perceived as the result of adaptation to the postglacial conditions of the Holocene (Binford 1968; Newell 1984; Kozlowski and Kozlowski 1986). In contrast, the term "Neolithic" came to stand for village-based agro-pastoral farming societies (Dennell 1983; Barker 1985; Whittle 1985; Lewthwaite 1986) whose roots—cultural or genetic—extended ultimately to the Near East (Childe 1925, 1957; Piggott 1965; Ammerman and Cavalli-Sforza 1984; Renfrew 1987; Hodder 1990).

Mesolithic hunter-gatherers and Neolithic farmers, then, have been defined by their mode of subsistence (Zvelebil 1996, but see Thomas 1988, 1991). On the basis of ethnographic analogies, hunter-gatherer societies such as those of the Mesolithic tend to be regarded as mobile groups with low population densities and simple social and economic organization, while Neolithic farmers are inevitably viewed as sedentary, village-based communities with limited mobility and an evolved symbolic, social, and economic structure. This difference has been accentuated by the exogenous origin of most—if not all—Neolithic cultigens and domesticates, which were imported into Europe from the East Mediterranean, appearing to leave little evidence for continuity in cultural and economic practices between the two periods. As a result, the disparity inherent in the original concepts of the Mesolithic and the

Neolithic grew into a major rift, pitting the early postglacial hunter-gatherers against the Neolithic farming societies as two typological extremes.

Such a perception of the Mesolithic masks important variation in the organization of the postglacial hunter-gatherer communities, and obscures continuities between the Mesolithic and the Neolithic. In recent years, this normative view of the Mesolithic has been increasingly challenged by evidence for variability in Mesolithic "adaptations" (Rowley-Conwy 1986), for sedentism (Rowley-Conwy 1983; Price 1985), for technological and economic complexity (Price 1985; Zvelebil 1986b, c; Rowley-Conwy and Zvelebil 1989; Zvelebil and Dolukhanov 1991; Mithen 1991, etc.), and for social elaboration (O'Shea and Zvelebil 1984; Clark and Neeley 1987; Zvelebil 1992a; Larsson 1989, 1993). This reconsideration of the archaeological evidence finds support in the reappraisal of the historical context of modern hunter-gather societies (Lee and DeVore 1968; Leacock and Lee 1982; Ingold et al. 1988, etc.), exposing the dangers of using modern hunter-gatherers too closely as analogues for prehistoric situations.

The work of the Palaeoeconomy school in the 1970s and 1980s contributed to this reassessment by bridging the gap between exploitation of wild resources and husbandry of domesticated ones (Higgs 1972, 1975; Jarman et al. 1982; Dennell 1983; Barker 1985). In regarding domestication as a long-term and continual process, and in drawing a clear distinction between *cultural* and *biological* domestication,[1] Higgs and Jarman (1972, 1975) have focused attention on the status of semi-domesticated species, on the actual process of domestication, and on the controlling, domesticatory potential of various hunter-gatherer strategies. This early lead was followed by a rapid growth of research on the subject, leading to the finer categorization of manipulated, but undomesticated, resources, and to the recognition that many societies, both ethnographic and prehistoric, filled the hitherto ill-defined gap between hunter-gatherers and farmers through a close management of their resources (see, e.g., Harris 1977; Rindos 1984; Harris and Hillman 1989; Williams and Hunn 1982).

In Mesolithic Europe, this change in research orientation has had only a limited impact so far. This must be due partly to the conviction that the indigenous food resources of Europe preclude full domestication (Rowley-Conwy 1986; Harris 1977; Zvelebil 1986c), and partly to the paucity of paleobotanical data. Above all, it must be due to the inclination to adopt Near Eastern agro-pastoral farming as a yardstick for any move to agriculture, and the consequent failure to recognize that postglacial hunter-gatherers in Europe could have produced their own system of intensive resource management, or some form of husbandry.[2]

Nevertheless, investigations of hunter-gatherer economies in postglacial Europe suggest several important developments. These include the specialized use of resources, particularly those of the water-edge and aquatic environments, as in Southern Scandinavia (Rowley-Conwy 1983; Price 1989), or the East Baltic (Zvelebil 1981, 1989, 1992b), the selective cull and possibly herding of red deer in Central Europe, Southern Scandinavia, and Britain (Jarman 1972; Chaplin 1975; Mithen 1987; but see Rowley-Conwy 1986), and the intensive use of plant foods, approaching "asexual horticulture and arboriculture" (Clarke 1976). Local domestication of caprines has been postulated in both the West and the East Mediterranean (Dennell 1983; Barker 1985), but, for the West Mediterranean at least, the idea has been convincingly refuted by Geddes (1985) on genetic, paleontological, and zoological evidence. The graduated variation in the size of the "wild" pig bones in both the Mediterranean and temperate Europe has led to suggestions of local domestication (e.g., Lepiksaar 1974; Markevitch 1974; see below); as did the evidence for the variation in the size of prehistoric cattle in Hungary and the former Yugoslavia (Bökönyi 1974). Barker (1985) and Dennell (1983) have argued the case for local domestication of wild cereals and pulses in the southeastern Balkans by the local hunter-gatherer communities.

Such evidence hints at the existence of management strategies in the Mesolithic, which may have formed the basis for local domestication of plants and animals, while at the same time remaining a part of a system of resource procurement where hunting and gathering prevailed. Such local systems varied from region to region, and involved varying degrees of resource control. In this study, I attempt a re-interpretation of Late Mesolithic hunter-gatherer economic strategies in North Temperate Europe as an interdependent, integrated system (Fig. 1). In this area we have evidence for several strategies of specialization and controlled management, which, in some regions, appear to have combined to form an integrated system of resource use serving as an alternative and an analogue to the agropastoral farming developed in the Near East.

The period in question covers the Late Mesolithic, between ca. 6000 and 2000 b.c. While the beginning of the period, marked traditionally by typological and technological changes in the lithic industry, ranges from ca. 6800 b.c. in Britain to ca. 6000 b.c. in Ireland and 5800 b.c. in Southern Scandinavia, the end of the period is marked by the introduction of agro-pastoral farming and associated changes in stone technology, settlement structures, and burial. In the western part of North Temperate Europe (Ireland, Britain, Southern Scandinavia, and the Low Countries) this transition occurred during the fourth millennium b.c.; in the east (southern Finland, Estonia, Latvia, Lithuania, northeast Poland, western Russia) the gradual adoption of agro-pastoral farming occurred principally at the end of the third and in the course of the second millennium b.c. (Price 1987; Zvelebil and Dolukhanov 1991). Hunter-gatherer communities in North Temperate

KEY

Marine shoreline zones ▤

Lacustrine zones ⋯

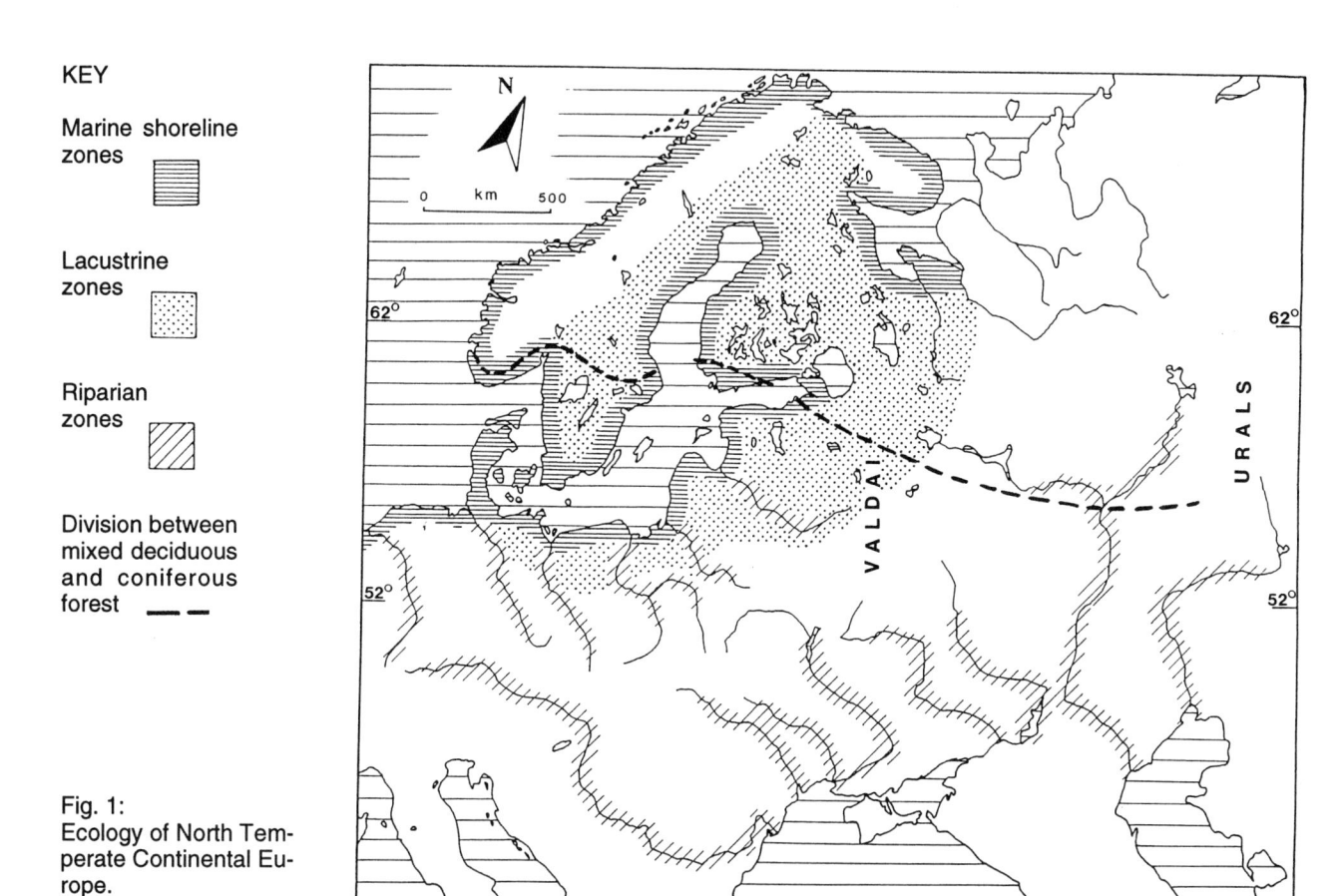

Riparian zones ▨

Division between mixed deciduous and coniferous forest — —

Fig. 1: Ecology of North Temperate Continental Europe.

Europe included some of the best prehistoric examples of "complex" or "affluent" foragers, despite some argument about the degree of complexity attained, and despite regional and temporal variation in the level of such complexity (Price 1985, 1987; Rowley-Conwy 1983; Zvelebil and Rowley-Conwy 1986; Larsson 1990; Fischer 1993; Andersen 1993, etc.). The "complexity" is expressed in increased residential permanence, logistic use of resources, technological developments such as the use of capture facilities, specialized tool-kits, and the adoption of pottery, development of trade and exchange, and social elaboration (for summary descriptions, see Zvelebil 1986b, c, 1992a, b; Price 1987; Larsson 1990; Morrison 1980; Simmons et al. 1981; Woodman 1978; Smith 1992; Dolukhanov 1979; Zvelebil and Dolukhanov 1991; for regional studies, see Mellars 1978; Gramsch 1981; Zvelebil 1981, 1986b, c; Rowley-Conwy 1983; Rowley-Conwy et al. 1987; Price and Brown 1985; Bogucki 1988; Bonsall 1989; Vermeersch and van Peer 1990; Zvelebil et al. in press and references therein).

North Temperate Europe covers the geographical zone in Europe approximately between 52 and 62 degrees latitude north, with the North European Plain being the prevailing landform. The area is fronted by the Caledonian mountain ranges of Ireland, Britain, and Norway to the west and northwest, the Hercynian and Carpathian mountain ranges to the south, while in the east, the lowlands continue across present-day Russia to the Valdai uplands and beyond to the Urals.

This is not, of course, an ecologically uniform zone. In the north and the east, the forested landscape consists of mainly conifers with some broad-leaved species, notably birch, alder, and hazel, with open landscape created by wetlands and peatlands. Elk, beaver, and fur animals such as bear predominate among terrestrial animals. In Southern Scandinavia, the British Isles, and on the North European Plain, deciduous or mixed-deciduous forests prevail. This is a more fertile zone with deeper soils and a greater range of food resources, which included wild cattle, wild pig, red deer, and roe deer, in addition to elk and beaver. The boundary between these two zones changed considerably during the climatic fluctuations of the last 10,000 years. In the Late Mesolithic, the deciduous forest zone, with its greater range of plants and animals, extended further north than it does today, reaching the 62-degree latitude in most lowland areas of northern Europe, and extending eastwards up to the Valdai uplands.

Within these two broad zones, we can distinguish coastal and inland regions. Coastal zones include marine shores, major river valleys, and lacustrine areas: they tend to have their resources enriched by shellfish, marine mammals, fish, and waterfowl. These areas also served as passage corridors for migratory species and as aggregation grounds for animals in winter. One of the most significant features of North Temperate Europe, therefore, is the concentration of resources near bodies of water. As a formerly periglacial or glacial zone, the entire area is relatively rich in lakes, rivers, and coastal environments.

North Temperate Europe is a highly seasonal place, with the type and quantity of resources varying from season to season. Much of this variation is due to the migratory nature of food resources, such as waterfowl, eel, salmon, and some seals. The pattern of migrations means that some species are available in abundance only for a brief period of the year, principally in the late spring and autumn. At other times of the year, particularly in winter and early spring, entire food webs "shut down" and food can be scarce.

The Gulf Stream along the western margins of the area acts as an enormous heating system and generates a comparatively mild climate in North Temperate Europe relative to its northerly location. The Gulf Stream also ensures high productivity in the north Atlantic and Baltic seas,

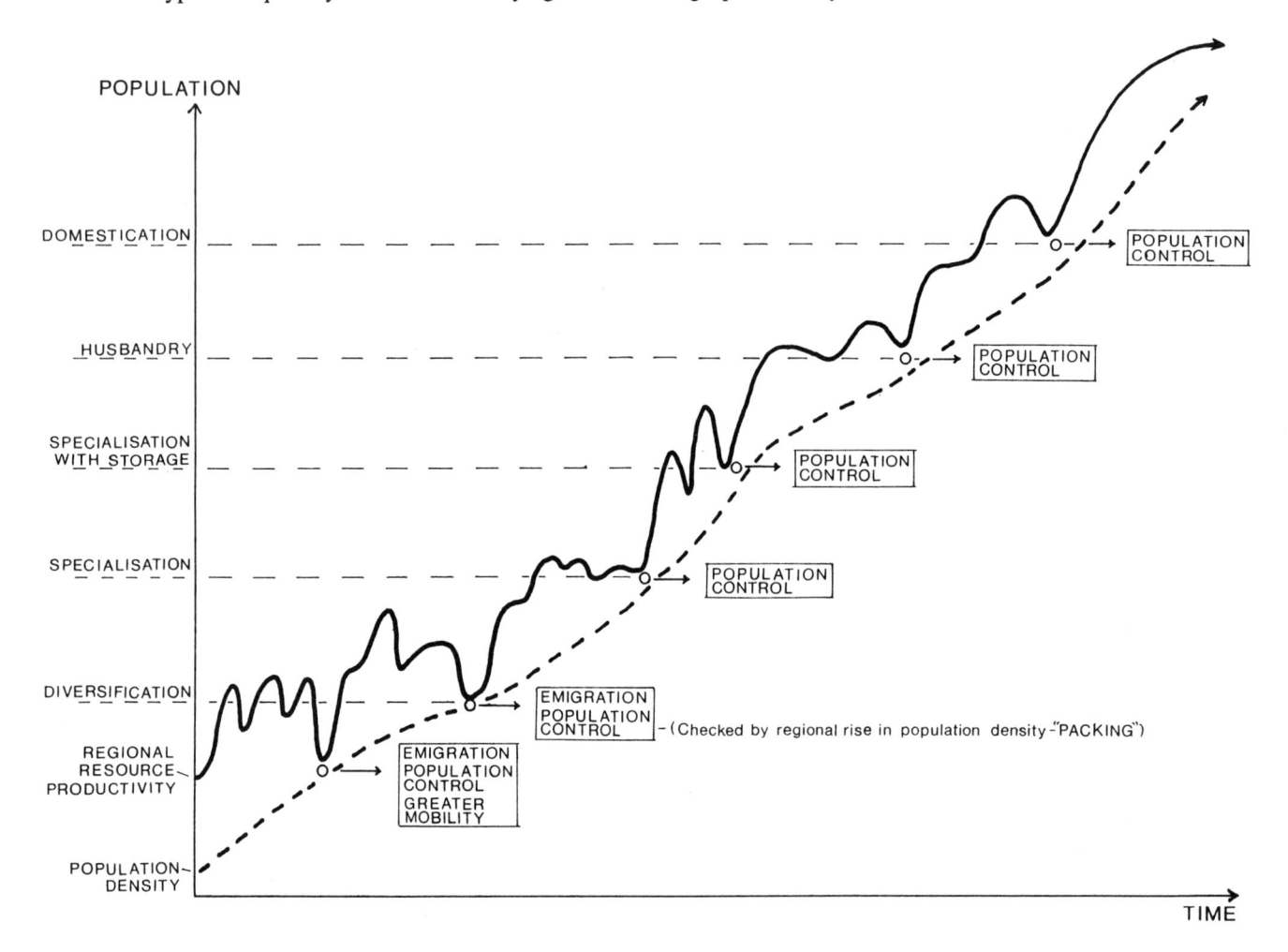

Fig. 2:
Population density, resource productivity, and resource-use strategies.
  In this figure, resource-use strategies are arranged in relation to regional resource productivity and population density. It is assumed that population density of a region will increase through time as a consequence of population growth, and by the drowning of coastal plains by sea-level rise (an assumption supported by empirical evidence in coastal areas of Mesolithic Europe). Whenever population density approaches the resource productivity ceiling, several strategic responses are likely to occur, which may be both intensive (such as specialization) and extensive in nature (boxed). In time, the recourse to extensive responses will be increasingly limited, and people will increasingly rely on economic intensification, marked by greater labor investment and the exercise of greater control over their resources. This is, however, only one possible historical scenario, based on the assumption of continual growth in population density. Ideology is expected to play a role in specifying which strategies will be implemented in response to the practical problems faced by the hunter-gatherer communities.

since its currents support extensive fish populations, which in turn provide food for marine mammals such as seal. Thus the presence of the Gulf Stream substantially increases the productivity of coastal regions. In summary, postglacial conditions in North Temperate Europe produced uneven distribution of resources in space and over seasons. For hunter-gatherer societies, the implications were two-fold: on the one hand, seasonal and longer term fluctuations increased survival risks in that people had to find their regular food supply from fluctuating resources; on the other hand, effective exploitation of seasonally aggregated food resources could generate a surplus and raise the population capacity of the area.

Late Mesolithic subsistence strategies in their socioeconomic context

When faced with the dilemma of securing a continuous food supply from resources that are unevenly distributed in space and time, people have two basic choices. They can either move around a landscape from one source of food to another, or they can develop technological, social, and economic means of coping with a periodic scarcity of resources.

At the same time, the changes in landmass in the early Holocene—the drowning of coastal areas by the rise in the sea level and the opening up of Scandinavia by deglaciation and isostatic rise of land—initiated shifts in population, which eventually led to an increase in population density along the lines described by Binford in his "packing model" (Binford 1983). Although the final Paleolithic and Early Mesolithic in North Temperate Europe is to a large extent a story of colonization of periglacial or recently deglaciated landscapes (e.g., Fisher 1991), continuing colonization, eustatic rise in the sea level, and probably population growth resulted in an increase in population density towards the end of the period (ca. 6000 b.c.). This is evidenced especially in the coastal zones of North Temperate Europe, and is marked by increasing permanency of residence (Vankina 1970; Rowley-Conwy 1983; Newell 1984; Price 1985, 1987; Zvelebil 1986a; Larsson 1990), the distribution of formalized burial areas, i.e., cemeteries (Constandse-Westermann et al. 1984; Zvelebil and Rowley-Conwy 1986; Larsson 1993), an increase in territorial definition (Petersen 1984; Larsson 1989), reduction in the size of territories (Rowley-Conwy 1995; Larsson 1990), and the decline and/or disappearance of preferred terrestrial fauna such as reindeer, elk, wild cattle, and, in Denmark, eventually, red deer (Petersen 1984). In some (but not all) regions of North Temperate Europe, then, increasing population density gradually constrained the mobility range of hunter-gatherer communities and created conditions for more intensive use of resources (Fig. 2).

Strategies of intensification, aimed at greater productivity or greater security of food supply, are arranged in Fig. 2 in chronological succession. It is necessary to emphasize that this is only one, generalized pathway of development, contingent on social and ideological factors. As in any other society, in hunter-gatherer societies ideology must have played a key role in guiding the choice of socioeconomic strategies and motivating social behavior (Fig. 3). It served as a selective force which could either promote or proscribe technological development or social change.

While developments toward greater social and economic complexity occurred in the Early Mesolithic in

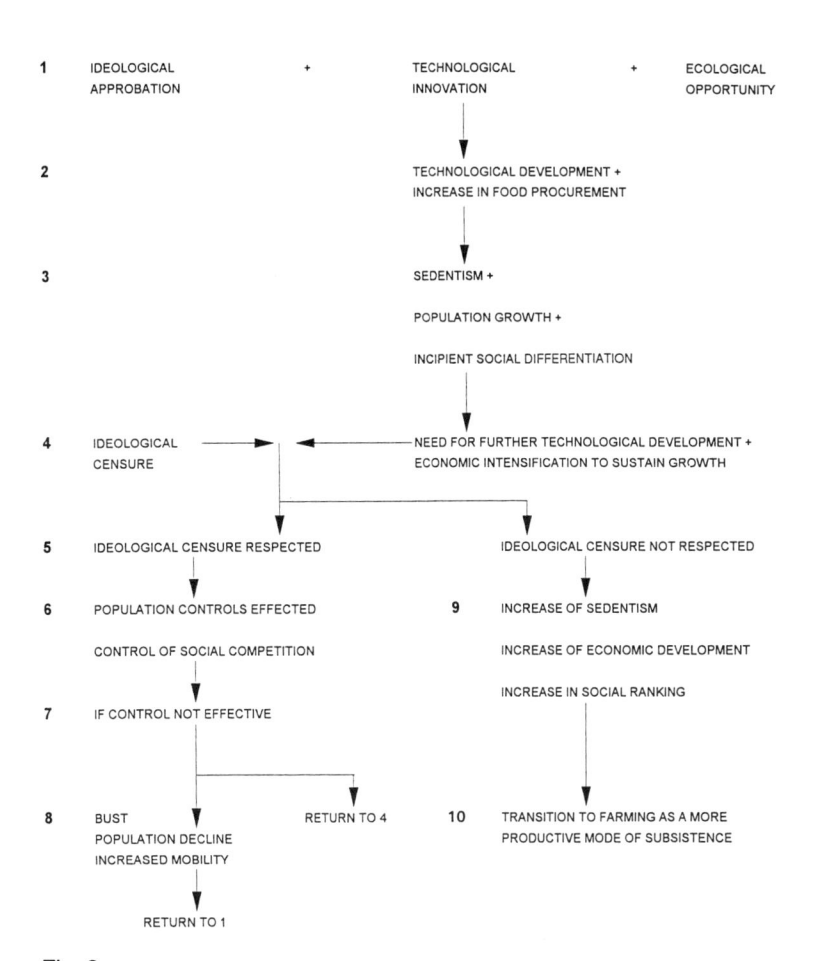

Fig. 3:
Ideology and the decision-making process.
This figure illustrates the role of ideological considerations in the decision-making process of prehistoric hunter-gatherer communities. Ideology is expected to specify which strategies will be implemented in response to the practical problems faced by prehistoric communities.

coastal and some inland lacustrine regions of North Temperate Europe, various stages of this progression are less evident in other areas. This may be for reasons of population density, or for social and ideological reasons. We also have evidence for increased mobility and reduced cultural "complexity" in some regions at the end of the Mesolithic, as, for example, in parts of Britain (Myers 1989) and Denmark. There is, then, nothing inevitable about the course towards increased cultural complexity and greater control of resources, but in my view this does represent one major trend in the historical process of development of Mesolithic hunter-gatherers.

Within this scheme, the more controlled use of plants and animals, leading possibly to husbandry and domestication, follows earlier technological and social strategies: specialization and diversification. In my view, time and resource stress, driven by resource seasonality inherent in the ecology of the northern part of Europe, and by the increasing population density, elicited a *dual* technological and economic response, which could be grouped under strategies of *diversification* and *specialization* (Fig. 4; see Zvelebil 1984, 1986c for further discussion of concepts of time stress and diversification; see also Vierra 1992; Torrence 1983). Economic diversification consisted of encounter foraging practiced by logistic task groups on a wide range of resources. This practice was reflected in faunal evidence by the "broad spectrum" of food remains characteristic of the Mesolithic since the Maglemosian period (ca. 7500–6000 b.c.).

Economic specialization consisted of interception of seasonally aggregated migratory resources such as seal, anadromous fish, and waterfowl. This activity was often carried out from seasonal camps, where the majority of faunal remains belong to a single species, as, for example, at Narva (Gurina 1966), Loona, Näakamäe in Estonia (Paaver 1965; Zvelebil 1989), or Laggersund, Vaenge Sø II, or Dyrholm in Denmark (Rowley-Conwy 1983).

Duality of economic practice was linked to duality of technology. The diversified strategy was served by multi-component, maintainable tools consisting of bone shafts—probably curated in advance of use—and of versatile microliths, which formed the expedient components for replacement. The microliths, then, can be seen at least

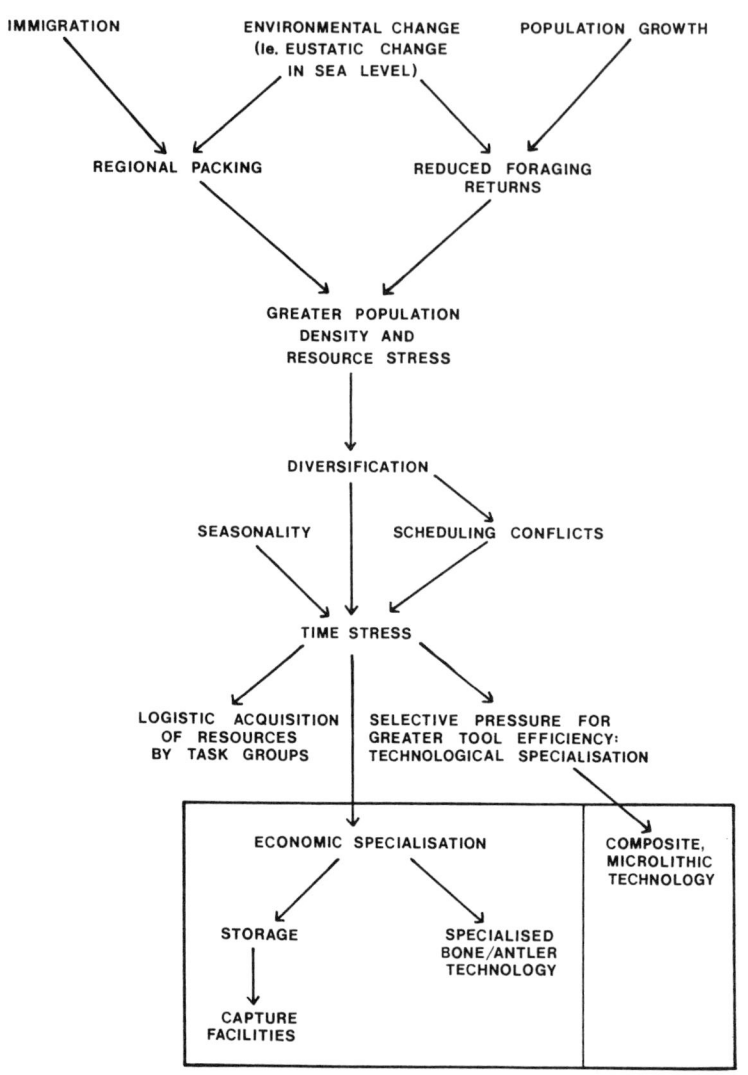

Fig. 4:
The decision-making process and the development of economic and technological specialization
This figure refers to the initial steps in the process of intensification (Fig. 2; Fig. 3, steps 1–4) in greater detail. The dual technological and economic response discussed in the text is boxed. (Partly based on Torrence 1983 and Vierra 1992.)

partly as the archaeological signature of a technology developed to meet the demands of a generalized use of resources under *resource stress*.

Economic specialization, on the other hand, was served by highly efficient, specialized tools, curated in advance of use and designed with some redundancy to ensure maximum efficiency in the exploitation of seasonal resources under *time stress*. Capture facilities (Fig. 5), as well as some antler and bone tool types, serve as archaeological signatures of this technology.

While hunter-gatherer communities appear to have employed both strategies concurrently from the onset of the Mesolithic, specialized strategies increase relative to

Fig. 5:
Capture facilities in northern Europe and the circum-Baltic area.

Site abbreviations:
USV   Usvyaty
SAR   Sarnate
ŠVE   Šventoji
KRE   Kreichi
KRI   Krivina
T.V. Tybrind Vig
AGE   Ageröd
Aerø Aerø Mollegabet I and II

KEY

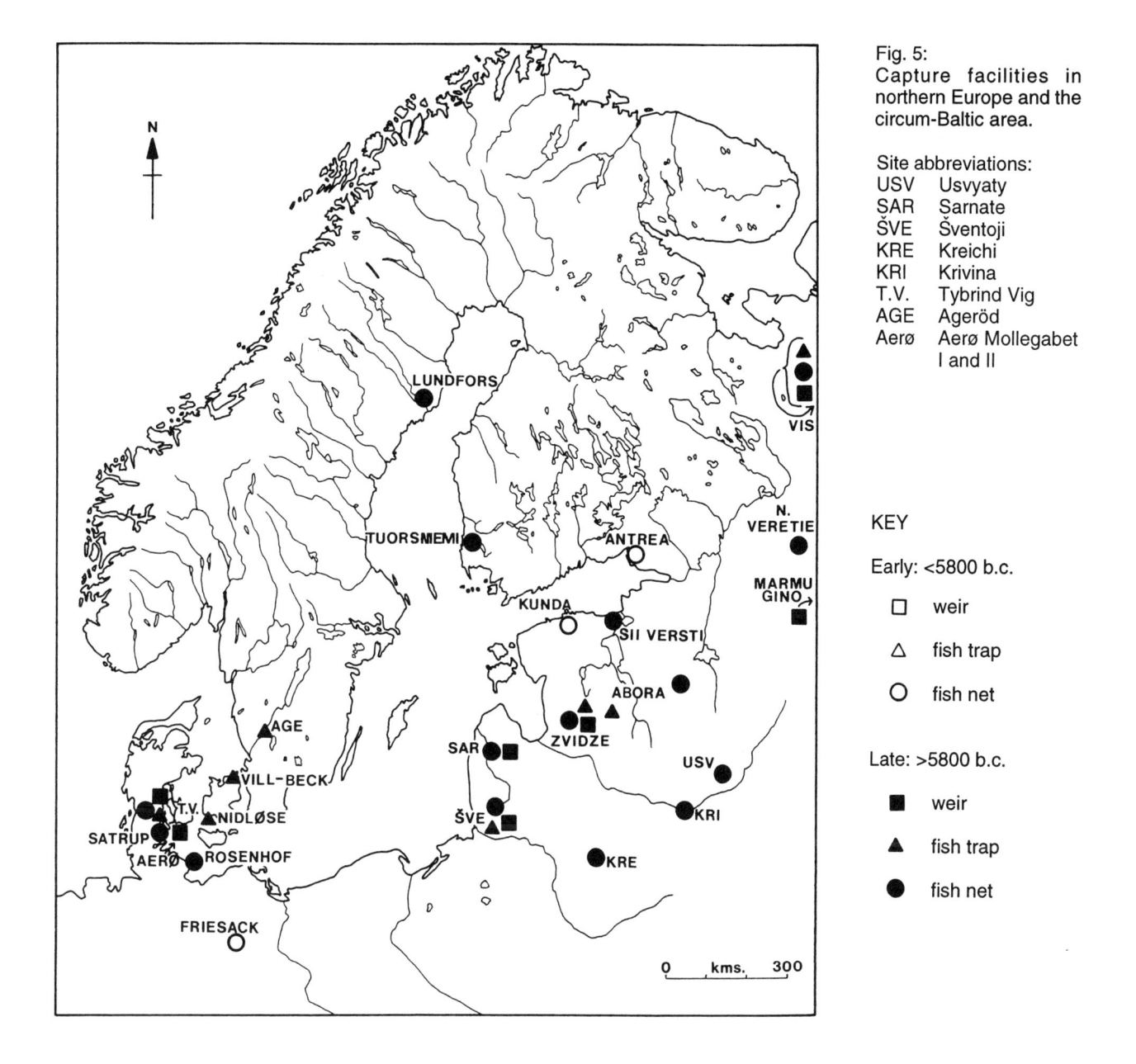

Early: <5800 b.c.
□ weir
△ fish trap
○ fish net

Late: >5800 b.c.
■ weir
▲ fish trap
● fish net

diversified ones as time goes on: a feature evident in the faunal remains from settlements of the fifth–third millennium b.c., and reflected, probably, in the relative decline of microlithic technology at the end of the Mesolithic. This may have reflected the decline in the availability of larger, terrestrial resources, which are more vulnerable to predation than seasonally exploited aquatic ones. The overall response to increasing population density, in some areas at least, is likely to have followed the pattern suggested in Fig. 2: a range of solutions leading to increased technological efficiency and increased labor investment until the introduction of farming. Within this framework, the development of local plant and animal management or husbandry practices can be seen as a crucial development foreshadowing the changes attendant on the introduction of agro-pastoral farming on the one hand, and providing a viable alternative to it on the other.

From specialization to husbandry?

At first it would appear that the scope for domestication in the temperate forest zone was limited by the range of resources. The development of a farming economy was unlikely to take place using only the indigenous resources, and the domestication of individual species such as pig or cattle alone, or the tending of nut trees, was likely to remain within the context of a hunting-gathering economy until the introduction of a more productive and balanced range of cultigens and domesticates (Zvelebil 1986c:174).

Within the context of a hunting-gathering economy, however, a range of subsistence practices may have developed which included elements of resource management or husbandry, and which together produced an alternative to the agro-pastoral farming characteristic of the Neolithic. In North Temperate Europe, there are indications that such an integrated system operated to a varying degree in some regions and that it was based on the intensive use of plant foods, aquatic resources, and wild pig.

The taming of wild boar by Mesolithic hunter-gatherers has been a recurrent theme in recent and not-so-recent literature. The domestication of local wild pigs has been discussed, in passing, with reference to the west Mediterranean (Lewthwaite 1986; Rowley-Conwy 1995), the Balkans (Bökönyi 1974; Shnirelman 1980, 1992), Crimea (Tringham 1971), Moldavia (David and Markevitch 1970; Markevitch 1974), Hungary (Bökönyi 1974), and Scandinavia (Pira 1909; Ekman 1974; Welinder 1982; Wyszomirska 1986, 1988; Lepiksaar 1974; Rowley-Conwy 1995).

Despite their popular image, wild swine, if captured young, can be tamed easily and they can reconvert just as easily to the wild state, leading to taxonomic problems in distinguishing between tamed boar and a free-ranging domesticate. In zooarchaeological terms, the usual criteria of size and shape for distinguishing between wild and domestic swine are equally precarious when trying to recognize early stages of domestication (Rowley-Conwy 1995; Jonsson 1986).

Among hunter-gatherers of temperate Europe, reliance on pigs would make sound economic sense. Because of the greater fat content of its meat, and because of its greater reproductive capacity, wild boar can support five times as many people as red deer hunting (5.65 as opposed to 0.91 individuals per sq. km [Jochim 1976]). In North Temperate Europe (as here defined), wild boar is close to its natural distribution limit and its numbers are dependent on the availability of food in winter and early spring. It is during this time that pig would be attracted to human settlements to scavenge for food.

Humans, in contrast, might be faced with seasonal abundance of nuts and aquatic resources (especially seal and anadromous fish) in the autumn and early spring, when major migratory fishing and sealing episodes take place. A tame pig or two would act as an efficient convertor of surplus food, as storage on the hoof for excess resources which could not be stored or consumed during the short harvesting periods. With the pig cast in the role of a tame scavenger around residential sites and a supplier of protein and fat, wild pig management could become a very productive element of an integrated hunter-gatherer economy, without necessarily leading to full biological domestication.

Does this theory find support in the archaeological evidence? We should expect to find evidence for:

1. Intensive use of plant foods, especially of nuts.
2. Widespread use of fish and sea mammals.
3. Specialized hunting of wild boar.
4. Killing of pigs in winter and early spring.
5. The presence of tame pigs.

Plant food in the Mesolithic

Recovery of plant remains depends on the seasonality of a site's occupation, the preservation conditions, the method of retrieval, and the method of processing. Despite the biases against finding evidence for plant use introduced by these factors, the body of information on the use of wild plants in Mesolithic Europe is growing (Clarke 1976; Simmons et al. 1981; Zvelebil 1994, etc.).

Nuts, such as hazelnuts, water chestnuts, and occasionally acorns, formed an important element in the diet and the food procurement strategies of Mesolithic hunter-gatherers (Clarke 1976). A recent re-examination of the paleobotanical evidence (Zvelebil 1994) indicates that plant use in the Mesolithic was far more extensive than hitherto acknowledged, and that accumulations of plant food, especially of nuts, point to their regular and extensive use (Figs. 6 and 7). In those areas, such as Britain, where a large number of fine-resolution palynological studies have been carried out, the incidence of burning and clearance phases seems to be too high to be explained by acts of nature alone. A good case can be made for deliberate forest clearance and the maintenance of more open landscapes by Late Mesolithic groups as a part of a promotional strategy to increase the productivity of nut and fruit trees, shrubs, wetland plants, and possibly native grasses (Zvelebil 1994; Clarke 1976; Bogucki 1988; Simmons and Innes 1985, 1987; Simmons et al. 1981).

Artifactual evidence points to a widespread distribution of soil-working tools (hoes and antler mattocks), especially in temperate Europe, and to a greater than expected presence of reaping and grinding equipment, lending conditional support for the existence of a specialized tool-kit for digging, reaping, and processing plants, at least in some regions of temperate Europe during the Late Mesolithic (Zvelebil 1994). A high rate of caries among the Late Mesolithic population of the west Mediterranean suggests a high use of starchy and carbohydrate foods (Meiklejohn and Zvelebil 1991), while in the Dnieper basin (east temperate Europe), recent analysis of skeletal remains suggests a shift to greater use of plant foods from the sixth millennium b.c. onwards (Jacobs 1993).

The growing awareness of a widespread and intensive use of plant food in Mesolithic Europe corresponds to the recognition of a wide range of promotional plant-management practices in pre-agricultural contexts elsewhere (Munson 1984; Harris and Hillman 1989, etc.). As ethnohistorical data accumulate about plant husbandry from Australia, Africa, and North America, the concept of domestication has been extended from its orthodox biological definition to embrace wider aspects of relationships between people and plants. Such a range of practices has given rise to the notions of incidental, specialized, and agricultural domestication, described by Rindos (1984); of domiculture by Hynes and Chase (1982); of cultivation and domestication stages of food production (Ford 1985); and to a four-fold scheme presented by Harris (1989), where a distinction is made between foraging, wild plant food production, cultivation, and agriculture. Of relevance to the Mesolithic is that all these schemes recognize a phase that involves practices more intensive than gathering. These practices are described in terms of the social relationship of humans to plants, the extractive technology used, and plant use and its effect on plant communities.

Bearing this in mind, I would like to outline five plant-using traditions, three of which have relevance to plant use in the Mesolithic (Zvelebil 1994).

1. *Opportunistic and incidental use of plant food.* This would not cause any adjustment in the overall organization of procurement activities, would proceed without technological specialization, and would leave little trace in the archaeological record. It corresponds to "casual gathering" as defined by Jarman et al. (1982). Mesolithic plant use has been regarded in this light by many archaeologists, either explicitly (Rozoy 1989; Bonsall 1989; Rowley-Conwy 1986) or implicitly in that wild plant use was not accorded a role to play in settlement-subsistence modeling or in the social organization of Mesolithic communities (Price 1987; Clark 1975, 1980; Morrison 1980, etc.).

2. *Systematic and intensive plant use.* If wild plants played a major role in the subsistence of Mesolithic communities, plant food should have been an important factor in locating settlements, in food-getting strategies, and in the organization of labor. Within such a tradition, people can be expected to engage in conservation of food resources, development of specialized tool-kits for plant processing, and storage of plant foods. In terms of previous frameworks, such a tradition would correspond to the systematic gathering of Jarman et al. (1982), the incidental domestication of Rindos (1984), and some aspects of the wild plant procurement of Harris (1989). Archaeologically, this would be discernible by the existence of tool-kits for plant use, stored plant food, and evidence for increased intake of plant food in skeletal remains. A number of scholars have already argued for heavy plant use in the Mesolithic (Clarke 1976; Woodman 1985; Simmons and Innes 1985, 1987; Simmons et al. 1981; Bogucki 1988; Smith 1992).

3. *Plant-food management, or husbandry.* This is marked by deliberate and planned promotional strategies designed to increase control over plant resources and improve conditions of habitat favorable to the propagation of targeted plants. Such practices include protective plant tending, selective burning of woodland, weeding, and soil modification. They do not necessarily include sowing or planting, but occasionally may. In my view, it is with these promotional practices that the change in social relations towards investment, delayed returns, and appropriation of resources and landscape begins to occur, well in advance of actual cultivation (Testart 1982; Hynes and Chase 1982; Yen 1989).

In terms of established frameworks, this tradition would fall between wild plant procurement and production as defined by Harris (1989); in its emphasis on social practice and control of the landscape, it conforms to the notion of husbandry as outlined by Chase (1989) and Yen (1989); it corresponds to the specialized domestication defined by Rindos (1984); and it subsumes the definition of husbandry of Higgs and Jarman (1972:8), based on plant-human relationships "where some form of intentional conservation was practised." In the archaeological record, such practices, although difficult to identify, should be reflected in repeated episodes of burning, maintenance of open landscapes, rise in the incidence of targeted species, and specialized tool-kits for plant tending and soil working.

4. *Cultivation of wild species.* This denotes husbandry with systematic sowing/planting added. Such practices may lead to domestication. Archaeologically, it would be difficult to recognize them, unless the presence of sown/planted wild plants can be attested (see Hillman and Davies 1992). In the Mesolithic of Europe, Dennell (1983) suggested that such cultivation may have occurred in the Balkans and in Britain, while Clarke (1976:480) spoke of "asexual horticulture and arboriculture" in temperate Europe.

5. *Cultivation of domesticated species.* This is predicated on "intentional selective purposeful breeding" of cultigens and domesticates (Higgs and Jarman 1972). While this process of plant domestication is well attested in the Near East (e.g., Reed 1977; Zohary and Hopf 1988; Hillman and Davies 1992), no evidence has so far been advanced for the indigenous domestication of plants in Mesolithic Europe.

It needs to be stressed that these plant-using traditions are not mutually exclusive. Indeed, it can be expected that several traditions were practiced simultaneously, making the recognition of each practice all the more difficult. Nor is it necessary to regard these traditions as steps in a cultural-evolutionary advance towards civilization, a view according to which hunter-gatherers are redeemed only by their "progress" towards agriculture.

Bearing in mind the evidence for plant use that is accumulating in the context of Mesolithic Europe, I suggest that three of these traditions were involved: intensive plant gathering, plant-food husbandry, and, possibly, cultivation of wild species. This suggestion is based on the following observations:

1. The widespread use of burning—to the point of creating a permanent change in the landscape in some areas of Britain, for example (Mellars 1975, 1976; Simmons 1975; Simmons et al. 1981, 1989; Simmons and Innes 1987; Thomas 1989)—supports the notion that Mesolithic people deliberately manipulated their environment as a part of an organized land-use strategy (Mellars 1975, 1976; Jacobi et al. 1976; Jacobi 1978; Simmons 1975; Simmons et al. 1981, 1989; Simmons and Innes 1987; Bogucki 1988; Welinder 1989; Gøransson 1988), with the effect of promoting the growth and reproduction of food plants such as hazel, forbs, and grasses.

   The development of hazel woodland, in some regions beyond the area of natural distribution, is thought to have been brought about by human clearance of land in Ireland, Britain (Smith 1970; Jacobi 1978; Edwards 1982), Holland (Smith 1970), Poland (Bogucki 1988), and Finland (Salmi 1963). The conspicuous increase in hazel woodlands in the vicinity of some hunter-gatherer settlements (Welinder 1989), and the extension of water chestnut beyond the area of its natural habitat (Larsson 1990), may have also been caused by human agency. Such symbiotic relationships would correspond to "specialised domestication," which is "mediated by the environmental impact of humans, especially in local areas in which they reside" (Rindos 1984), and would reflect "spatially focused, labour-demanding and ecologically interventionist activities," which characterize the wild plant procurement system of Harris (1989:20). Such practices would correspond to plant-food husbandry as defined here.

2. The use of mattocks (made of wood and antler), hoes, and picks on the scale suggested by their distribution (Zvelebil 1994) indicates interference with the soil; this may indicate either preparation for planting and/or harvesting of root crops on a regular basis. The match in the distribution of antler mattocks and the temperate forest, where roots and tubers occur in profusion (Clarke 1976), makes the latter a stronger possibility. Harvesting, storage, and processing of water chestnut are demonstrated in the East Baltic (Vankina 1970; Zvelebil 1981; Dolukhanov 1992). Harvesting, storing, and soil working are activities that characterize plant-food husbandry.

3. The presence of large-grained cereal-type pollen in pollen diagrams dating to the Late Mesolithic (Edwards and Hirons 1984; Edwards 1988, 1989, 1993; Zvelebil 1994 with references) either indicates anthropogenic selection of certain species of native grasses (even though there is no evidence for their domestication as in the Near East), or, more likely, is the result of fire-assisted forest clearance by Mesolithic groups. Again, this suggests implementation of promotional strategies, which characterize plant-food management or husbandry as defined here.

Within this broad context of plant-using traditions in the Late Mesolithic, which were practiced with different emphasis in different regions of Europe (Zvelebil 1994), the Mesolithic communities in temperate Europe appear to have placed emphasis on arboreal and shrub vegetation bearing nuts and fruits, and also on roots, with seeds assuming a secondary role. Some of these plants were capable of producing a remarkable quantity of food.[3] The paleobotanical evidence, particularly for hazelnut and water chestnut (Figs. 6 and 7), and the distribution of antler mattocks as digging tools, provide some support for the use

Table 1. Site information for Fig. 6

Site	Date b.c.	Plant remains
NORWAY		
Dysvikja	6100–5600	Hazelnuts
Torkop	*6590–6180*	Hazelnuts
Viste	6000–3000	Hazelnuts
Hå Old Vic	6480–6000	Hazelnuts
Stora Mosvatnet	3090±100	Hazelnuts
Sola	6420±120	Hazelnuts
Lego I	*5640±120*	Hazelnuts
Lego II	*5730±150*	Hazelnuts
SWEDEN		
Bredasten	4500–4000	Hazelnuts
Ageröd 5	4910–4500	Hazelnuts, water chestnuts, goosefoot, sorrel, waterlily, raspberry, meadowsweet
Skateholm		Hazelnuts, water chestnuts
Ageröd 1 B/D	6200–4500	Hazelnuts
Nymölla 3	Meso/TRB transition ca. 3000 b.c.	Hazelnuts
Sjövreten	4600–4200	Hazelnuts
Vaalby	4200	Hazelnuts
Darlarlstorp	4500	Hazelnuts
Överäda	2250–2085	Hazelnuts
Högby (Räa)	7020–5150 5900–4600	Hazelnuts
Lövas	*6020–6280*	Hazelnuts
Huseby Klev	6400–6650	Hazelnuts, apple
Balltorp	7130–6315	Hazelnuts, blackberries, rowan berries, polygonum seeds
FINLAND		
Kolvidja	Säter III ceramics: 2350–2200 b.c.	Hazelnuts
Järvensuo	Combed Ware	Hazelnuts, water chestnuts
Orimattila	3420	Water chestnuts
Pennala	3360	Water chestnuts
Humpilanjärvi	3000–2500	Polygonum seeds

DENMARK			LATVIA		
Ertebølle	3810–3160	Hazelnuts	Sarnarte	2700–2490	Water chestnut
Ringkloster	3600–3200	Hazelnuts, acorns	Iča	Late Neolithic	Hazelnuts, water chestnuts
Tybrind Vig	4500–3200	Hazelnuts, acorns	Piestina	2510	Hazelnuts, water chestnuts
Holmegaard	4500–6450	Yellow waterlily			
Ulkestrup	6030–6370	Hazelnuts	Kreichi	2250–2070	Water chestnuts
Flådet	Preboreal	Hazelnuts	Leimaniski	1879	Water chestnuts
Melsted	6240	Hazelnuts	Osa	3800–3700	Hazelnuts, water chestnuts
Aerø Mollegabet I and II	3960±75	Hazelnuts, acorns, hawthorn			
Angus Bank Småland Bight	4900	Hazelnuts, black- or raspberry	NORTHWEST RUSSIA		
			Naumovo	2050	Hazelnuts, water chestnuts
Muldbjerg		Raspberries	Usvyaty	2360–2100	Hazelnuts, water chestnuts
NORTH GERMANY					
Duvensee	Late Mesolithic	Hazelnuts	Krivina	2000–1600	Hazelnuts, water chestnuts, acorns
Friesack	6200–2450	Hazelnuts			
LITHUANIA			Serteya	4250–4050	Hazelnuts, water chestnuts, waterlily, Ceratophyllum
Šventoji 1 & 2	2690–2450	Hazelnuts, water chestnuts			
Kreutonas	2470–1620	Hazelnuts, water chestnuts	NORTHERN POLAND		
			Pobiel	*6370*	Hazelnuts

Fig. 6: Plant use in North Temperate Europe: Scandinavia and the circum-Baltic area. Site information in Table 1. For further details and references, see Zvelebil (1994), Wigforss (1995), and Bang-Andersen (1995). Italicized dates are of the plant remains themselves; others are dates for the sites.

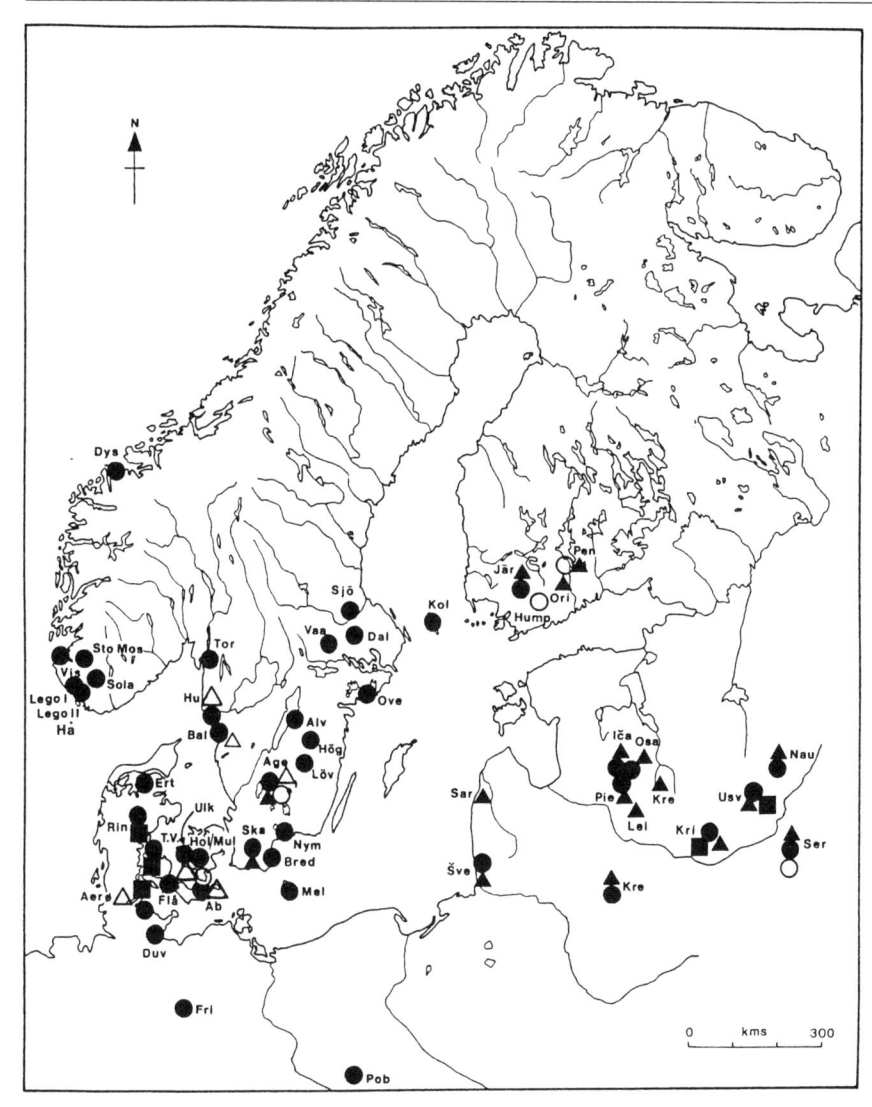

KEY
- ● hazelnuts
- ○ seeds
- ▲ waterchestnuts
- △ fruits
- ■ acorns
- □ roots

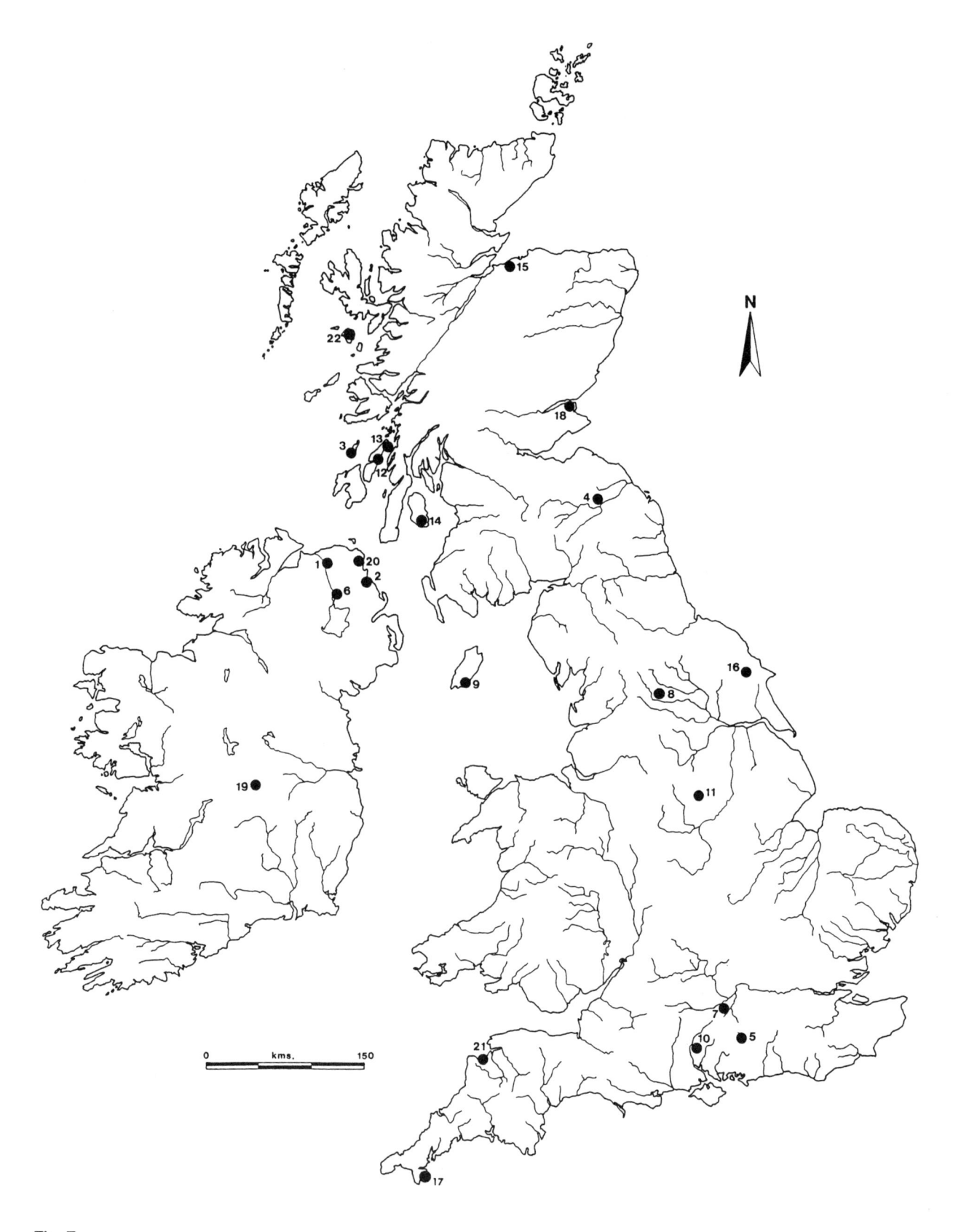

Fig. 7:
Plant use in North Temperate Europe: the British Isles. Site information in Table 2. Italicized dates are of the plant remains themselves, others are dates for the sites. For further details and references, see Zvelebil (1994).

Table 2. Site information for Fig. 7

No.	Site	Date b.c.	Plant remains
1	Mount Sandel	7010±70	Hazelnuts
		6840±185	
		6775±115	
		6605±70	
		6490±60	
		6845±135	Vetches, goosegrass seed, wild pear/apple, white waterlily
		6270±100	
2	Carnlough	Late Mesolithic	Hazelnuts
3	Cnoc Coig	3345±75	Hazelnuts
		3585±140	
4	Derravaragh	3410	Hazelnuts, yellow waterlily seeds
5	Oakhanger	4350–4430	Hazelnuts
6	Newferry	5500–3500	Raspberry seeds
7	Thatcham	7150±80	Hazelnuts
8	Blubberhouses Moor		Hazelnuts
9	Cass Ny Hawin	7660±100	Hazelnuts
10	Broom Hill	5270±120	Hazelnuts
11	Thorpe Common	4500–3700	Hazelnuts
12a	Lussa Wood	6013	Hazelnuts
12b	Lussa River	3450–2980	Hazelnuts, acorn husks, barren strawberry, chickweed, lead shot fungus, bog myrtle
13	Carn Southern	3000	Pear fruit pip, hazelnut shells
14	Auchareoch	5350±90	Hazelnuts
		6110±90	
15	Kingsteps Quarry		Hazelnuts
16	Star Carr		Reeds, bog bean, hazelnuts
17	Poldowrian	4500±110	Hazelnuts
18	Morton A	5350±200	Hazelnuts
18	Morton B	4197±90	Iron root, fat hen, knottgrass, annual knavel, corn spurrey, chickweed, silver birch
		4432±120	
19	Lough Boora	6400±70	Hazelnuts
		6525±75	
20	Cushendun	5720±140	Microbotanical remains of edible plants: *Eurhynchium hylcomium, Nechara complanata, Thamnobryum alopercurum, Thuidium tamariscinum*
21	Westward Ho!	4860±140	Hazel nuts, fruits, seeds, prickle, thorn
		5005±140	
		4635±130	
22	Kinloch Rhum	6640±95	Hazelnuts

of these two major elements in the plant diet. Such plant-food strategies focused on the exploitation of the forest ecosystem (Bogucki 1988, also this volume) within an integrated economy that was characterized by the specialized use of several animal resources. In North Temperate Europe, particularly in coastal and lacustrine zones, these included pig, seal, and fish.

The aquatic resources

The concentration of Mesolithic settlement in coastal zones of Europe is well known. David Clarke (1976:468) spoke of a saucer-like distribution of dense Mesolithic settlement "along the coastal and glaciated rim" of Europe. In the last twenty years, additional evidence has only reinforced this view (Mellars 1978; Rowley-Conwy 1983; Larsson 1990; Zvelebil 1986a, etc.). Lacustrine and riverine zones in the interior of the continent, too, attracted Mesolithic settlement (Dolukhanov 1979; Zvelebil and Dolukhanov 1991; Woodman 1978, 1985, etc.). One of the principal reasons for such a settlement pattern must have been the seasonal availability of food resources connected to water, both vegetal and animal. Migratory fish (salmon, eel, sea trout), seal, shellfish, and waterfowl were the principal animal resources increasing the productivity of coastal and lacustrine regions (Rowley-Conwy 1983; Bailey 1978, 1983; Zvelebil 1981).

Aquatic species, such as seal, waterbirds, or fish would be difficult to domesticate owing to the restricted nature of their habitat, and, in some cases, the migratory nature of their life cycle. Fish, moreover, have a cumulative, rather than sigmoid rate of growth (McCullough 1970). As a consequence, various forms of selective cull which would effectively increase production among mammals would not be effective on fish.

The exploitation of aquatic resources, however, could be increased by employing labor-demanding mass-capture facilities, such as nets, fish traps, and fish weirs. Some resources, because of their migratory lifestyle, are less sensitive to predation than stationary, territorial species, allowing for sustained specialization during the restricted periods of the year, if the appropriate level of technology is developed.

There is little doubt that fishing, fowling, and specialized hunting of sea mammals formed an important element of the economy among the Late Mesolithic and Neolithic communities in many coastal zones of Europe (Clark 1952; Rowley-Conwy 1983; Zvelebil 1981, 1986a, 1992a, b; Mellars 1978; Paaver 1965; Vankina 1970; Siiriäinen 1980; Matiskainen 1989, 1990; Nygaard 1989; Welinder 1975; Andersen 1987, 1993; Price 1989; Tauber 1981, etc.). The distribution of fish weirs, fish traps, and nets in the Baltic Sea basin shown in Fig. 5, although by no means exhaustive, shows that the employment of delayed-capture facilities was a common practice, at least since the Late Mesolithic in this part of Europe, although fish nets had already been in use since the early Mesolithic (Clark 1975), and possibly earlier. The fishing/sea hunting tool-kits also included equipment for more individual hunting by fish hook, fish spear (leister), and harpoon. Remains of watercraft, boats, and paddles, are common on sites with good preservation of organic materials (e.g., Vankina 1970; Andersen 1987; Clark 1975). The development of specialized fishing, sealing, and fowling finds confirmation also in the faunal remains, showing that specialized sites for fowling (for example, Narva in Estonia [Gurina 1966] and Aggersund in Denmark [Andersen 1979]), sealing (for example, Nääkämäe and Loona in Estonia [Paaver 1965] and Pitted Ware sites in eastern Sweden [Welinder 1976]), or fishing (for example, Dyrholm [Rowley-Conwy 1983]) formed a part of the logistic system of resource procurement in the circum-Baltic zone (Rowley-Conwy 1983; Rowley-Conwy and Zvelebil 1989).

Given this marked orientation towards aquatic resources, it may be the case that during the seasonal peaks in their exploitation, people were faced with a surplus which would have been difficult to consume or to preserve. In such a situation, by-products of fishing and sealing could be fed to pigs, or left for pigs to scavenge on or near the settlements. This might be especially the case where seasonal kills of seals, salmon, and eels were made in late winter and early spring, a period marked by a shortage of food for wild boar.

The pig

Turning now to the evidence for pig exploitation itself, I have summarized the faunal data for the use of pigs and sea mammals in the coastal zones of the Baltic during the Late Mesolithic or transitional stages to the Neolithic, covering broadly the period 6000–2000 b.c. (Figs. 8, 9, and 10). The standardization and representation of the evidence drawn from a number of disparate sources presented a major problem in this endeavor. First, the percentage ratios are calculated from a total sample that includes fur animals, some of which may or may not have been used for food. Second, I have chosen bone fragments out of the total mammal bone sample as the basis for my calculations, in order to broaden the sample and to make it compatible with counts for sea mammals. Pig bones are strongly susceptible to attrition. Had I used MNI (minimum number of individuals) or calculated the percentages out of meat-bearing ungulates, the values for pig would have been higher, indeed, in some cases, such as Ringkloster, they would have doubled. In contrast, in those instances where pigs were brought onto the site whole, as opposed to meat joints for other ungulates, the bone-fragment count for pigs would result in their over-representation (Blankholm, pers. comm.). So the bone count can provide only an approximate estimation of the relative importance of a resource in the economy. Given the range of sources used and the variation in the calculations of faunal remains, the choice of identifiable bone fragments in this study is the only option that would maintain a reasonably broad sample. The results, therefore, should be taken as illustrative and approximate rather than accurate.

Several things can be noted from the graph in Fig. 8:
1. There seems to be a qualitative increase in the use of pigs on coastal sites from about 4500 b.c.
2. There seems to be a gradual increase in the exploitation of sea mammals from about 4000 b.c., leading to a strong specialization on sea mammals between 2500 and 1500 b.c. in the central and eastern Baltic (but not in the southwest Baltic, where agro-pastoral farming was adopted ca. 3000 b.c.).
3. There seems to be an increase in the use of pigs on inland sites from about 4000 b.c. The chronological and geographical distribution of these patterns is illustrated in Figs. 9 and 10. During the Late Mesolithic, pig becomes a key resource on a number of sites in the Ertebølle culture, while seal-dominated sites occur in peninsular Scandinavia. Apart from Vaenge Sø and Visby, there is no evidence for co-dominance of seal and pig in the osteological remains, although artifactual evidence points to a marked sea-hunting and -fishing orientation.

During the third millennium b.c., we can see the emergence of a specialized resource-use pattern, where pig and seal are the dominant elements, within the context of the Pitted Ware culture and similar settlements in the East Baltic. Pig is the main resource on some inland East Baltic sites, while in Finland the tradition of specialized sealing communities continues into the Bronze Age (Zvelebil 1981; Siiriäinen 1981; Matiskainen 1989).

At the same time, in both the Ertebølle culture of Denmark, and in the East Baltic during the third millennium b.c., there are other sites where pig is *not* the dominant element in the faunal assemblage (Paaver 1965; Rowley-Conwy 1980). Red deer and elk are the principal components.

Fig. 8:
Percentages of wild-pig and sea-mammal bones on coastal and inland sites in southern Scandinavia and the circum-Baltic zone between ca. 6500 and 1500 b.c.
   The sample comes from sites with hunter-gatherer economies (Late Mesolithic or Forest Neolithic). The sample is not comprehensive: some sites, although belonging to Early or Middle Neolithic farming cultures, contained predominantly bones of wild animals, emphasizing the gradual nature of the transition to farming. For example, Sølager 2 and 3, dated to the Early and Middle Neolithic respectively, contained only 5 and 14% domesticates each, with no domestic pig, and wild pig values of 17 and 32%, respectively (Skaarup 1973). For references to individual sites, see Paaver (1965) for the East Baltic sites, and Rowley-Conwy (1980) and Andersen et al. (1990) for the Scandinavian sites. The figure has been prepared following these sources.

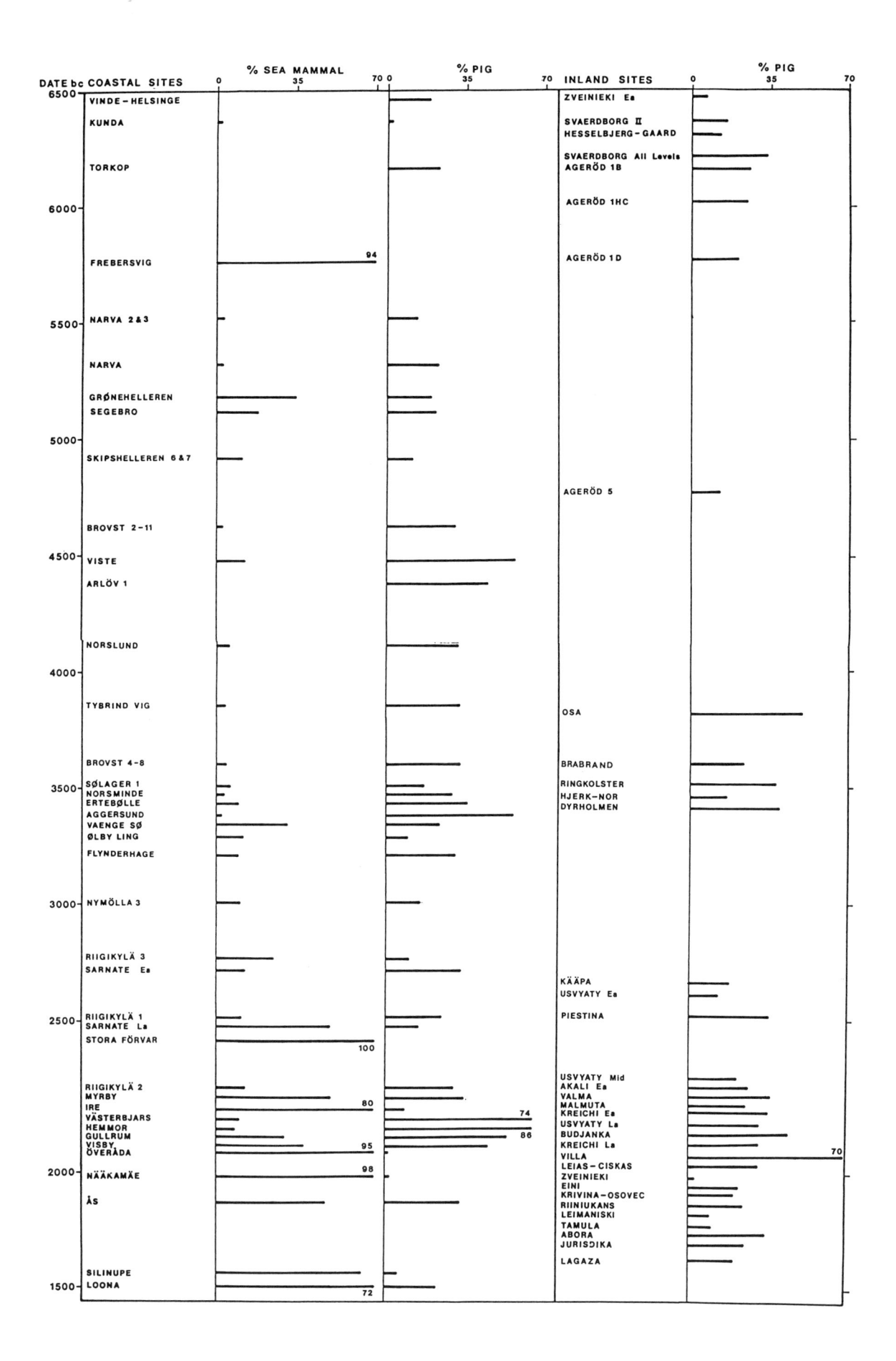

DATE bc	COASTAL SITES	% SEA MAMMAL	% PIG	INLAND SITES	% PIG
6500	VINDE-HELSINGE			ZVEINIEKI Ea	
	KUNDA			SVAERDBORG II	
				HESSELBJERG-GAARD	
	TORKOP			SVAERDBORG All Levels	
				AGERÖD 1B	
6000				AGERÖD 1HC	
	FREBERSVIG	94		AGERÖD 1D	
5500	NARVA 2 & 3				
	NARVA				
	GRØNEHELLEREN				
	SEGEBRO				
5000					
	SKIPSHELLEREN 6 & 7			AGERÖD 5	
	BROVST 2-11				
4500	VISTE				
	ARLÖV 1				
	NORSLUND				
4000					
	TYBRIND VIG			OSA	
	BROVST 4-8			BRABRAND	
3500	SØLAGER 1			RINGKOLSTER	
	NORSMINDE			HJERK-NOR	
	ERTEBØLLE			DYRHOLMEN	
	AGGERSUND				
	VAENGE SØ				
	ØLBY LING				
	FLYNDERHAGE				
3000	NYMÖLLA 3				
	RIIGIKYLÄ 3				
	SARNATE Ea			KÄÄPA	
				USVYATY Ea	
2500	RIIGIKYLÄ 1			PIESTINA	
	SARNATE La				
	STORA FÖRVAR	100			
	RIIGIKYLÄ 2			USVYATY Mid	
	MYRBY	80		AKALI Ea	
	IRE		74	VALMA	
	VÄSTERBJARS			MALMUTA	
	HEMMOR			KREICHI Ea	
	GULLRUM		86	USVYATY La	
	VISBY	95		BUDJANKA	
	ÖVERÅDA			KREICHI La	
				VILLA	70
				LEIAS-CISKAS	
2000	NÄÄKAMÄE	98		ZVEINIEKI	
				EINI	
	ÅS			KRIVINA-OSOVEC	
				RIINIUKANS	
				LEIMANISKI	
				TAMULA	
				ABORA	
				JURISDIKA	
	SILINUPE			LAGAZA	
1500	LOONA	72			

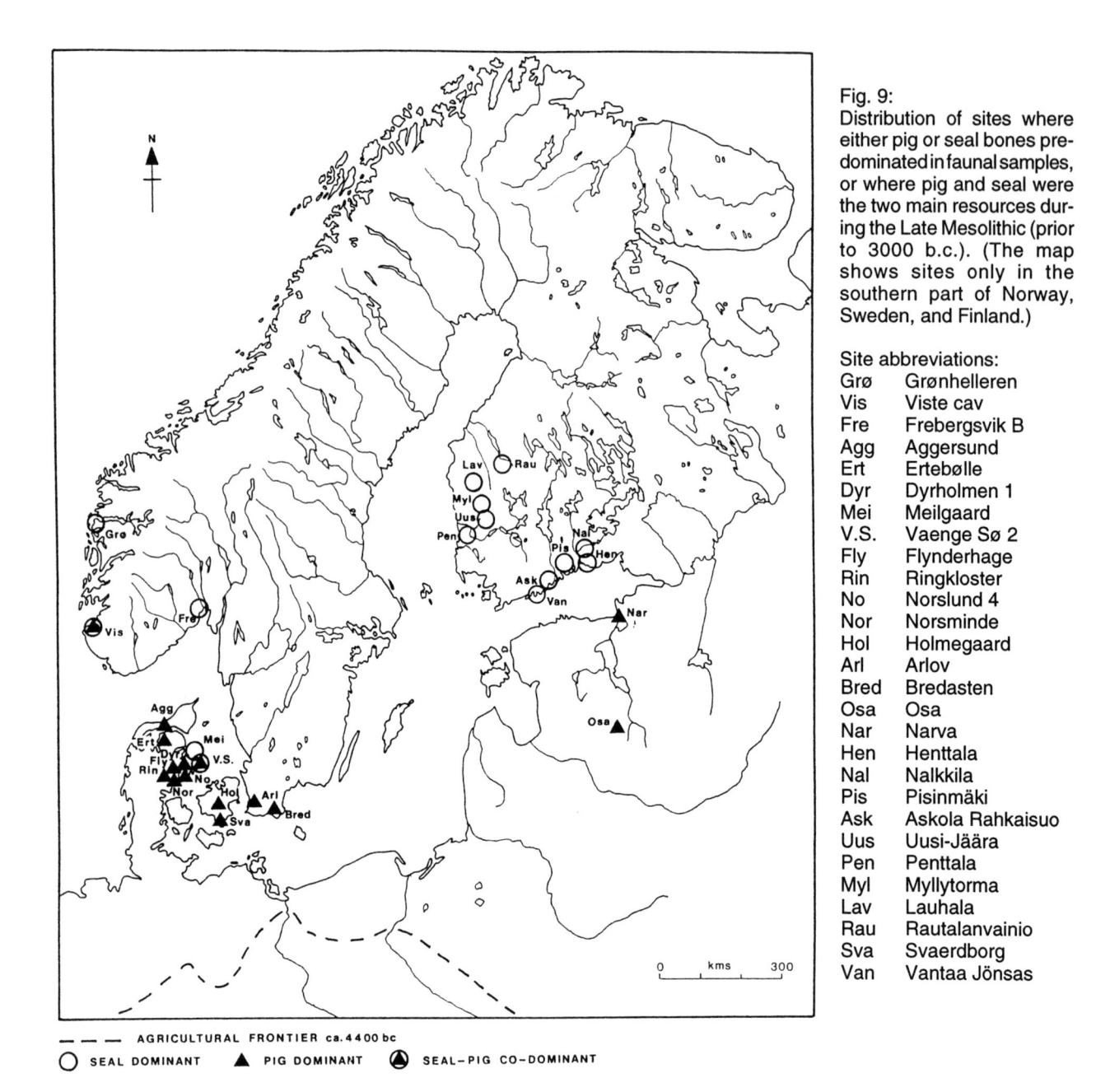

Fig. 9:
Distribution of sites where either pig or seal bones predominated in faunal samples, or where pig and seal were the two main resources during the Late Mesolithic (prior to 3000 b.c.). (The map shows sites only in the southern part of Norway, Sweden, and Finland.)

Site abbreviations:
Grø	Grønhelleren
Vis	Viste cav
Fre	Frebergsvik B
Agg	Aggersund
Ert	Ertebølle
Dyr	Dyrholmen 1
Mei	Meilgaard
V.S.	Vaenge Sø 2
Fly	Flynderhage
Rin	Ringkloster
No	Norslund 4
Nor	Norsminde
Hol	Holmegaard
Arl	Arlov
Bred	Bredasten
Osa	Osa
Nar	Narva
Hen	Henttala
Nal	Nalkkila
Pis	Pisinmäki
Ask	Askola Rahkaisuo
Uus	Uusi-Jäära
Pen	Penttala
Myl	Myllytorma
Lav	Lauhala
Rau	Rautalanvainio
Sva	Svaerdborg
Van	Vantaa Jönsas

— — — AGRICULTURAL FRONTIER ca. 4400 bc
○ SEAL DOMINANT ▲ PIG DOMINANT ⬤ SEAL-PIG CO-DOMINANT

At which point within this development can we speak of a specialized use of wild boar? The variation in the level of pig exploitation can reflect local availability of pig in the natural environment. It also can be related to the seasonality of the settlement: winter-occupied sites can be expected to contain more pig bones than those occupied in the summer half of the year. The duration of the settlement, and its function as a base camp or a seasonal site, can also be expected to have an effect on the composition of faunal samples. These considerations emphasize the preliminary and coarse-grained nature of the pattern observed in my sample.

However, it appears significant that dependence on pigs *increases* in the third millennium b.c., a time of climatic deterioration and decline in the distribution of deciduous woodland, both of which should have had an adverse effect on the numbers of wild boar in North Temperate Europe.

Investigations into the kill patterns of wild pigs on Ertebølle sites, carried out by Møhl (1971), Bay-Petersen (1978), and Rowley-Conwy (1980), indicate that there seems to be selection for juvenile pigs,[4] and that in most cases pigs were killed in the winter half of the year, as at Aggersund, Ringkloster, Brovst 4-8, and Dyrholm 1. Even where year-round killing of pigs was noted, as at Ertebølle or Norslund, the majority of kills still occurred in the winter. Winter kills of young pigs also occurred on Gotland, at sites such as Ire, where most individuals were killed

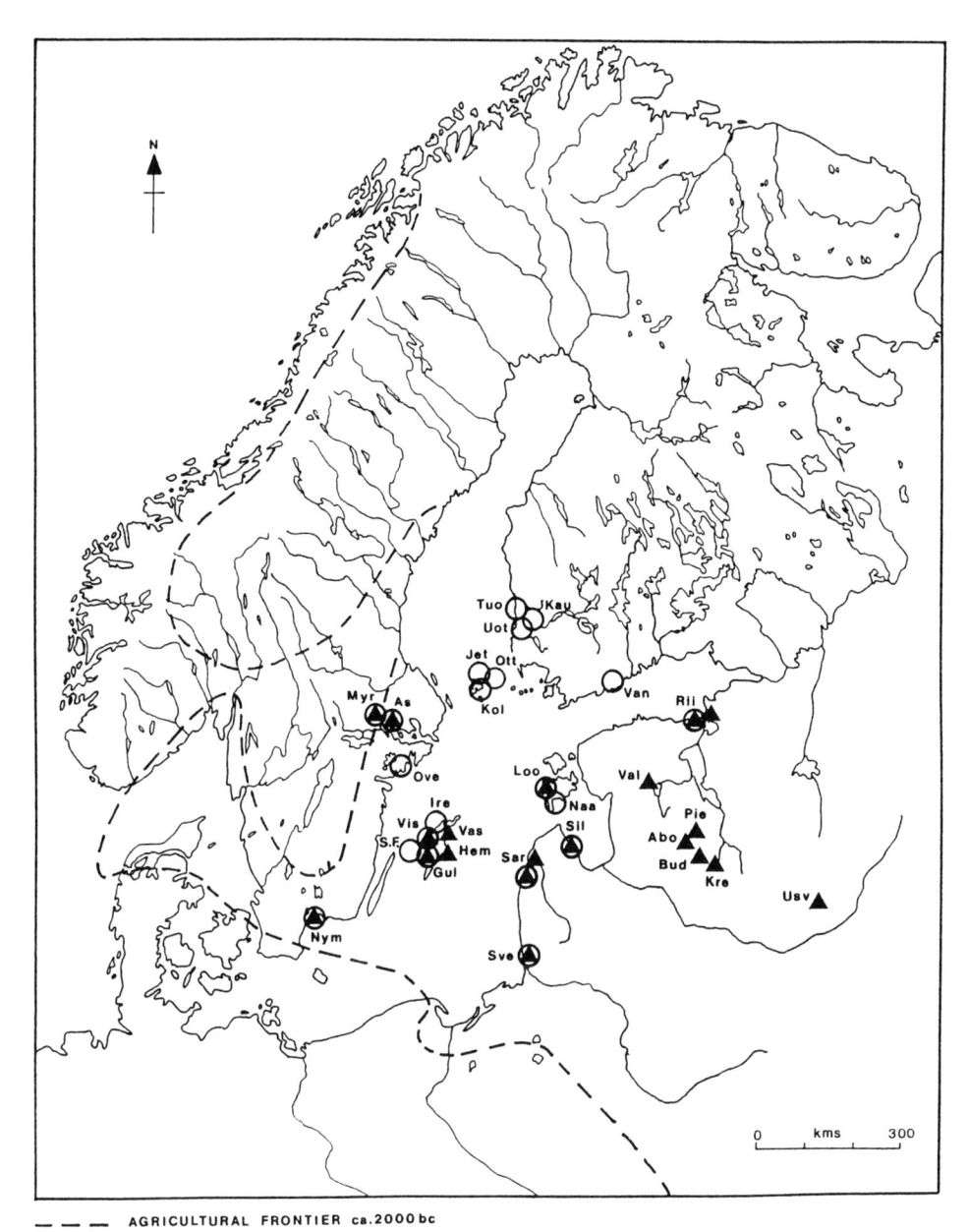

Fig. 10:
Distribution of sites where either pig or seal bones predominated in faunal samples, or where pig and seal were the two main resources between 3000 and 1500 b.c.

Site abbreviations:
Nym	Nymölla
Myr	Myrby
As	Ås
Ove	Overäda
Ire	Ire
Vis	Visby
Vas	Västebjers
Gul	Gullrum
S.F.	Stora Förvar
Sar	Sarnate
Sve	Šventoji
Sil	Silnyupe
Loo	Loona
Naa	Nääkamäe
Usv	Usvyaty
Kre	Kreichi
Bud	Budyanka
Abo	Abora
Pie	Piestina
Val	Valma
Rii	Narva Riigiküla
Van	Vantaa Comb Ceramic II Sites
Jet	Jettböle
Kol	Kolisvidja
Ott	Kökar Otterböte
Tuo	Tuorsniemi
Kau	Kaunismäki
Uot	Uotinmäki
Hem	Hemmor

— — — AGRICULTURAL FRONTIER ca.2000 bc
○ SEAL DOMINANT   ▲ PIG DOMINANT   ⊕ SEAL-PIG CO-DOMINANT

between October and March.

There is also strong correspondence between increased residential permanence and increased pig exploitation in Ertebølle and later settlements. In the Ertebølle, pigs dominate in the fauna of major base camps and on seasonal winter sites, which were nevertheless occupied for a considerable period of the year. Ringkloster is a case in point: although a seasonal site, it must have been occupied between November and May (Rowley-Conwy 1983). Wild pigs also dominate the fauna of what was apparently a permanently occupied settlement at Viste in western Norway (Degerbol 1951, Nygaard 1989) and of a winter base camp at Arlöv in Scania.

The question to be addressed now is the domestication status of the pigs—were they wild, tame, or domesticated? Up to this point, we have some evidence for increasing specialization, selective cull of young pigs, winter kills, and correspondence between increasing pig exploitation and residential permanence. On coastal sites, this coincides with increased marine specialization. Although generally in conformity with our expectations, none of this amounts to behavioral or biological domestication of wild pigs.

Changes in body size, morphology of the facial region, and dentition are the main criteria for distinguishing between wild and domestic pigs. All of these are subject to variation that has nothing to do with domestication, such as temperature, diet, and genetic isolation (Bökönyi 1974; Payne and Bull 1988). Nevertheless, the size of the lower

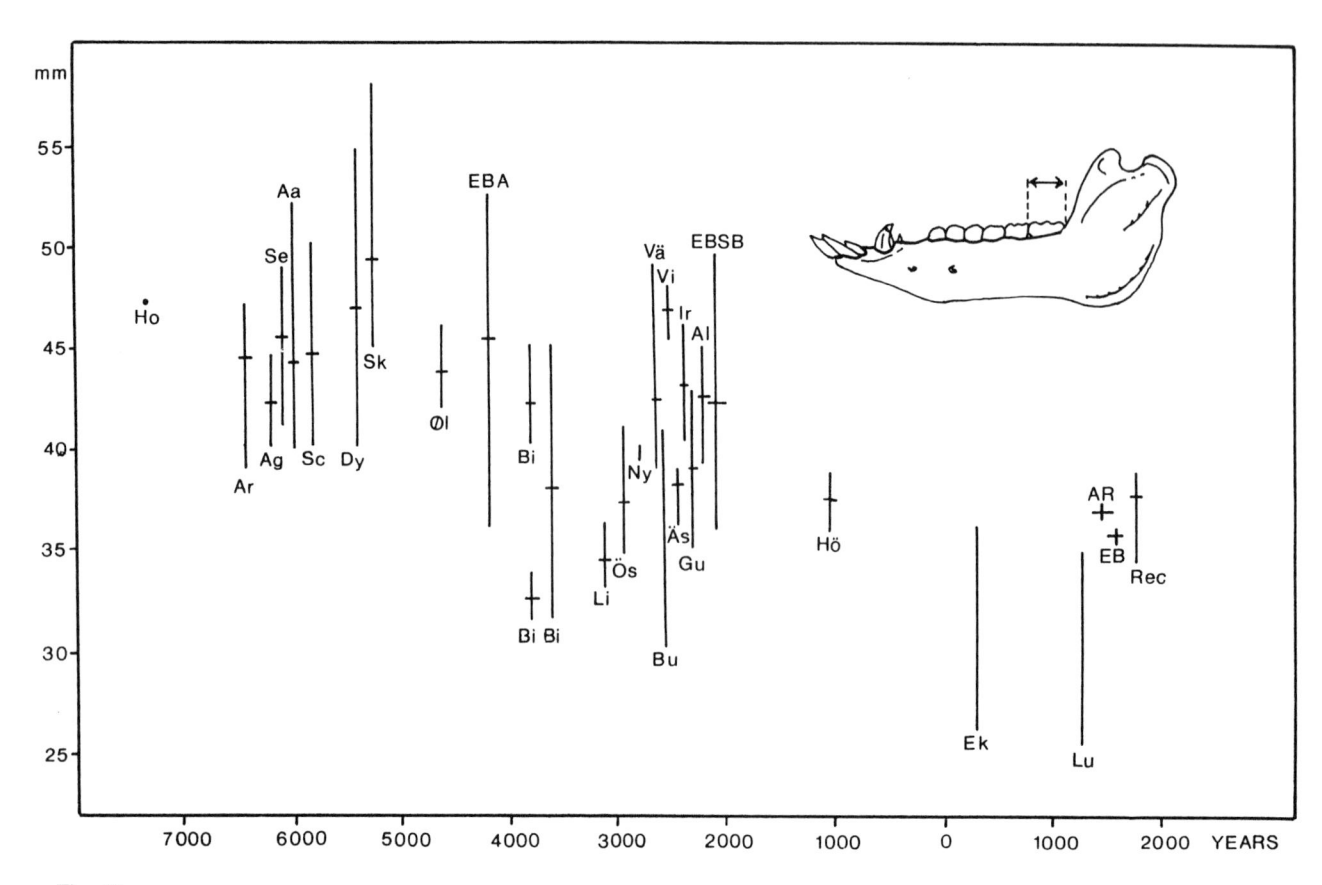

Fig. 11:
Size of the lower third molar of pigs from south Scandinavian and circum-Baltic sites. (After Jonsson 1986, data from Paaver 1965 added and shown in capitals.)

Site abbreviations: Ho: Hornborgarsjon; Ar: Arlöv; Ag: Ageröd; Se: Segebro; Aa: Aamosen; Sc: Scania; Dy: Dyrholm; Sk: Skateholm; Øl: Ølby Lyng; Bi: Bistoft (values for total, "wild," and "domestic" shown); Li: Lidsø; Ös: Östra Vemmenhog; Ny: Nymölla; Vä: Västerbjers; Bu: Bundsø; Vi: Visby; Äs: Äs; Ir: Ire; Gu: Gullrum; Al: Alvastra; Hö: Hötofta; Ek: Eketorp; Lu: Lund; Rec: recent western Europe (after Jonsson 1986); EBA: East Baltic Atlantic sample; EBSB: East Baltic Sub-Boreal sample; AR/EB: Early Medieval samples from ancient Russia (AR) and East Baltic (EB) (calculated from Paaver 1965).

third molar has been commonly used to distinguish wild from domestic pigs.

Figure 11, redrawn after Jonsson (1986), with the East Baltic data added (Paaver 1965), illustrates the situation in the circum-Baltic area. The sample appears to divide into three groups: clearly wild Mesolithic remains from Dano-Scania, a group dating to the third millennium b.c. with the three smallest cases belonging to the Neolithic TRB culture (Bistoft, Lidsø, and Östra Vemmenhog), and a more recent sample of clearly domestic animals from Dano-Scania, the East Baltic, and Russia.

It is the third millennium sample which is of interest here. Values within this group are clearly in the intermediate position. Although regarded by Jonsson (1986) as belonging to domestic pigs, Paaver (1965) and Lepiksaar (1974) regard the same range of values as belonging to wild pigs; they suggest that the reduction in size in the third millennium b.c. may indicate the local domestication of wild boar, or crossbreeding between imported domestic pig and local boar. The same trend could also occur as a result of stress imposed by the increasingly marginal conditions of habitat for wild pig in the third millennium b.c. as climatic deterioration sets in. In summary, then, although the analysis of dentition indicates some change in the lifestyle of pigs in the third millennium b.c., it is not clear whether the change can be taken as an indication of taming or domestication.

Can we see any evidence for taming or behavioral domestication of morphologically wild pigs? Close contact with pigs in the Ertebølle is suggested by stray finds of injured pigs who survived human efforts to get their bacon: the sample is evenly divided between those hit by a blunt instrument, probably axe, and those wounded by the penetration of a projectile point (Noe-Nygaard 1974). Dolukhanov (1986) reports finds of pig feces at Usvyaty in northwest Russia, which contained many bones of fish. If indeed these belong to morphologically wild pigs, this would be one of the clearest indications of taming.

Porcine colonization of islands provides another puzzling aspect of the story. Wild pig remains were found on Bronholm, Saaremaa, and Gotland. The Bronholm finds have been dated to the late Preboreal and Boreal ages (Aaris-Sørenson 1988); the Gotland and Saaremaa sites date to 2500–1500 b.c. All of these islands are thought to have been isolated from the mainland during the Younger Dryas or Preboreal periods (Clark 1975), and, although pigs can swim, it is unlikely they could make a journey of 15–20 miles across the sea or brackish water, even if they knew where they were going. We are faced with the same dilemma when attempting to explain the widespread presence of wild pigs in Ireland from about 7000 b.c. onwards: although the date for the separation of Ireland from Britain has not been fully agreed upon, most authorities believe that Ireland had become an island before 8000 b.c. (Mitchell 1986; Woodman 1978). One explanation, of course, would be that pigs were brought to the islands by humans as tame beasts.

Finally, linguistic evidence for the terminology denoting pig in Celtic, Germanic, and Baltic languages points to a wide range of pig-handling practices reflected in developed vocabulary for different types of pig. Hamp (1987) discusses the non-Indo-European terms for pig in Celtic, Germanic, and Lithuanian, and suggests that pig played a special role in the pre-Indo-European communities of North Temperate Europe. If, as Renfrew (1987) and others claim, the Indo-European languages were introduced to Europe by Neolithic agro-pastoral farmers, and if the pre-Indo-European terminology belonged to the indigenous Mesolithic hunter-gatherers (Zvelebil 1995), then we have linguistic support for some form of pig management by these groups.

In summary, although the evidence for the taming of pigs remains circumstantial, it does, in my view, suggest some form of management, probably in association with intensive plant use or plant husbandry, and specialized use of aquatic resources. When compared to other schemes introduced to account for the domestication of animals, for example, the four-part model of ovicaprid domestication in the Near East proposed by Horwitz (1989), the evidence from the circum-Baltic part of North Temperate Europe for the specialized and selective use of wild pig populations, matched perhaps by some restriction on their movement, goes beyond generalized hunting and suggests incipient domestication, either through intensive hunting (B1 in Horwitz's scheme) or population isolation (B2, Horwitz 1989).

The current evidence, preliminary as it is, leaves room for two historical explanations:
1. With increasing sedentism, pigs were attracted to the vicinity of human settlement as scavengers. This resulted in increased predation, especially during the winter, a pattern reflected in bone samples. The introduction of farming and its spread in southern Scandinavia in the Early Neolithic (3200–2600 b.c.) introduced domesticates to the area. Along the margins of the agricultural frontier zone, surviving hunter-gatherers developed a lifestyle partly dependent on exchange with the farming groups further inland (Funnel Beaker and Single Grave cultures). Intensive seal exploitation and seal products played a role in this exchange for products of farming. Domesticated pigs were introduced at this stage but crossbred with wild boar to produce large-sized animals (the intermediate group in Fig. 11). This explanation does not envisage the existence of tame pigs prior to ca. the third millennium b.c., when a remarkable sea-hunting and pig-husbanding culture emerged in the eastern part of North Temperate Europe under the influence of the agricultural frontier. It also does not explain some features of the archaeological record, such as the presence of pigs on islands.
2. Pigs scavenging or being fed surplus food during the winter half of the year (November–April) resulted in restrictions imposed on animal movements and a certain amount of population isolation, leading to an increased rate of random morphological change in the population (Horwitz 1989). The variation in size of pigs can perhaps be explained by this means. It also may have led to the taming of at least a part of the population, accounting for the presence of pigs on the Baltic islands, and other indications of close contact (see above). During the Early Neolithic, the conventional domesticates replaced this form of pig husbandry with some interbreeding between the local and introduced pig populations. The old form of pig husbandry continued in eastern Sweden and the coastal East Baltic in a more developed form as a part of an economy based on sealing, fishing, and pig-keeping. A full agro-pastoral farming economy was finally introduced into this area between 1800 and 1200 b.c.

Conclusions

The case I have presented here for intensive plant use and wild pig husbandry in the Late Mesolithic of North Temperate Europe is based on circumstantial evidence. Most if not all of the phenomena discussed here can be individually explained by other means. Together, they present a coherent explanation pointing towards the existence of an integrated resource-use system which, in terms of management and control, may perhaps be regarded as husbandry: a set of practices intermediate in intensity between hunting and gathering on the one hand, and keeping domestic livestock on the other. While there is little use in forcing such an explanation on the evidence, which is often inconclusive, there are, in my view, enough indicators of the special status of nuts, aquatic resources, and wild pig to consider the plant-pig management hypothesis seriously.

Acknowledgments

This paper was completed while I was a Fellow at the Netherlands Institute for Advanced Studies in Humanities and Social Sciences (NIAS). I am grateful to the Institute for logistical assistance and financial support. I would also like to express my thanks to Dr. Peter Rowley-Conwy, Dr. Hans-Peter Blankholm, and Dr. Anders Fisher for reading and commenting on earlier versions of this paper. Even though I failed to follow their advice in many cases, without their helpful criticisms this paper would have been even more speculative. I remain solely responsible for any errors or omissions.

Notes

1. Cultural domestication involves the keeping or tending of morphologically undomesticated plants and animals. Some of these tending or handling strategies interfere with the natural propagation or reproduction of the resources, and this may in time result, through the process of selection, in biological changes in the plants or animals in question, and therefore in biological domestication. There is, then, a span of time when biologically undomesticated resources are semi-wild, tame, or culturally domesticated in terms of their control and behavior.

2. Husbandry is defined in this paper as the planned and deliberate application of promotional strategies to plants or animals designed to increase their productivity and to gain greater control over them.

3. An experiment in Sondermaland (central Sweden) has shown that wild hazelnut yields vary between 200 and 540 kg/ha, and that a person can easily collect about a kilogram in an hour (Lindquist 1988). Since hazelnut has double the energy value of cereals, the total caloric yield of a hectare of hazelnut woodland would be about 660,000 kcal, enough to support a person through the winter with enough left over for two pigs as well. This means that a relatively small area, such as the Kolsvidja island on Aland, with its 250 ha of hazel woodland (Lindquist 1988), could support 100 people and 400 pigs through the winter. This example suggests that there were enough nut crops for people to meet their needs and for pigs to convert the rest into an alternative source of energy.

4. Rowley-Conwy (pers. comm.) notes that higher wild-pig fecundity will be reflected in a higher number of juvenile pigs in faunal samples, irrespective of selection for immature pigs. Only further and more detailed studies of the age and sex structure of the pig kills can determine whether additional selection was operating. See also Rowley-Conwy 1995.

References

Aaris-Sørenson, K. 1988. *Danmarks forhistoriske Dyreverden, Fra Istid til Vikingetid.*

Ammerman, A. J., and L. L. Cavalli-Sforza. 1984. *The Neolithic Transition and the Genetics of Populations in Europe.* Princeton University Press, Princeton, NJ.

Andersen, S. T. 1979. Identification of Wild Grass and Cereal Pollen. *Danmarks geologiske Undesogelse* 1978:69–92.

Andersen, S. H. 1987. Tybrind Vig: A Submerged Ertebølle Settlement in Denmark. In *European Wetland in Prehistory*, ed. J. M. Coles and A. J. Lawson, pp. 253–281. Clarendon Press, Oxford.

_____ 1993. Mesolithic Coastal Settlement. In *Digging into the Past: 25 Years of Archaeology in Denmark,* ed. S. Hvass and B. Storgaard, pp. 65–68. The Royal Society of Northern Antiquities and Jutland Archaeological Society, Copenhagen.

Andersen, S. H., A. Bietti, C. Bonsall, N. D. Broadbent, G. A. Clark, B. Gramsch, R. M. Jacobi, L. Larsson, A. Morrison, R. R. Newell, J.-G. Rozoy, L. G. Strauss, and P. C. Woodman. 1990. Making Cultural Ecology Relevant to Mesolithic Research. I: A Database of 413 Mesolithic Assemblages. In *Contributions to the Mesolithic in Europe*, ed. P. M. Vermeersch and P. van Peer. Papers presented at the Fourth International Symposium "The Mesolithic in Europe." Leuven University Press, Leuven.

Bailey, G. N. 1978. Shell Middens as Indicators of Postglacial Economies: A Territorial Perspective. In *The Early Postglacial Settlement of Northern Europe*, ed. P. Mellars, pp. 37–63. Duckworth, London.

_____ (ed.) 1983. *Hunter-gatherer Economy in Prehistory: A European Perspective.* Cambridge University Press, Cambridge.

Bang-Andersen, S. 1995. The Mesolithic Man and the Rising Sea Spotlighted by Three Tapes-transgressed Sites in SW Norway. In *Man and Sea in the Mesolithic*, ed. A. Fisher, pp. 113–122. Oxbow Monograph 53. Oxford.

Barker, G. 1985. *Prehistoric Farming in Europe.* Cambridge University Press, Cambridge.

Bay-Petersen, J. L. 1978. Animal Exploitation in Mesolithic Denmark. In *The Early Postglacial Settlement of Northern Europe*, ed. P. Mellars, pp. 115–146. Duckworth, London.

Binford, L. R. 1968. Post-Pleistocene Adaptations. In *New Perspectives in Archaeology*, ed. S. Binford and L. R. Binford, pp. 313–341. Aldine, Chicago.

_____ 1983. *In Pursuit of the Past.* Thames and Hudson, London.

Bogucki, P. I. 1988. *Forest Farmers and Stockherders: Early Agriculture and its Consequences in North-central Europe.* Cambridge University Press, Cambridge.

Bökönyi, S. 1974. *History of Domestic Mammals in Central and Eastern Europe.* Akadémiai Kiadó, Budapest.

Bonsall, C. (ed.) 1989. *The Mesolithic in Europe.* John Donald, Edinburgh.

Brown, A. 1893. On the Continuity of the Neolithic and

Palaeolithic Periods. *Journal of the Royal Anthropological Institute* 22:66–98.

Chaplin, R. E. 1975. The Ecology and Behavior of Deer in Relation to their Impact on the Environment of Prehistoric Britain. In *The Effect of Man on the Landscape: The Highland Zone*, ed. J. G. Evans, S. Limbrey, and H. Cleere, pp. 40–42. CBA Research Report 11. Council for British Archaeology, London.

Chase, A. K. 1989. Domestication and Domiculture in Northern Australia: A Social Perspective. In *Foraging and Farming: The Evolution of Plant Exploitation*, ed. D. R. Harris and G. C. Hillman, pp. 42–53. Unwin Hyman, London.

Childe, V. G. 1925. *The Dawn of European Civilisation*. Kegan Paul, London.

_____ 1957. *The Dawn of European Civilisation*, 6th ed. Kegan Paul, London.

Clark, G. A., and M. Neeley. 1987. Social Differentiation in European Mesolithic Burial Data. In *Mesolithic Northwest Europe: Recent Trends*, ed. P. Rowley-Conwy, M. Zvelebil, and H. P. Blankholm, pp. 121–130. University of Sheffield, Sheffield.

Clark, J. G. D. 1936. *The Mesolithic Settlement of Northern Europe*. Cambridge University Press, Cambridge.

_____ 1952. *Prehistoric Europe: The Economic Basis*. Methuen, London.

_____ 1975. *The Earlier Stone Age Settlement of Scandinavia*. Cambridge University Press, Cambridge.

_____ 1978. Neothermal Orientations. In *The Early Postglacial Settlement of Northern Europe*, ed. P. Mellars, pp. 1–10. Duckworth, London.

_____ 1980. *Mesolithic Prelude: The Palaeolithic-Neolithic Transition in Old World Prehistory*. Edinburgh University Press, Edinburgh.

Clarke, D. L. 1976. Mesolithic Europe: The Economic Basis. In *Problems in Economic and Social Archaeology*, ed. I. Sieveking, I. J. Longworth, and K. E. Wilson, pp. 449–481. Duckworth, London.

Constandse-Westermann, T. S., R. R. Newell, and C. Meiklejohn. 1984. Human Biological Background of Population Dynamics in the Western European Mesolithic. *Human Palaeontology Proceedings* B 87(2).

David, A. I., and V. I. Markevitch. 1970. Khozajstvo i fauna neoliticheskikh poselenij Severnogo Podnestrovija. In *Fauna Kajnozoja Moldavii*, Shiintsa, Kishinev 53–72.

Degerbol, M. 1951. *Harald Egenaes Lund Fangst-Boplassen I Vistehulen*. Utgitt av Stavanger Museum, Stavanger.

Dennell, R. 1983. *European Economic Prehistory*. Academic Press, London.

Dolukhanov, P. M. 1979. *Ecology and Economy in Neolithic Eastern Europe*. Duckworth, London.

_____ 1986. Natural Environment and the Holocene Settlement Pattern in the Northwestern Part of the USSR. *Fennoscandia archaeologica* 3:3–16.

_____ 1992. Evolution of Lakes and Prehistoric Settlement in Northwestern Russia. In *The Wetland Revolution in Prehistory*, ed. B. Coles. pp. 93–98. WARP, Exeter.

Edwards, K. J. 1982. Man, Space and the Woodland Edge—Speculation on the Detection and Interpretation of Human Impact in Pollen Profiles. In *Archaeological Aspects of Woodland Ecology*, ed. B. M. Bell and S. Limbrey, pp. 5–22. British Archaeological Reports, Oxford.

_____ 1988. The Hunter-gatherer/Agricultural Transition and the Pollen Record in the British Isles. In *The Cultural Landscape—Past, Present and Future*, ed. H. H. Birks, H. J. B. Birks, P. E. Kaland, and D. Moe, pp. 255–266. Cambridge University Press, Cambridge.

_____ 1989. The Cereal Pollen Record and Early Agriculture. In *The Beginnings of Agriculture*, ed. D. Milles, D. Williams, and N. Gardner, pp. 113–135. British Archaeological Reports, Oxford.

_____ 1993. Models of Mid-Holocene Forests Farming for North-west Europe. In *Climatic Change and Human Impact on the Landscape*, ed. F. M. Chambers, pp. 132–145. Chapman and Hale, London.

Edwards, K. J., and K. R. Hirons. 1984. Cereal Pollen Grains in Pre-elm Decline Deposits: Implications for the Earliest Agriculture in Britain and Ireland. *Journal of Archaelogical Science* 11:71–80.

Ekman, J. 1974. Djurbensmaterialet från stenålderslokalen Ire, Hangvar sn. Gotland. In *Gotlands mellaneolotiska gravar. Acta Universitatis Stockholmiensis*, ed. G. O. Janzon, pp. 212–246. Studies in North-European Archaeology 6. Stockholm.

Fischer, A. 1993. The Late Palaeolithic. In *Digging into the Past: 25 Years of Archaeology in Denmark*, ed. S. Hvass and B. Storgaard, pp. 51–57. The Royal Society of Northern Antiquaries, Copenhagen.

Fisher, A. 1991. Pioneers in Deglaciated Landscapes: The Expansion and Adaptation of Late Palaeolithic Societies in Southern Scandinavia. In *The Late Glacial in North-west Europe: Human Adaptation and Environmental Change at the End of the Pleistocene*, ed. N. Barton, A. J. Roberts, and D. A. Roe, pp. 100–121. CBA Research Report 77. Council for British Archaeology, London.

Ford, R. I. 1985. The Processes of Plant Food Production in Prehistoric North America. In *Prehistoric Food Production in North America*, ed. R. I. Ford, pp. 1–18. Anthropological Paper 75. University of Michigan, Museum of Anthropology, Ann Arbor.

Geddes, D. S. 1985. Mesolithic Domestic Sheep in West Mediterranean Europe. *Journal of Archaeological Science* 12:25–48.

Gøransson, H. 1988: Comments on Remodelling the Neolithic in Southern Norway. On Analytical Myths. *Norwegian Archaeological Review* 21(1):33–37.

Gramsch, B. (ed.) 1981. *Mesolithikum in Europe*. Des Museums für Ur- und Frühgeschichte, Potsdam and VEB Deutscher Verlag der Wissenschaften, Berlin.

Gurina, I. I. (ed.) 1966. *Sources of Ancient Culture (Mesolithic Epoch)*. Mat. Issled. po Arkh. SSSR no. 126.

Hamp, E. P. 1987. The Pig in Ancient Northern Europe. In *Proto-Indo-European: The Archaeology of a Linguistic Problem*, ed. S. N. Skomal and L. E. C. Polomé, pp. 185–190. Institute for the Study of Man, Washington, DC.

Harris, D. R. 1977. Alternative Pathways towards Agriculture. In *Origins of Agriculture*, ed. C. Reed, pp. 179–244. Mouton, The Hague.

―――― 1989. An Evolutionary Continuum of People-Plant Interaction. In *Foraging and Farming: The Evolution of Plant Exploitation*, ed. D. R. Harris and G. C. Hillman, pp. 11–24. Unwin Hyman, London.

Harris, D. R., and G. C. Hillman (eds.) 1989. *Foraging and Farming: The Evolution of Plant Exploitation*. Unwin Hyman, London.

Higgs, E. S. (ed.) 1972. *Papers in Economic Prehistory*. Cambridge University Press, Cambridge.

―――― (ed.) 1975. *Palaeoeconomy*. Cambridge University Press, Cambridge.

Higgs, E. S., and M. R. Jarman. 1972. The Origins of Animal and Plant Husbandry. In *Papers in Economic Prehistory*, ed. E. S. Higgs, pp. 3–13. Cambridge University Press, Cambridge.

―――― 1975. Palaeoeconomy. In *Palaeoeconomy*, ed. E. S. Higgs, pp. 1–7. Cambridge University Press, Cambridge.

Hillman, G. C., and M. S. Davies. 1992. Domestication Rate in Wild Wheats and Barley under Primitive Cultivation: Preliminary Results and Archaeological Implications of Field Measurements of Selection Coefficient. In *Préhistoire de l'agriculture: Nouvelles approches expérimentales et ethnographiques*, ed. P. C. Anderson, pp. 113–158. Monographie du CRA no. 6. Editions de CNRS, Paris.

Hodder, I. 1990. *The Domestication of Europe*. Blackwell, Oxford.

Horwitz, L. 1989. A Reassessment of Caprovine Domestication in the Levantine Neolithic: Old Questions, New Answers. In *People and Culture in Change. Proceedings of the Second Symposium on Upper Palaeolithic, Mesolithic and Neolithic Populations of Europe and the Mediterranean Basin*, ed. I. Hershkovitz, pp. 153–181. BAR International Series 508 (i). British Archaeological Reports, Oxford.

Hynes, R. A., and A. K. Chase. 1982. Plants, Sites and Domiculture, Aboriginal Influence upon Plant Communities in Cape York Peninsula. *Archaeology in Oceania* 17:38–50.

Ingold, T., D. Riches, and J. Woodburn (eds.) 1988. *Hunters and Gatherers*. Berg, Oxford.

Jacobi, R. M. 1978. Northern England in the Eighth Millennium bc: An Essay. In *The Early Postglacial Settlement of Northern Europe*, ed. P. Mellars, pp. 295–332. Duckworth, London.

Jacobi, R. M., J. H. Tallis, and P. A. Mellars. 1976. The Southern Pennine Mesolithic and the Ecological Record. *Journal of Archaeological Science* 3:307–320.

Jacobs, K. 1993. Human Postcranial Variation in the Ukrainian Mesolithic-Neolithic. *Current Anthropology* 34:311–324.

Jarman, M. 1972. European Deer Economies and the Advent of the Neolithic. In *Papers in Economic Prehistory*, ed. E. Higgs, pp. 125–147. Cambridge University Press, Cambridge.

Jarman, M., G. N. Bailey, and H. N. Jarman. 1982. *Early European Agriculture*. Cambridge University Press, Cambridge.

Jochim, M. A. 1976. *Hunter-gatherer Subsistence and Settlement*. Academic Press, London.

Jonsson, L. 1986. From Wild Boar to Domestic Pig—A Reassessment of Neolithic Swine of Northwestern Europe. *Nordic Late Quaternary Biology and Ecology* 24:125–129.

Kozlowski, J. K., and S. K. Kozlowski. 1986. Foragers of Central Europe and their Acculturation. In *Hunters in Transition: Mesolithic Societies of Temperate Eurasia and their Transition to Farming*, ed. M. Zvelebil, pp. 95–108. Cambridge University Press, Cambridge.

Larsson, L. 1989. Ethnicity and Traditions in Mesolithic Mortuary Practices of Southern Scandinavia. In *Archaeological Approaches to Cultural Identity*, ed. S. J. Shennan, pp. 210–218. Unwin Hyman, London.

―――― 1990. Dogs in Fraction—Symbols in Action. In *Contributions to the Mesolithic in Europe*, ed. P. M. Vermeersch and P. van Peer, pp. 153–160. Papers presented at the Fourth International Symposium "The Mesolithic in Europe." Leuven University Press, Leuven.

―――― 1993. The Skateholm Project: Late Mesolithic Coastal Settlement in Southern Sweden. In *Case

Studies in European Prehistory, ed. P. Bogucki, pp. 31–62. CRC Press, Ann Arbor, MI.

Leacock, E., and R. B. Lee 1982. *Politics and History in Band Societies*. Cambridge University Press, Cambridge.

Lee, R. B., and I. DeVore. 1968. Problems in the Study of Hunters and Gatherers. In *Man the Hunter*, ed. R. B. Lee and I. DeVore, pp. 3–12. Aldine, Chicago.

Lepiksaar, J. 1974. Bone Remains from the Mesolithic Settlements Ageröd I:B and I:D. In *Ageröd I:B–Ageröd I:D, A Study of Early Atlantic Settlements in Scania*, pp. 234–244. Acta Archaeologica Lundendsia Series in 4°, 12. Lund.

Lewthwaite, J. 1986. The Transition to Food Production: A Mediterranean Perspective. In *Hunters in Transition: Mesolithic Societies of Temperate Eurasia and Their Transition to Farming*, ed. M. Zvelebil, pp. 53–66. Cambridge University Press, Cambridge.

Lindquist, C. 1988. A Carbonized Cereal Grain (*Hordeum* sp.) and Faunal Remains of e.g. Harp Seal (*Phoca groenlandica*), Cod (*Gadus morhua*) and Herring (*Clpea harengus*), from the Kolsvidja Upper Stone Age Habitation Sites on Aland. *Finskt Museum* 95:5–40.

Markevitch, V. I. 1974. *Bugodnestrovskaya kultura na territorii Moldavii*. Shiintsa, Kishinev.

Matiskainen, H. 1989. Studies on the Chronology, Material Culture and Subsistence Economy of the Finnish Mesolithic, 10000–6000 BP. *Iskos* 8.

—— 1990. Mesolithic Subsistence in Finland. In *Contributions to the Mesolithic in Europe*, ed. H. Vermeersch and P. van Peer, pp. 211–214. Papers presented at the Fourth International Symposium "The Mesolithic in Europe." Leuven University Press, Leuven.

McCullough, S. 1970. Secondary Production of Birds and Mammals. In *Temperate Forest Ecosystems*, ed. E. D. Reiche, pp. 107–130. Ecological Studies 1. Springer Verlag, Berlin.

Meiklejohn, C., and M. Zvelebil. 1991. Health Status of European Populations at the Agricultural Transition and the Implications for the Adoption of Farming. In *Health in Past Societies: Biocultural Interpretations of Human Skeletal Remains in Archaeological Contexts*, ed. H. Bush and M. Zvelebil, pp. 129–145. BAR International Series 567. British Archaeological Reports, Oxford.

Mellars, P. 1975. Ungulate Populations, Economic Patterns, and the Mesolithic Landscape. In *The Effect of Man on the Landscape: The Highland Zone*, ed. J. G. Evans, S. Limbrey, and H. Cleere, pp. 49–63. CBA Research Report 11. Council for British Archaeology, London.

—— 1976. Fire Ecology, Animal Populations and Man: A Study of Some Ecological Relationships in Prehistory. *Proceedings of the Prehistoric Society* 42:15–45.

—— (ed.) 1978. *The Early Postglacial Settlement of Northern Europe*. Duckworth, London.

—— 1981. Towards a Definition of the Mesolithic. *Mesolithic Miscellany* 2(2):13–16.

Mitchell, F. 1986. *Reading the Irish Landscape*. Amach Faoin Aer Teo, Dublin.

Mithen, S. J. 1987. Prehistoric Red Deer Hunting Strategies: A Cost-Risk–Benefit Analysis with Reference to Upper Paleolithic Northern Spain and Mesolithic Denmark. In *Mesolithic Northwest Europe: Recent Trends*, ed. P. Rowley-Conwy, M. Zvelebil, and H. P. Blankholm, pp. 93–108. University of Sheffield, Sheffield.

—— 1991. A Cybernetic Wasteland: Rationality, Emotion and Mesolithic Foraging. *Proceedings of the Prehistoric Society* 57(2):9–14.

Møhl, U. 1971. Oversigt over dyreknoglerne från Ølby Lyng. *Aarböger*, 43–77.

Morrison, A. 1980. *Early Man in Britain and Ireland*. Croom Helm, London.

Munson, P. J. (ed.) 1984. *Experiments and Observations on Aboriginal Wild Plant Food Utilization in Eastern North America*. Indiana Historical Society VI(2). Indianapolis.

Myers, A. M. 1989. Reliable and Maintainable Technological Strategies in the Mesolithic of Mainland Britain. In *Time, Energy and Stone Tools*, ed. R. Torrence, pp. 78–91. Cambridge University Press, Cambridge.

Newell, R. R. 1984. On the Mesolithic Contribution to the Social Evolution of Western European Society. In *European Social Evolution: Archaeological Perspectives*, ed. J. Bintliff, pp. 69–82. Bradford University Press, Bradford.

Noe-Nygaard, N. 1974. Mesolithic Hunting in Denmark Illustrated by Bone Injuries Caused by Human Weapons. *Journal of Archaeological Science* 1:217–248.

Nygaard, S. E. 1989. The Stone Age of Northern Scandinavia: A Review. *Journal of World Prehistory* 3(1):72–116.

O'Shea, J., and M. Zvelebil. 1984. Oleneostrovskii Mogilnik: Reconstructing Social and Economic Organisation of Prehistoric Hunter-fishers in Northern Russia. *Journal of Anthropological Archaeology* 3:1–40.

Paaver, K. C. 1965. *Formirovaniye Teriofauny i Izmenchivost Mlekopytayushchikh Pribaltiki v Goltsene*. Akademiya Nauk Estonskoii SSR, Tartu.

Payne, S., and G. Bull. 1988. Components of Variation in Measurements of Pig Bones and Teeth, and the

Use of Measurements to Distinguish Wild from Domestic Pig Remains. *Archaeozoologia* 2:27–66.

Petersen P. Vang. 1984. Chronological and Regional Variation in the Late Mesolithic of Eastern Denmark. *Journal of Danish Archaeology* 3:7–18.

Piggott, S. 1965. *Ancient Europe*. Edinburgh University Press, Edinburgh.

Pira, A. 1909. Studien zur Geschichte der Schweinerassen inbesondere derjenigen Schwedens. *Zoologisch Jahrbuch Supplement* 10(2):233–426.

Price, T. D. 1985. Affluent Foragers of Mesolithic Southern Scandinavia. In *Prehistoric Hunter-gatherers: The Emergence of Cultural Complexity*, ed. T. D. Price and J. A. Brown, pp. 341–360. Academic Press, Orlando.

―――― 1987. The Mesolithic of Western Europe. *Journal of World Prehistory* 1:225–305.

―――― 1989. The Reconstruction of Mesolithic Diets. In *The Mesolithic in Europe*, ed. C. Bonsall, pp. 48–59. John Donald, Edinburgh.

Price, T. D., and J. A. Brown (eds.) 1985. *Prehistoric Hunter-gatherers: The Emergence of Cultural Complexity*. Academic Press, Orlando.

Reed, C. A. (ed.) 1977. *Origins of Agriculture*. World Anthropology Series. Mouton, The Hague.

Renfrew, C. 1987. *Archaeology and Language. The Puzzle of Indo-European Origins*. Jonathan Cape, London.

Rindos, D. 1984. *The Origins of Agriculture, An Evolutionary Perspective*. Academic Press, New York.

Rowley-Conwy, P. 1980. *Continuity and Change in the Prehistoric Economies of Denmark, 3700–2300 BC*. Unpubl. Ph.D. diss., Cambridge.

―――― 1983. Sedentary Hunters: The Ertebølle Example. In *Hunter-gatherer Economy in Prehistory: A European Perspective*, ed. G. Bailey, pp. 111–126. Cambridge University Press, Cambridge.

―――― 1986. Between Cave Painters and Crop Planters: Aspects of the Temperate European Mesolithic. In *Hunters in Transition: Mesolithic Societies of Temperate Eurasia and their Transition to Farming*, ed. M. Zvelebil, pp. 17–32. Cambridge University Press, Cambridge.

―――― 1995. Wild or Domestic? On the Evidence for the Earliest Domestic Cattle and Pigs in South Scandinavia and Iberia. *International Journal of Osteoarchaeology* 5:115–126.

Rowley-Conwy, P., and M. Zvelebil. 1989. Saving it for Later: Storage by Prehistoric Hunter-gatherers in Europe. In *Bad Year Economics*, ed. P. Halstead and J. O'Shea, pp. 40–56. Cambridge University Press, Cambridge.

Rowley-Conwy, P., M. Zvelebil, and H. P. Blankholm (eds.) 1987. *Mesolithic Northwest Europe: Recent Trends*. University of Sheffield, Sheffield.

Rozoy, J.-G. 1989. The Revolution of the Bowmen in Europe. In *The Mesolithic in Europe*, ed. C. Bonsall, pp. 13–28. John Donald, Edinburgh.

Saint-Exupéry, A. de. 1943. *The Little Prince*, trans. K. Woods. Harcourt, Brace, and Co., New York.

Salmi, M. 1963. On the Distribution of Corylus. *Bulletin Commentationes Geologicae Finlandiae* 207:1–67.

Shnirelman, V. A. 1980. Proiskhozdneije Skotovodstva. Academy of Sciences USSR, Moscow.

―――― 1992. The Emergence of Food Producing Economy in the Steppe and Forest-steppe Zones of Eastern Europe. *The Journal of Indo-European Studies* 20:123–143.

Siiriänen, A. 1980. On the Cultural Ecology of the Finnish Stone Age. *Suomen Museo* 87:5–40.

―――― 1981. On the Cultural Ecology of the Finnish Stone Age. *Suomen Museo* 87:5–40.

Simmons, I. G. 1975. Towards an Ecology of Mesolithic Man in the Uplands of Great Britain. *Journal of Archaeological Science* 2:1–15.

Simmons, I. G., G. W. Dimbleby, and C. Grigson. 1981. The Mesolithic. In *The Environment in British Prehistory*, ed. I. G. Simmons and M. J. Tooley, pp. 82–124. Duckworth, London.

Simmons, I. G., and J. B. Innes. 1985. Late Mesolithic Land Use and its Impact in the English Uplands. *Biogeographical Monographs* 2:7–17.

―――― 1987. Mid-Holocene Adaptations and Mesolithic Forest Disturbance in Northern England. *Journal of Archaeological Science* 14:385–403.

Simmons, I. G., J. Turner, and J. B. Innes. 1989. An Application of Fine-resolution Pollen Analysis to Later Mesolithic Peats of an English Upland. In *The Mesolithic in Britain*, ed. C. Bonsall, pp. 206–217. John Donald, Edinburgh.

Skaarup, J. 1973. *Hesselo-Sølager*. Akademisk Forlag, Copenhagen.

Smith, A. G. 1970. The Influence of Mesolithic and Neolithic Man on British Vegetation: A Discussion. In *Studies in the Vegetational History of the British Isles*, ed. D. Walker and R. G. West, pp. 81–96. Cambridge University Press, Cambridge.

Smith, C. 1992. *Late Stone Age Hunters of the British Isles*. Routledge, London.

Tauber, H. 1981. 13C Evidence for Dietary Habits of Prehistoric Man in Denmark. *Nature* 292:332–333.

Testart, A. 1982. *Les chasseurs-cueilleurs ou l'origine des inégalités*. Société d'Ethnographie, Paris.

Thomas, J. 1988. Neolithic Explanations Revisited: The Mesolithic-Neolithic Transition in Britain and South Scandinavia. *Proceedings of the Prehistoric Society* 54:59–66.

_____ 1991. *Rethinking the Neolithic*. Cambridge University Press, Cambridge.

Thomas, K. D. 1989. Vegetation of the British Chalklands in the Flandrian Period: A Response to Bush. *Journal of Archaeological Science* 16:549–553.

Torrence, R. 1983. Time Budgeting and Hunter-gatherer Technology. In *Hunter-gatherer Economy in Prehistory: A European Perspective*, ed. G. Bailey, pp. 11–22. Cambridge University Press, Cambridge.

Tringham, R. 1971. *Hunters, Fishers and Farmers of Eastern Europe 6000–3000 BC*. Hutchinson, London.

Vankina, L. V. 1970. *Torfyanikovaya Stonanka Sarnate*. Zinatne, Riga.

Vermeersch, P. M., and P. van Peer (eds.) 1990. *Contributions to the Mesolithic in Europe*. Papers presented at the Fourth International Symposium "The Mesolithic in Europe." Leuven University Press, Leuven.

Vierra, B. D. 1992. *Subsistence Diversification and the Evolution of Microlithic Technologies: A Study of the Portuguese Mesolithic*. Ph.D. diss., University of New Mexico.

Welinder, S. 1975: Agriculture, Inland Hunting, and Sea Hunting in the Western and Northern Region of the Baltic, 6000–2000 BC. In *Prehistoric Maritime Adaptations of the Circumpolar Zone*, ed. W. Fitzhugh, pp. 21–39. Mouton, Paris/The Hague.

_____ 1976. The Economy of the Pitted Ware Culture in Eastern Sweden. *Meddelanden Fran Lunds Universitets Historika Museum* 1975–76 n.s. 1:20–30.

_____ 1982. The Hunting-gathering Component of the Central Swedish Neolithic Funnel-beaker Culture (TRB) Economy. *Fornvännen* 77:154–166.

_____ 1989. Mesolithic Forest Clearance in Scandinavia. In *The Mesolithic in Europe*, ed. C. Bonsall, pp. 362–366. John Donald, Edinburgh.

Westropp, H. M. 1872. *Pre-historic Phases*. London.

Whittle, A. 1985. *Neolithic Europe: A Survey*. Cambridge University Press, Cambridge.

Wigforss, J. 1995. West Swedish Settlements Containing Faunal Remains—Aspects of the Topography and Economy. In *Man and Sea in the Mesolithic*, ed. A. Fischer, pp. 197–206. Oxbow Monograph 53. Oxford.

Williams, N. M., and E. S. Hunn (eds.) 1982. *Resource Managers: North America and Australian Hunter-gatherers*. Westview Press, Boulder, CO.

Woodman, P. C. 1978. The Chronology and Economy of the Irish Mesolithic: Some Working Hypotheses. In *The Early Postglacial Settlement of Northern Europe*, ed. P. Mellars, pp. 333–369. Cambridge University Press, Cambridge.

_____ 1985. *Excavations at Mount Sandel 1973–77*. Northern Ireland Archaeological Monographs No. 2. Her Majesty's Stationery Office, Belfast.

Wyszomirska, B. 1986. The Nymolla Project: A Middle Neolithic Settlement and Burial Complex in Nymolla, North east Scania. *Meddelanden Fran Lunds Universitets Historika Museum* 1985–86:115–138.

_____ 1988. *Ekonomisk Stabilitet vid Kusten*. Acta Archaeologica Lundendsia Series 8(17). Lund.

Yen, D.E. 1989. The Domestication of Environment. In *Foraging and Farming: The Evolution of Plant Exploitation*, ed. D. R. Harris and G. C. Hillman, pp. 53–75. Unwin Hyman, London.

Zohary, D., and M. Hopf (eds.) 1988. *Domestication of Plants in the Old World*. Clarendon Press, Oxford.

Zvelebil, M. 1981. *From Forager to Farmer in the Boreal Zone*. BAR International Series 115. British Archaeological Reports, Oxford.

_____ 1984. Clues to Recent Human Evolution from Specialised Technologies? *Nature* 307:314–315.

_____ (ed.) 1986a. *Hunters in Transition: Mesolithic Societies of Temperate Eurasia and their Transition to Farming*. Cambridge University Press, Cambridge.

_____ 1986b. Mesolithic Prelude and Neolithic Revolution. In *Hunters in Transition: Mesolithic Societies of Temperate Eurasia and their Transition to Farming*, ed. M. Zvelebil, pp. 5–17. Academic Press, London.

_____ 1986c. Mesolithic Societies and the Transition to Farming: Problems of Time, Scale and Organisation. In *Hunters in Transition: Mesolithic Societies of Temperate Eurasia and their Transition to Farming*, ed. M. Zvelebil, pp. 167–188. Cambridge University Press, Cambridge.

_____ 1989. Economic Intensification and Postglacial Hunter-gatherers in North Temperate Europe. In *The Mesolithic in Europe*, ed. C. Bonsall, pp. 80–88. John Donald, Edinburgh.

_____ 1992a. Les chasseurs pêcheurs de la Scandinavie préhistorique. *La Recherche* 246(23):982–990.

_____ 1992b. Hunting in Farming Societies; The Prehistoric Perspective. *Anthropozoologica* 16:7–17.

_____ 1994. Plant Use in the Mesolithic and the Implications for the Transition to Farming. *Proceedings of the Prehistoric Society* 60:95–134.

_____ 1995. Indo-European Origins and the Agricultural Transition in Europe. In *Whither Archaeology? Festschrift for E. Neustupný*, ed. M. Kuna and N. Venclova, pp. 173–202. Institute of Archaeology, Prague.

_____ 1996. Farmers Our Ancestors. In *European Communities: Archaeology and the Construction of Cultural Identity*, ed. S. Jones, C. Gamble, and P. Graves, pp. 145–166. Routledge, London.

Zvelebil, M., R. Dennell, and L. Domanska (eds.) in press. *The Origins of Farming in the Baltic Region*.

Sheffield Academic Press, Sheffield.

Zvelebil, M., and P. Dolukhanov. 1991. Transition to Farming in Eastern and Northern Europe. *Journal of World Prehistory* 5(3):233–278.

Zvelebil, M., and P. Rowley-Conwy. 1986. Foragers and Farmers in Atlantic Europe. In *Hunters in Transition: Mesolithic Societies of Temperate Eurasia and Their Transition to Farming*, ed. M. Zvelebil, pp. 67–93. Cambridge University Press, Cambridge.

PRELUDE TO AGRICULTURE IN NORTH-CENTRAL EUROPE

Peter Bogucki

School of Engineering and Applied Science, Princeton University, ACE-23 Engineering Quadrangle, Princeton, NJ 08544-5263

Introduction

Most treatments of the transition to agriculture over the last century have viewed this process as a shift between two stages of subsistence organization. While this perspective may reflect the beginning and end points of the process, it does not adequately address the middle phase, in which a population that had previously relied on collected and hunted resources adopts cultivation and animal husbandry. Moreover, it forces the process to be seen in a linear sense, in which the introduction of domesticated plants and animals so transforms the subsistence economy that no return to foraging is possible. Again, while eventually this may have happened in many cases, such an assumption suppresses consideration of the more interesting period in which this process occurred.

The view of foraging and farming as two "stages" is particularly ingrained in European prehistory, in which the concepts of "Mesolithic" and "Neolithic" are firmly rooted in economic terms. Despite a rise in the status of Mesolithic foragers over the last two decades from pathetic folks waiting for agriculture to masters of the forest environment, the Mesolithic economy is generally considered to have been a dead end once crops and livestock made their appearance—if not immediately, then over the next few centuries. This contrast is heightened by the fact that most of the crops and some of the animals were not indigenous domesticates but had their roots, literally and figuratively, in the Near East and perhaps southeastern Europe.

An important and influential attempt to deal with this problem was made by Zvelebil and Rowley-Conwy (1984, 1986; Zvelebil 1986), who model the Mesolithic/Neolithic frontier as a process having three phases: availability, in which foragers are in contact with farmers; substitution, in which foraging replaces farming; and consolidation, in which the agrarian economy is fully established. This model of the Mesolithic/Neolithic frontier is much more appropriate for areas such as the North European Plain and western Mediterranean basin than other models which view the spread of agriculture as a "wave-of-advance" or as a pioneer colonization. Yet Zvelebil and Rowley-Conwy's "availability model" is predicated on just that—availability of domesticated plants and animals—to trigger human behavior that leads to the adoption of food production.

My goal in this paper is to take a different slant on the transition to agriculture in northern Europe, with special reference to the part of Poland where I have been working for a number of years. Rather than conceptualizing this transition in terms of stages, I would instead like to argue that during the period between 8,000 and 5,000 b.p.[1] subsistence strategies in this area were composed of a complex of resource exploitation and land management techniques into which it was possible to integrate cultivated plants and livestock without significant dislocation. Inspiration for this perspective came from discussions of subsistence strategies of foragers, foraging cultivators, and small-scale agriculturalists in the world today, which indicate that such groups are keen experimenters and extremely open to the adoption of new subsistence "tools." Moreover, they are not hesitant to revert to previously used strategies or to have several concurrent approaches to resource management. When one considers the wealth of comparative ethnological data on societies that are on the margin between foraging and farming economies, the static categories of "Mesolithic" and "Neolithic" begin to fade as useful characterizations of actual subsistence adaptations. These terms continue to have utility as chronological markers or technical shorthand, but they obscure the complex shifts in subsistence behavior that must have been repeated in countless different ways around the world throughout the Holocene.

Taking such an approach and drawing on ethnological data require the use of some measure of "uniformitarianism," a practice which recently has come in for much criticism (e.g., Thomas 1991). Thomas (1991:3) refers to this approach as "Past-as-Same," under the uniformitarian assumption that the same processes operated in the past as in the present. The criticism is that this approach is at best constraining and at worst ethnocentric. My position is that this critique is flawed by a misunderstanding of the uniformitarian principle, as first applied in earth sciences and extended by analogy to prehistory. Gould (1965) distinguishes between "substantive uniformitarianism" and the "methodological principle of uniformitarianism." Substantive uniformitarianism is the direct explanation of the past by reference to present situations, events, and processes as a one-to-one correspondence, which is clearly inappropriate for the understanding of prehistoric behavior. The "methodological principle of uniformitarianism," on the other hand, "serves as a means of organizing our knowledge of the past by serving as an *a priori* method of limiting the interpretations that can be used to explain a given set of data (Ryder 1978:249)." Although processes which operated under conditions that existed in the past may not operate now, they can be related to processes that do act now in a regular and systematic way. For that reason, applications of the "methodological principle of uniformitarianism," whether through the use of ethnographic analogues or "middle-range theory," continue to have considerable validity for prehistoric research.

The North European Plain, 7000–5000 b.p.

The flat lowlands of the North European Plain stretch from northeastern France, Belgium, and the Netherlands, across Germany and Poland, into the Baltic states and Belarus. Its relief and soils are products of late Quaternary glacial and periglacial processes. Major features include the glacial outwash plains of the northern Netherlands, Niedersachsen, and central Poland; the morainic plateaus of Mecklenburg, Great Poland, and Kuyavia; the glacial meltwater valleys on the lines between Warsaw and Berlin and Toruń and Eberswalde; and the North Sea and Baltic coasts which have undergone eustatic change in response to postglacial sea-level adjustments. The area that forms the particular focus of this discussion falls between the lower courses of the Elbe and the Vistula rivers (Fig. 1).

The period under discussion here falls within the postglacial climatic optimum referred to as the Atlantic period. Of course, whether or not it was really "optimum" depends on one's perspective. On the North European Plain, indications point to warmer and moister climatic conditions with climax forest conditions. Much of the North European Plain would have been covered by linden-oak-elm forest associations, with hazel as a subordinate species along forest edges (Birks 1986:26).

Although variations existed in forest composition, within the forest there was reduced heterogeneity. According to Birks (1986:27), "shade was maximal, and only shade-tolerant taxa grew within the forest. Many light-demanding shrubs may have persisted as 'fugitives' in transient open habitats such as gaps and forest edges." Each spring, the forest floor would have come alive with leafy plants that were adapted to flowering during the brief vernal florescence before the leaves of the forest canopy deployed to shade them out.

The forests of the North European Plain were not uniform. Instead, they were spatially heterogeneous, composed of many different micro-habitats. Variation in the forest cover would have been produced by differences in altitude (of which there was little on the North European Plain), soil moisture and nutrients, and natural disturbances such as storm damage and disease. Every tree fall opens a break in the canopy, allowing understory herbs and shrubs to flourish before the canopy closes again. These natural disturbances also would have been the foci for rich terrestrial animal life, including the productive food species of red deer, roe deer, aurochs, and wild boar.

The structural heterogeneity of the forest ecosystem would have resulted in great overall productivity of which the foragers could take advantage. Working against the foragers, however, would have been the fact that mobile resources (i.e., game animals) would have been spatially unpredictable within this heterogeneous ecosystem, particularly in the inland zones which lacked the rich estuarine and lacustrine habitats. The characteristics of the brief vernal florescence and the focus of animal species at edges and in disturbances would have been particularly striking to the foraging peoples of the inland parts of northern Germany and Poland when contrasted with the usual condition of the forest ecosystem.

The prehistory of northern Poland and Germany during the period between 7000 and 5000 b.p. requires careful explanation. There are several important distinctions to be drawn between coastal and inland foragers and between farmers who represent intrusive elements at first and those who only later show continuity from the indigenous populations. The quality of archaeological evidence varies among these different elements, further complicating comparisons.

Inland foraging groups during this period are known primarily from stone tools recovered from sand sites in major river valleys, the Warsaw-Berlin and Toruń-Eberswalde meltwater valleys, and the outwash plains of central Poland. Here, the later Mesolithic is represented by the Janisławice culture in central Poland, the Chojnice and Pienki groups in northern and western Poland, and the Jühnsdorf group in eastern Germany. Chojnice, Pienki, and Jühnsdorf are seen as related to

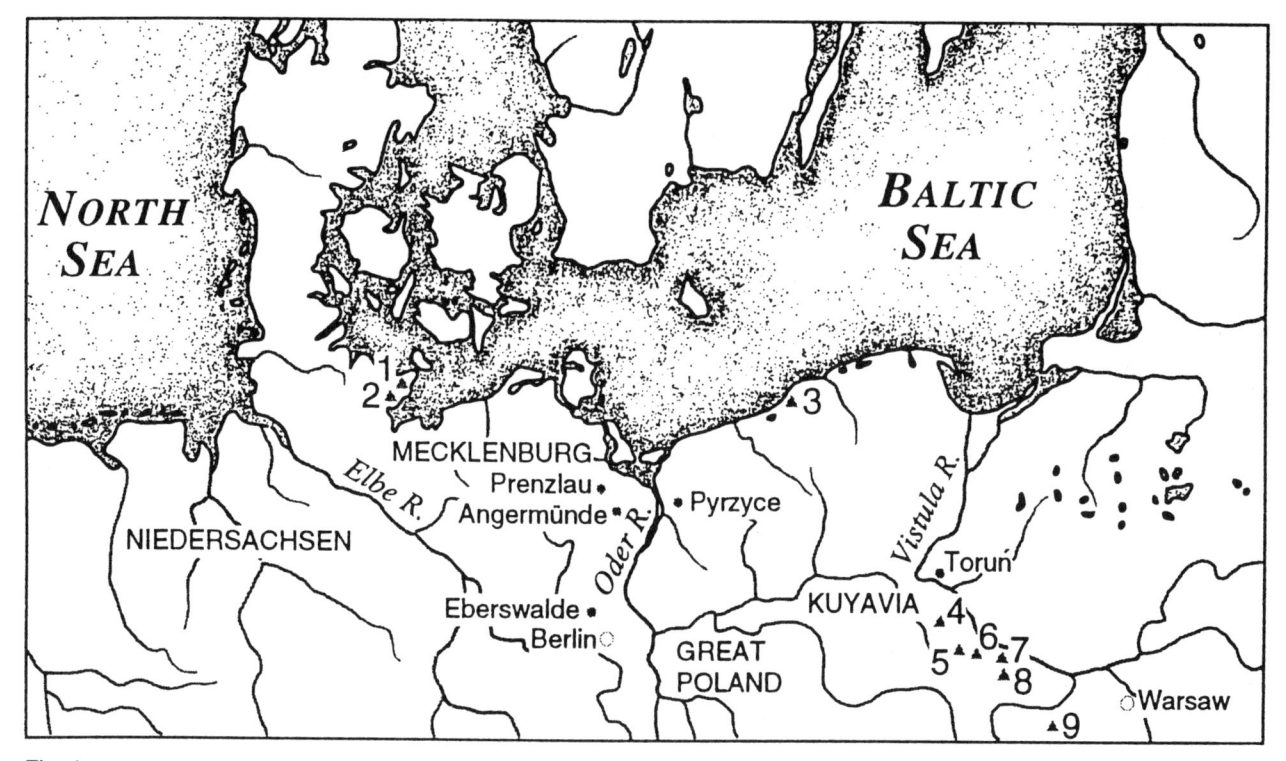

Fig. 1:
Map of northern Germany and Poland showing key sites mentioned in text: (1) Siggeneben-Süd; (2) Rosenhof; (3) Dąbki; (4) Dęby 29; (5) Osłonki; (6) Brześć Kujawski; (7) Wistka Szlachecka; (8) Lake Gościąż; (9) Janisławice.

the post-Maglemosian cultures of the western Baltic zone (Kozłowski and Kozłowski 1986; Domańska 1989; Gramsch 1989). Janisławice, on the other hand, has distinctive characteristics suggesting a specific inland adaptation to the outwash plains and meltwater valleys. Important Janisławice sites include the eponymous burial site at Janisławice in central Poland (Sulgostowska 1990) with a radiocarbon date of 6580±80 b.p. (Gd-2432) and the settlement at Wistka Szlachecka along the Vistula river (Schild et al. 1975) dated to 6555±45 b.p. (GrN-7051). Of particular significance for Janisławice is the broad distribution of high quality "chocolate" flint from its source in the Holy Cross Mountains of central Poland. For instance, at the site of Dęby 29 in north-central Poland, 99% of the flint tools are made of "chocolate" flint, over 200 km from its source (Willis 1990).

Coastal and estuarine adaptations after about 6500 b.p. have yielded sites with rich data, particularly about subsistence (see below). In northern Germany and along the Polish coast, particularly in estuarine habitats, a number of sites are known that have material remains similar to the Ertebølle culture of Denmark and southern Sweden. In Schleswig-Holstein and northeastern Germany, these are known as the Ellerbek (or Ertebølle-Ellerbek) culture (Schwabedissen 1981; Gramsch 1989), while in northern Poland, the variant of this adaptation is hitherto unnamed and known only from a single site at Dąbki (Ilkiewicz 1989). At Dąbki are both evidence of cultural continuity from the earlier Mesolithic (e.g., Chojnice-Pienki) and broad regional similarities both in artifact inventory and in subsistence behavior. A series of radiocarbon dates places this site between 6200 and 5200 b.p. (unrecalibrated).

By 6400–6200 b.p., Neolithic communities of the Linear Pottery culture had been established on the loess soils of the central European uplands, and small enclaves of Linear Pottery settlement also appeared on the North European Plain. There are three important localities for these initial agricultural settlements beyond the loess: the Kuyavia region of central Poland, the area north of the city of Toruń along the Vistula river in northern Poland, and the triangle bounded by the Polish city of Pyrzyce and the German towns of Prenzlau and Angermünde along the lower Oder. The Linear Pottery settlement in these cells is contemporaneous with that of the loess and potentially has considerable importance for the introduction of domestic plants and animals to the foragers of the North European Plain. These Linear Pottery sites have yielded significant samples of bones of domestic animals, especially cattle (Bogucki 1989; Bogucki and Grygiel 1993), as well as impressions of domestic plants in the pottery (Heussner 1989).

The Linear Pottery settlement cells of the North European Plain do not persist much past ca. 6000 b.p., after which there are very few traces of pottery-using Neolithic peoples in the areas north of Toruń and along the lower Oder. Only in Kuyavia is there significant continuity of settlement through a post–Linear Pottery phase to the emergence of the local variant of the Lengyel culture, the Brześć Kujawski Group, about 5700/5600 b.p. The Brześć Kujawski Group, named after the type site at Brześć Kujawski, represents an intensive agricultural occupation of sedentary hamlets, much like the Linear Pottery settlements of the loess almost a millennium earlier. It has a complex subsistence and settlement system with longhouses and domesticated plants and livestock, along with great investment in burial rites and trade for exotic flint and copper (Bogucki 1982, 1989; Bogucki and Grygiel 1993). The distribution of the Brześć Kujawski Group is currently confined to Kuyavia, especially in two relatively small settlement cells, one around the town of Brześć Kujawski and the other near Lake Pakość. The Brześć Kujawski Group represents an anomaly when considered from the perspective of the entire breadth of the North European Plain at this time. It is really a belated, but elaborate, development from the tradition of nucleated settlements with longhouses, livestock, and domesticated plants that began with the Linear Pottery culture over a millennium earlier in central Europe.

Almost immediately after the *floruit* of the Brześć Kujawski Group, the earliest sites of the Funnel Beaker culture (*Trichterbecher*, or TRB) are found across northern Germany and Poland (Midgley 1992). In north-central Poland, the flint work of the earliest Funnel Beaker communities, at sites such as Sarnowo, shows apparent continuity from the Mesolithic assemblages of the Janisławice culture (Niesiołowska-Śreniowska 1986). Although there is a radiocarbon date from Sarnowo of 5570±60 b.p. (GrN-5035), dates for the earliest Funnel Beaker materials elsewhere in northern Germany and Poland fall around 5200–5000 b.p. Numerous Funnel Beaker sites occur on the sandy soils of inland meltwater valleys and outwash plains, in situations reminiscent of Mesolithic settlement locations. They generally have poor preservation of architecture and faunal remains, but the presence of pottery fragments makes them very visible archaeologically. Along the Baltic coast in northern Germany, a number of rich early Funnel Beaker sites, often in estuarine and lacustrine habitats, have yielded large samples of artifacts, animal bones, and botanical remains (e.g., Johansson 1979; Schwabedissen 1981; Meurers-Balke 1983). In a number of cases, there is antecedent Ertebølle/Ellerbek settlement on the same site with evidence of continuity between the two occupations (or on adjacent sites, such as at the Ertebølle site of Rosenhof and the Funnel Beaker site of Siggeneben-Süd [Meurers-Balke 1983].)

With the exception of the Linear Pottery pioneers and the sedentary agriculturalists of the Brześć Kujawski Group, the first farmers of northern Poland and Germany were the last foragers (a point made also for southern Scandinavia by Price and Gebauer [1992].) The domestic plants and livestock that formed the basis of the agrarian economy were largely introduced from the outside, with the Linear Pottery and later the Brześć Kujawski farmers playing a crucial role in their transmission (Bogucki 1987). Beyond the enclaves of the earliest Neolithic settlement, however, the people who became the first farmers in most parts of the North European Plain outside of the Early Neolithic settlement cells were descended from local hunter-gatherers. Populations were not replaced. Instead, domesticated plants and livestock were integrated into existing patterns of land use and transformed a way of life that had persisted already for centuries.

Late Mesolithic subsistence and land use

Data on Mesolithic subsistence on the North European Plain, particularly that after 8,000 b.p., is quite elusive, given the fact that most inland Mesolithic sites in northern Germany and Poland lie on sandy glacial outwash that does not provide good conditions for the preservation of bone. This is in marked contrast to sites in the western Baltic zone which have provided rich data on late Mesolithic subsistence (Price and Gebauer 1992). All available indications (and drawing on data from sources further afield, in Holland, for instance), suggest that Mesolithic foragers pursued a wide range of forest resources. Data from several sites in Germany and Poland provide a glimpse of this, although each has its own difficulties for interpretation. The overall picture that emerges, however, is of the opportunistic exploitation of a broad range of forest flora and fauna.

Late Meolithic sites with faunal remains are known from the morainic lake belt of northern Mecklenburg between the modern towns of Schwerin and Neubrandenburg (Keiling 1985; Gehl 1976). The stratification on these sites is often difficult to sort out, and frequently there are both Mesolithic and Neolithic components mixed together. Nonetheless, the overall impression that one gets from sites like Stinthorst (Gehl 1976) is of a widespread exploitation of forest herbivores, especially red deer and roe deer, along with a range of smaller fur-bearing species. It is important to note that this pattern continues into the early Neolithic sites of the Funnel Beaker culture of this area (Johansson 1979; Nobis 1983; Lehmkuhl 1989; Bogucki 1989) with the addition of domestic animals.

In the well-known burial of Janisławice in central Poland, an assemblage of worked and unworked bone was found that came from a range of forest species

(Lasota-Moskalewska et al. 1985). These include aurochs, red deer, roe deer, wild boar, beaver, and a representative of *Mustelida* sp. A necklace is made from the teeth of at least four aurochs and more than one red deer, while the beaver and red deer postcranial bones are quite large. The presence of such a variety of species again reflects the relationship of Mesolithic peoples with the other denizens of the forest and the diverse behavioral repertoire required to interact with them.

At the site of Dąbki on the Baltic coast, an assemblage with similarities to the Ertebølle materials of the Danish littoral has been excavated along with a wealth of subsistence and paleoenvironmental data (Ilkiewicz 1989). Forty-nine species of animals were represented in the Dąbki assemblage, including 20 species of mammals, 15 birds, 13 fish, and 1 reptile. The fish assemblage yielded a minimum of 716 individuals, the mammals 103, the birds 28, and the reptiles 2. Most of the fish were freshwater species. Among the mammals, beavers were the most common, followed by deer, wild boar, and aurochs. Along with dogs, a number of specimens were identified as belonging to domestic livestock including pigs (minimum of 3 individuals) and cattle (minimum of 8 individuals), although the criteria for discriminating these from their wild counterparts are not provided.

As Price (1989:49) notes, the frustrating aspect of Mesolithic subsistence is that we know very little about the contribution of the different classes of food to the total diet. This is particularly true with regard to the contribution of plant food, although it is presumed to have been substantial, based on analogies with other foragers who occupy forested habitats. In temperate North America, where deciduous forests and a similar history of glaciation/deglaciation provide an environmental analog to Europe, an extraordinary range of plants was used not only for food but also for medicine, dyes, cordage, and textiles (Watson 1989).

Data on European Mesolithic plant use are difficult to find, due largely to conditions of preservation. Almost two decades ago, David Clarke argued that plants probably constituted the major part of the Mesolithic diet, especially tubers and rhizomes which would not be preserved archaeologically (Clarke 1976). Hillman (1989:220) points out that a common denominator in ethnographic studies of plant food choice among foragers is the preference for root foods over seed foods, which echoes Clarke's position. The most commonly occurring plant remains found on Mesolithic sites are the hazelnut shells found in hearths and pits. The large volume of refuse in proportion to the actual edible parts that hazel generates may provide a misleading view of its importance on any given site. The ubiquity of hazel fragments, however, indicates that it was a widely used resource, perhaps a better reflection of its importance on a regional scale. Since nuts can be stored over long periods, hazel also provided a resource that could outlast the perishable tubers and rhizomes gathered during the warmer months.

Decisions and risk

The number of terrestrial and aquatic species available to Mesolithic foragers suggests also that they needed to manage a large corpus of information about seasonality, behavior, technology of hunting and catching, rates of return, and labor allocation. The use of plants also required many decisions and alternative patterns of behavior, depending on the season and local ecology. In terms of both the amount of information and the complexity of its organization, the system of knowledge that this implies was perhaps as elaborate, if not perhaps more so, than that of a Neolithic farmer. The decisions made by each population might have been different, but the degree of information required can be argued to have been of a similar order of magnitude. Decisions about the allocation of time and labor are made under conditions of risk and uncertainty, based on the information available to the individual or group making the decision.

Discussions of hunter-gatherer decision-making are increasing in frequency in archaeology (e.g., Torrence 1989; Myers 1989; Mithen 1990, 1991). Rather than recapitulating these studies here, the main point that emerges from them is that much hunter-gatherer behavior, both in technology and in subsistence, can be viewed as a means of managing risk. Torrence (1989:59) points out the key dimensions of risks associated with subsistence: the variability of abundance of resources in time and space and the mobility of potential sources of food so that their presence at a set location is not guaranteed. Myers (1989) examines changes in Mesolithic procurement strategies in the British Isles with specific reference to lithic technology. Employing Binford's (1978) distinction between "intercept" and "encounter" hunting, Myers proposes that mid-Holocene climatic amelioration would have resulted in vegetation changes that might have led to a shift from using an "intercept" strategy of hunting relatively predictable terrestrial fauna in fixed locations to an "encounter" strategy exploiting unpredictable faunal resources over a broader landscape. Such a shift would change the risks associated with hunting and the approaches to their amelioration, which Myers argues is reflected in the changing microlithic tool-kits of this period in the British Isles.

Myers' model is hypothetical and to extend it to the North European Plain may be too great a stretch, despite similar shifts in lithic technology about 8000 b.p. Nonetheless, he makes some important points. I believe that this discussion, hypothetical as it is, can be extended beyond lithic technology to think about other approaches to resource management. The development of the closed forest of the Atlantic period would have called for additional adjustments in resource procurement.

The decline in spatial concentration of terrestrial fauna (or, to put it differently, increasing spatial heterogeneity in the distribution of various species) would have been keenly felt in inland parts of the North European Plain during the Atlantic climatic optimum, ca. 7000–5000 b.p. In coastal and estuarine habitats, the openings in the forest and the adjacent bodies of water would have provided ample spatial concentrations of many different resources. By 6500 b.p. the Ertebølle culture exploited a diverse range of terrestrial but especially marine resources along the Baltic coast in a complex foraging adaptation.

In the inland zones of meltwater valleys and outwash plains, such natural spatial foci would have been lacking. The distribution of game would have become increasingly unpredictable. If the Mesolithic foragers in the inland zone could exert greater control over the spatial and temporal distribution of game, they could dampen the effects of this unpredictability and the risk that a hunting session would be unproductive. One way of doing this would have been to alter the vegetation in such a way as to create analogues to the spatial foci of the estuaries and coasts found further north and to maintain parts of it in this open state. To do this would create patches of dense productivity, particularly of large herbivores that flourish in broken landscapes, reducing search area and time and thus risk. If they could not have the estuaries and coasts, the late Mesolithic foragers of inland northern Europe could at least cope with the forest by modifying it to suit their needs. But did they?

Foragers as experimenters

The traditional view of foraging populations as conservative and unchanging is not borne out by ethnographic studies of extant populations today. Instead, they are open to the adoption of new behavioral patterns, if not inveterate experimenters themselves. While they do not capriciously change things that work, they are usually always tinkering with their adaptive strategies to make them work *better*. The results of these experiments are incorporated into their practices as part of a system of knowledge about their environment. Griffin (1989:69) notes that the Agta of the Philippines "are constantly experimenting with different emphases in food procurement." The Kumeyaay of southern California has a complex understanding of plant biology and ecology that was acquired by experimentation and maintained over time (Shipek 1989:165). Just on the other side of the forager-farmer divide, Dwyer and Minnegal (1990:184) report that among the Kubo, non-intensive New Guinea agriculturalists who hunt and gather forest products, "agricultural intensification and experimentation are current" and that "archaic practices that in their origins were domesticatory rather than agricultural . . . may survive within a repertoire that is being reassessed as it is diversified."

One area where ecological knowledge is manifested regularly among foraging societies is their use of fire to create and maintain plant associations that are economically productive. Lewis (1991) has discussed the patterns of burning among Aboriginal populations in the Northern Territories of Australia (as he has on earlier occasions with reference to the Native American populations of California and Alberta) as a reflection of a complex system of ecological knowledge. The Aborigines' knowledge, presumably gained over millennia of observation and experimentation, of the causes and effects of various patterns of burning enables them to manage a complex ecosystem to maximize a broad spectrum of resources.

Mills (1986) has documented the practice of environmental manipulation by foragers through burning on a global scale. In her view, "it is clear that hunter-gatherer populations understand at least the effects of the successional process, if not the specific principles" (Mills 1986:14). In most cases of temperate zone burning, increasing primary production was the central goal of forager burning. Mills, however, points out an important temporal effect, in that grasses and herbaceous plants may appear two to three weeks earlier on burned areas because the blackened soil absorbs and retains heat. In regions with strong seasonality and the short vernal florescence of herbaceous plants in the unaltered deciduous forest, such manipulation of the spring verdure would have had a direct effect on subsistence.

Artificial glades

Evidence of pre-Neolithic alteration of the natural vegetation, most probably through burning, has come from a number of sites in the British Isles. The evidence for such burning, and its implications, were discussed extensively in the 1970s by Mellars (1975; Mellars and Reinhardt 1978) and more recently by Edwards (1988, 1990). Further east, Welinder (1989) has discussed the evidence at several sites in southern Scandinavia. Although in the 1970s, the evidence was largely palynological, macroscopic charcoal layers or horizons of charcoal dust have been increasingly identified in association with changes in pollen spectra which seem irregular.

Evidence of pre-Neolithic vegetation manipulation from the North European Plain has been hitherto elusive, although there have been hints. Isopollen maps of Poland show an advance of hazel between 6000 and 5000 b.p. (Ralska-Jasiewiczowa 1983). Hazel is not a climax species and should be quickly closed out in a natural succession. In many diagrams, however, it persists, suggesting that vegetation was deliberately maintained at a sub-climax level. Many decades ago, Rawitscher (1945) suggested that if fire had been extensively used by the Mesolithic inhabitants of central Europe, "a prevalent hazel vegetation would not be unexpected."

Recently, a multidisciplinary paleoecology project at Lake Gościąż in central Poland (Ralska-Jasiewiczowa 1993) has recovered traces of anthropogenic vegetation disturbance at ca. 6700 b.p. (Ralska-Jasiewiczowa and van Geel 1992), which would place it coeval with the Late Mesolithic settlement of the region. The palynological data record several early disturbance phases in which open-habitat plants increase along with overall species diversity, suggesting openings in the closed forest. Paleobotanical evidence consists of charred pieces of wood and plants, including grass epidermal fragments. About 4.5 km northwest of Lake Gościąż in the Vistula valley is the Janisławice site of Wistka Szlachecka, so there is clearly forager settlement in this area at the time of these disturbances. The richness of the Lake Gościąż data suggests that this is not an isolated case either temporally or geographically. Future multidisciplinary studies of the smaller lake basins of inland northern Europe should show similar pre-Neolithic vegetational disturbances.

What effect would these disturbance have had on Mesolithic subsistence? It is possible to presume that the benefits enumerated by Mellars (1975), particularly the spatial concentration of game, its increased biomass, and improved reproductive biology, would be most appreciated by the foragers, as well as the production of economically useful herbaceous species, including hazel, for basketry and traps. Most studies of Mesolithic burning have taken place in "pristine" contexts with Neolithic economies either many kilometers or many centuries away. What might have happened, however, if there were communities with domesticated plants and animals a few kilometers away, as was the case in Kuyavia and along the lower Oder and Vistula rivers beginning about 6400 b.p.?

Feral Neolithic animals

Artificial glade communities of sub-climax vegetation created by Mesolithic burning also would have provided ideal habitats for livestock that had escaped from human control in Linear Pottery and subsequently Rössen and Lengyel communities along the Neolithic frontier between 6400 and 5000 b.p. The question is not "if" Neolithic livestock escaped, but rather "how many?" Keepers of livestock invest tremendous effort to control them and to keep them from wandering off. In recent centuries, technological developments (not the least of which are barbed wire and the helicopter) have made this easier, but nonetheless, livestock continue to stray. In colonial New England, every town had its animal pound in which wandering livestock were confined until claimed by their owners. Neolithic cattle, sheep, goat, and pigs were no less inclined to behave independently and probably wandered off regularly into the forests of northern Europe.

There are a number of recent examples which illustrate the degree to which livestock can become feral on an agricultural frontier. Davidson (1988), in writing about the introduction of food production to Spain, has drawn on the example of the colonization of Australia and the contact between foragers and fishers on one hand and farmers and herders on the other. He notes that the first things to cross the frontier between Aborigines and colonists in Australia were domestic animals, particularly cattle. Hallam argues that the anthropogenic grasslands of southwestern Australia were particularly suited for domestic livestock. She reports (1975:71) that one family of early Australian settlers in the 1830s, the Bussells, "built their house (called 'Cattle Chosen') on the grassland by the Vasse where they found their cow, Yulika, who had been lost in the bush for a year."

Other well-documented cases come from the southeastern United States. Stewart (1991) has described the keeping of livestock in colonial Georgia, and the number of animals that became feral is astonishing. For instance, 25 out of 30 cattle brought by German settlers in 1734 went wild. They remained in the vicinity of the settlement when forage was good in spring but ran off into the hinterland when it was either very cold or very warm. Large numbers of cattle moved across the landscape: former Spanish herds from Florida moving north, feral livestock from the Carolinas moving south. In the Carolina woodlands, an elaborate system of cattle exploitation developed during the seventeenth and eighteenth centuries that was geared to the management of free-range unfenced branded cattle and the collecting of unmarked "wild cattle" (Otto 1987:19).

The information presented by Stewart and Otto illustrates how well feral cattle can flourish and readily fill an ecological niche. The pine woods of the Southeast were apparently very hospitable to feral livestock. Apparently, cattle and cervids (in this case, white-tailed deer) can happily co-exist in the same habitat, as they did in the canebrakes of the Georgia coast. Although the deciduous forests of temperate Europe probably provided less browse than the pine barrens of the southeastern U.S. or the grasslands of Australia, such woodlands can support grazing and browsing at low stocking rates (Adams 1975). It is worth noting, however, that both the Australian and eastern American ecosystems were heavily modified by fire. Forest fires in the southeastern U.S.

had created patches of grassland, colloquially called "savannas," which were used by both penned and feral stock (Otto 1987:15). The Australian ecosystem had been heavily modified by fires which had been set by aborigines for many millennia (Hallam 1975; Lewis 1991).

Wace (1978:225) points out that the "success and abundance of naturalized species depends in large part on the competitive context into which they are introduced." From the ethnohistoric data, it is clear that escaped domestic animals flourish in natural grassland and in artificial open habitats. It seems reasonable to expect that artificial glade habitats in the primeval forests of temperate Europe would also be attractive to escaped livestock seeking grazing and browse. A feral cow from Brześć Kujawski would have been able to negotiate the 30 or so kilometers southeast to the shores of Lake Gościąż in a matter of days—there are no water barriers that could not be forded—and over time a small resident population might have been able to be established. If the reported co-existence of deer (albeit white-tailed) and cattle in the Georgia canebrakes is believed, then the appearance of a new type of animal in an artificial glade community would not have caused major disruption. Indeed, the aurochs that were indigenous to the European forests also would have been drawn to the artificial glades, so domestic cattle would have found conspecific individuals with whom to mate.

The suggestion that feral domesticated animals would have been among the first items to pass through the sieve that was the mythical "Mesolithic-Neolithic frontier" should in no way be taken as support of the argument for the early appearance of domestic animals at the site of Dęby 29 in north-central Poland ca. 7200–7100 b.p. (unrecalibrated) made by Domańska (1987, 1989, 1991). Dęby 29 is a site of the Janisławice culture, located in eastern Kuyavia. Of about 3,000 bone fragments, mostly burned, it was possible to identify only about 20 (Domańska 1987:2). A full list has not been published, but several first phalanges and teeth are claimed to be from sheep/goat, and the presence of pig is also suggested (Domańska 1991:34). The possibility that the bones might be those of roe deer, which are anatomically similar, is dismissed.

It is difficult to accept the validity of the Dęby 29 material on several grounds. First, in the absence of a properly presented faunal report there is no way to assess the validity of the identifications. (It should be noted, however, that the identifications were made by an outstanding faunal analyst, Alicja Lasota-Moskalewska, who has many years of experience.) Second, the site is on sand, and despite the claims by the excavator for contextual homogeneity, the possibility that the bones are intrusive cannot be excluded. There is a later Neolithic occupation on the site of the Globular Amphora culture (ca. 4600 b.p.), and my (as yet unpublished) work on the Globular Amphora assemblage from Brześć Kujawski 5 indicates that sheep/goat can be a significant component of such assemblages. Third, there are no other sites with documented sheep or goat bones within several hundred kilometers at this period. In fact, the nearest ones are those of the Starčevo-Criş-Körös complex of the Balkans. While one might expect sheep and goat to be traded over short distances between farmers and foragers, the large distance without intervening occurrences makes the Dęby claim implausible. A Crimean origin for the Dęby fauna and stone tool types is claimed (Domańska 1987), which is an even greater distance.

Several possible things could be wrong with the Dęby 29 data. Either the radiocarbon dates are faulty, or the faunal identifications are in error, or the contexts are mixed. It would be wonderful to find a number of single-component Mesolithic sites with radiocarbon dates of 6500–6000 b.p. in several parts of the North European Plain with clearly identifiable samples of bones of domestic animals. Unfortunately, the claims based on the meager Dęby data only cloud the picture.

Artificial glades as "domestilocalities"

Smith (1987) has coined the term "domestilocality" with reference to incipient plant cultivation in the midwestern United States during the Archaic period. The "domestilocalities" envisioned by Smith are the anthropogenic habitats around Archaic floodplain settlements in which the selection of seed species could take place, leading to domestication. Another construction that could be put on the term "domestilocality," however, is that it describes a "continually disturbed anthropogenic habitat patch" (Smith 1987:41). Such a description would also fit artificial glade communities in northern Europe, such as the ones suggested by the data from Lake Gościąż. The major differences would be (1) that in the Archaic Midwest the cause of the disturbance was human habitation, while on the North European Plain it would have been forest clearance or burning, and (2) that the pioneer species in such habitats on the North European Plain would have been feral domestic livestock, not the sumpweed and *Chenopodium* of the Midwestern floodplains (although there is some evidence for the dietary use of *Chenopodium* in prehistoric temperate Europe as well: see Renfrew 1973). The selection processes that took place with the seeds in the Midwestern "domestilocalities" would have already been essentially completed with the feral European livestock who would already have been selected for desirable domestic traits. Instead, the artificial glade habitats would have provided the localities for what probably was initially the hunting and eventually the capture and control of the feral livestock by Mesolithic communities.

In such a model, the insinuation of domestic livestock into the Mesolithic subsistence system can thus be seen as an opportunistic response to enriched habitats. Of course, the analogy between the Midwestern Archaic case and the Mesolithic European situation can only be drawn so far, but in both cases a foraging adaptation in temperate woodlands resulted in the creation of disturbed habitats which new species could colonize and flourish. The initial human intervention, either deliberate or inadvertent, would have been in the creation of these disturbed habitats,

What about domestic plants, specifically wheat and barley? In the part of the North European Plain under discussion here, the earliest evidence for the use of domestic plants is found at sites of the Linear Pottery culture in Kuyavia and the area north of Toruń which are dated ca. 6400–6200 b.p. Subsequently, there is extensive evidence of localized domestic plant use at sites of the Brześć Kujawski Group in Kuyavia, ca. 5400 b.p., with the eventual widespread distribution in northern Poland and Germany (and eventually into Denmark) of domestic plants by ca. 5000 b.p. The question is, what happened with domestic plants on the North European Plain during the millennium between ca. 6400 and 5000 b.p., the "availability" phase of Zvelebil and Rowley-Conwy?

Obviously, plants cannot walk in the same way the feral livestock can, so their transfer from the artificial cultivated field landscape of the Linear Pottery and Lengyel communities to the artificial glade landscape of the postglacial foragers would have required some sort of human intervention. Models to explain the introduction of domestic plants to the indigenous foragers of northern Europe would have to focus more on intentional human behavior rather than on opportunistic exploitation of a situation that can be hypothesized to have developed from existing practices. Exchange between foragers and farmers is a likely mechanism (e.g., Bogucki 1987), perhaps part of a complex of exchange relationships that also involved trade in stone axes and the transfer of pottery technology.

The question then arises: why, about 5000 b.p. or perhaps a bit earlier, did the indigenous foraging peoples of the North European Plain make the commitment to the sort of "risk-prone" economy (Wills 1992) that sedentary agriculture involves? Explaining this transition is beyond the scope of this paper, but it may involve the changes in climate that occurred on a global scale at the end of the Atlantic period or it may have been an inevitable result of the competitive success of a complex of domestic plants and animals in the glades of north-central Europe.

Conclusion

This paper has suggested that new ways of looking at the transition from foraging to farming on the North European Plain are needed. In particular, it is instructive to examine similar situations in which economies with domestic livestock encountered new habitats and indigenous populations, such as in the English colonies of North America and Australia.

At present, the chronology and spatial distribution of the relevant data have been documented through several decades of research. The establishment of communities with economies based on domesticated plants and animals across the length and breadth of the North European Plain ca. 5000 b.p. did not happen suddenly. Enclaves of farming villages, such as in Kuyavia in Poland, had existed in a world otherwise populated by indigenous foraging populations for a millennium or more. New evidence indicates that even prior to this period, the foragers of the North European Plain had modified their environment on a local scale, largely through the creation of openings in the vegetation to maintain sub-climax plant communities.

From this foundation, it is possible to move to a more speculative model which suggests that the first things to pass through the frontier between foragers and farmers were escaped livestock, particularly cattle, who found congenial habitats in the artificial glades created and maintained by the foragers. Exchange between foragers and farmers, perhaps involving domestic plants, may have followed. When the indigenous foragers of the North European Plain finally made, for whatever reason, the transition to economies based on domestic plants and animals, it came after a millennium of behavioral adaptation to the ways of domestic livestock and the agronomy of crops. Instead of when or why did the foragers of the North European Plain begin to farm and to keep livestock, the key question then becomes why did they eventually assume the risk that a full, sedentary, mixed-farming economy entails.

Notes

1. Since this paper deals in large measure with paleoecological data, dates are given in unrecalibrated radiocarbon years before present, as is the convention in Quaternary research.

References

Adams, S. N. 1975. Sheep and Cattle Grazing in Forests: A Review. *Journal of Applied Ecology* 12:143–152.

Binford, L. 1978. *Nunamuit Ethnoarchaeology. A Case Study in Archaeological Formation Processes.* Academic Press, New York.

Birks, H. 1986. Late-Quaternary Biotic Changes in Terrestrial and Lacustrine Environments, with

Particular Reference to North-west Europe. In *Handbook of Holocene Palaeoecology and Palaeohydrology*, ed. B. E. Berglund, pp. 3–65. John Wiley and Sons, Chichester and New York.

Bogucki, P. 1982. *Early Neolithic Subsistence and Settlement in the Polish Lowlands*. BAR International Series 150. British Archaeological Reports, Oxford.

────── 1987. The Establishment of Agrarian Communities on the North European Plain. *Current Anthropology* 28:1–24.

────── 1989. The Exploitation of Domestic Animals in Neolithic Central Europe. In *Early Animal Domestication and its Cultural Context*, ed. P. J. Crabtree, D. Campana, and K. Ryan, pp. 119–134. MASCA Research Papers in Science and Archaeology Vol. 6, Supplement. MASCA, University of Pennsylvania Museum, Philadelphia.

Bogucki, P., and R. Grygiel. 1993. The First Farmers of Central Europe. *Journal of Field Archaeology* 20:399–426.

Clarke, D. 1976. Mesolithic Europe: The Economic Basis. In *Problems in Economic and Social Archaeology*, ed. G. de G. Sieveking, I. H. Longworth, and K. E. Wilson, pp. 449–481. Duckworth, London.

Davidson, I. 1988. Escaped Domestic Animals and the Introduction of Agriculture to Spain. In *The Walking Larder. Patterns of Domestication, Pastoralism, and Predation*, ed. J. Clutton-Brock, pp. 59–71. Unwin Hyman, London.

Domańska, L. 1987. Studies on the Caucasian–Black Sea Component in the Neolithization of Mesolithic Communities in the Basins of the Odra and Vistula Rivers. *Mesolithic Miscellany* 8:1–5.

────── 1989. Elements of a Food-producing Economy in the Late Mesolithic of the Polish Lowland. In *The Mesolithic in Europe*, ed. C. Bonsall, pp. 447–455. John Donald Publishers, Edinburgh.

────── 1991. *Obozowisko Kultury Janisławickiej w Dębach, woj. Włocławskie, Stanowisko 29*. University of Poznań-University of Łódź, Poznań-Inowrocław.

Dwyer, P. D., and M. Minnegal. 1990. Yams and Megapode Mounds in the Lowland Rain Forest of Papua New Guinea. *Human Ecology* 18:177–185.

Edwards, K. J. 1988. The Hunter-gatherer/Agricultural Transition and the Pollen Record in the British Isles. In *The Cultural Landscape—Past, Present, and Future*, ed. H. H. Birks, H. J. B. Birks, P. E. Kaland, and D. Moe, pp. 255–266. Cambridge University Press, Cambridge.

────── 1990. Fire and the Scottish Mesolithic: Evidence from Microscopic Charcoal. In *Contributions to the Mesolithic in Europe*, ed. P. M. Vermeersch and P. van Peer, pp. 71–79. Leuven University Press, Leuven.

Gehl, O. 1976. Die steinzeitliche Siedlung Stinthorst bei Waren/Müritz im Spiegel des Säugetierfundgutes. *Bodendenkmalpflege in Mecklenburg* 1975:39–53.

Gould, S. J. 1965. Is Uniformitarianism Necessary? *American Journal of Science* 5:223–228.

Gramsch, B. 1989. Archäologische Kulturen des Mesolithikums. In *Archäologie in der Deutschen Demokratischen Republik*, ed. J. Herrmann, pp. 55–64. Konrad Theiss, Stuttgart.

Griffin, P. B. 1989. Hunting, Farming, and Sedentism in a Rain Forest Foraging Society. In *Farmers as Hunters. The Implications of Sedentism*, ed. S. Kent, pp. 60–70. Cambridge University Press, Cambridge.

Hallam, S. 1975. *Fire and Hearth. A Study of Aboriginal Usage and European Usurpation in South-Western Australia*. Canberra: Australian Institute of Aboriginal Studies.

Heussner, K.-U. 1989. Bandkeramische Funde von Zollchow, Kreis Prenzlau. *Bodendenkmalpflege in Mecklenburg* 1988:7–23.

Hillman, G. C. 1989. Late Palaeolithic Plant Foods from Wadi Kubbaniya in Upper Egypt: Dietary Diversity, Infant Weaning, and Seasonality in a Riverine Environment. In *Foraging and Farming. The Evolution of Plant Exploitation*, ed. D. R. Harris and G. C. Hillman, pp. 207–239. Unwin Hyman, London.

Ilkiewicz, J. 1989. From Studies in Cultures of the 4th Millennium B.C. in the Central Part of the Polish Coastal Area. *Przegląd Archeologiczny* 36:17–55.

Johansson, F. 1979. Die Knochenfunde von Säugetieren und Vögeln von Bistoft LA 11. In *Socio-ekonomiska Strukturer i Tidigt Neolithikum och deras Förutsättingar*, ed. L. Johansson, pp. 98–111. Institute of Archaeology, University of Göteborg, Göteborg.

Keiling, H. 1985. *Steinzeitliche Jäger und Sammler in Mecklenburg*. Museum für Ur- und Frühgeschichte, Schwerin.

Kozłowski, J. K., and S. K. Kozłowski. 1986. Foragers of Central Europe and their Acculturation. In *Hunters in Transition. Mesolithic Societies of Temperate Eurasia and their Transition to Farming*, ed. M. Zvelebil, pp. 95–108. Cambridge University Press, Cambridge.

Lasota-Moskalewska, A., H. Kobryń, and K. Świeżyński. 1985. Zabytki pochodzenia zwierzęcego z grobu mezolitycznego w Janisławicach, woj. skierniewickie. *Archeologia Polski* 30:287–309.

Lehmkuhl, U. 1989. Erste Ergebnisse der Tierknochenuntersuchungen von der neolithischen Siedlung Parchim (Löddigsee). *Bodendenkmalpflege in Mecklenburg* 1988:47–83.

Lewis, H. T. 1991. Technological Complexity, Ecological Diversity, and Fire Regimes in Northern

Australia. In *Profiles in Cultural Evolution*, ed. A. T. Rambo and K. Gillogly, pp. 261–288. Anthropological Papers 85. Museum of Anthropology, University of Michigan, Ann Arbor.

Mellars, P. 1975. Fire Ecology, Animal Populations, and Man: A Study of Some Ecological Relationships in Prehistory. *Proceedings of the Prehistoric Society* 42:15–45.

Mellars, P., and S. C. Reinhardt. 1978. Patterns of Mesolithic Land-use in Southern England: A Geological Perspective. In *The Early Postglacial Settlement of Northern Europe. An Ecological Perspective*, ed. P. C. Mellars, pp. 243–293. University of Pittsburgh Press, Pittsburgh, PA.

Meurers-Balke, J. 1983. *Siggeneben-Süd. Ein Fundplatz der frühen Trichterbecherkultur and der holsteinischen Ostseeküste.* Karl Wachholtz, Neumünster.

Midgley, M. 1992. *TRB Culture. The First Farmers of the North European Plain.* Edinburgh University Press, Edinburgh.

Mills, B. J. 1986. Prescribed Burning and Hunter-gatherer Subsistence Systems. *Haliksa'i. UNM Contributions to Anthropology* 5:1–26.

Mithen, S. 1990. *Thoughtful Foragers. A Study of Prehistoric Decision Making.* Cambridge University Press, Cambridge.

_____ 1991. "A Cybernetic Wasteland"? Rationality, Emotion, and Mesolithic Foraging. *Proceedings of the Prehistoric Society* 57(2):9–14.

Myers, A. 1989. Reliable and Maintainable Technological Strategies in the Mesolithic of Mainland Britain. In *Time, Energy, and Stone Tools*, ed. R. Torrence, pp. 78–91. Cambridge University Press, Cambridge.

Niesiołowska-Śreniowska, E. 1986. Osada z fazy AB kultury pucharów lejkowatych na stanowisku 1A w Sarnowie, wojewódstwo włocławskie, w świetle materiałów krzemiennych i niektóre problemy z nią związane. *Prace i Materiały Muzeum Archeologicznego i Etnograficznego w Łodzi, seria archeologiczna* 30:201–265.

Nobis, G. 1983. Wild- und Haustierknochen des Fundplatzes Siggeneben-Süd. In *Siggeneben-Süd. Ein Fundplatz der frühen Trichterbecherkultur and der holsteinischen Ostseeküste*, ed. J. Meurers-Balke, pp 115–119. Karl Wachholtz, Neumünster.

Otto, J. S. 1987. Livestock-raising in Early South Carolina, 1670–1700: Prelude to the Rice Plantation Economy. *Agricultural History* 61(4):13–24.

Price, T. D. 1989. The Reconstruction of Mesolithic Diets. In *The Mesolithic in Europe*, ed. C. Bonsall, pp. 48–59. John Donald Publishers, Edinburgh.

Price, T. D., and A. B. Gebauer. 1992. The Final Frontier: Foragers to Farmers in Southern Scandinavia. In *Transitions to Agriculture in Prehistory*, ed. A. B. Gebauer and T. D. Price, pp. 97–116. Prehistory Press, Madison, WI.

Ralska-Jasiewiczowa, M. 1983. Isopollen Maps for Poland: 0–11000 years BP. *New Phytologist* 94:133–175.

_____ (ed.) 1993. *Jezioro Gościąż—Stan Badań nad Osadami Dennymi i Środowiskiem Współczesnym.* Polish Botanical Studies, Guidebook Series No. 8. W. Szafer Institute of Botany, Kraków.

Ralska-Jasiewiczowa, M., and B. van Geel. 1992. Early Human Disturbance of the Natural Environment Recorded in Annually Laminated Sediments of Lake Gościąż, Central Poland. *Vegetation History and Archaeobotany* 1:33–42.

Rawitscher, F. 1945. The Hazel Period in the Postglacial Development of Forests. *Nature* 156:302–303.

Renfrew, J. 1973. *Palaeoethnobotany.* Columbia University Press, New York.

Ryder, L. 1978. The Use of Uniformitarianism and Analogy in Palaeoecology, Particularly Pollen Analysis. In *Biology and Quaternary Environments*, ed. D. Walker and J. C. Guppy, pp. 245–257. Australian Academy of Science, Canberra.

Schild, R., M. Marczak, and H. Królik. 1975. *Późny Mezolit. Próba Wieloaspektowej Analizy Otwartych Stanowisk Piaskowych.* Ossolineum, Wrocław.

Schwabedissen, H. 1981. Ertebølle/Ellerbek—Mesolithikum oder Neolithikum? In *Mesolithikum in Europa*, ed. B. Gramsch, pp. 129–142. Museum für Ur- und Frühgeschichte, Potsdam.

Shipek, F. 1989. An Example of Intensive Plant Husbandry: The Kumeyaay of Southern California. In *Foraging and Farming. The Evolution of Plant Exploitation*, ed. D. R. Harris and G. C. Hillman, pp. 159–170. Unwin Hyman, London.

Smith, B. D. 1987. The Independent Domestication of Indigenous Seed-bearing Plants in Eastern North America. In *Emergent Horticultural Economies of the Eastern Woodlands*, ed. W. F. Keegan, pp. 3–47. Occasional Paper 7. Center for Archaeological Investigations, Carbondale, IL.

Stewart, M. 1991. Whether Wast, Deodand, or Stray: Cattle, Culture, and the Environment in Early Georgia. *Agricultural History* 65(3):1–28.

Sulgostowska, Z. 1990. The Janisławice Burial from Poland: Radiocarbon Dating. *Mesolithic Miscellany* 11(2):2–5.

Thomas, J. 1991. *Rethinking the Neolithic.* Cambridge University Press, Cambridge.

Torrence, R. 1989. Re-tooling: Towards a Behavioral Theory of Stone Tools. In *Time, Energy and Stone Tools*, ed. R. Torrence, pp. 57–66. Cambridge University Press, Cambridge.

Wace, N. M. 1978. Human Modification of the Natural Ranges of Plants and Animals. In *Biology and Quaternary Environments*, ed. D. Walker and J. C. Guppy, pp. 225–244. Australian Academy of Science, Canberra.

Watson, P. J. 1989. Early Plant Cultivation in the Eastern Woodlands of North America. In *Foraging and Farming. The Evolution of Plant Exploitation*, ed. D. R. Harris and G. C. Hillman, pp. 555–571. Unwin Hyman, London.

Welinder, S. 1989. Mesolithic Forest Clearance in Scandinavia. In *The Mesolithic in Europe*, ed. C. Bonsall, pp. 362–366. John Donald Publishers, Edinburgh.

Willis, R. 1990. Dęby 29—The Functional Analysis of a Late Mesolithic Site in Poland, and its Significance in the Polish Context. In *Contributions to the Mesolithic in Europe*, ed. P. M. Vermeersch and P. van Peer, pp. 295–297. Leuven University Press, Leuven.

Wills, W. H. 1992. Plant Cultivation and the Evolution of Risk-prone Economies in the Prehistoric American Southwest. In *Transitions to Agriculture in Prehistory*, ed. A. B. Gebauer and T. D. Price, pp. 153–176. Prehistory Press, Madison, WI.

Zvelebil, M. 1986. Mesolithic Prelude and Neolithic Revolution. In *Hunters in Transition. Mesolithic Societies of Temperate Eurasia and their Transition to Farming*, ed. M. Zvelebil, pp. 5–15. Cambridge University Press, Cambridge.

Zvelebil, M., and P. Rowley-Conwy. 1984. Transition to Farming in Northern Europe: A Hunter-gatherer Perspective. *Norwegian Archaeological Review* 17:104–28.

——— 1986. Foragers and Farmers in Atlantic Europe. In *Hunters in Transition. Mesolithic Societies of Temperate Eurasia and their Transition to Farming*, ed. M. Zvelebil, pp. 67–93. Cambridge University Press, Cambridge.

MASCA Research Papers in Science and Archaeology

Supplement to Volume 12, 1995

Series Editor
Kathleen Ryan

Production Editors
Helen Schenck
Jennifer Quick

Advisory Committee
Stuart Fleming, Chairman
Philip Chase
Patrick McGovern
Henry Michael
Naomi F. Miller
Vincent Pigott

Design and Layout
Helen Schenck

Graphics
Paul Zimmerman

**Customer Service/
Subscriptions Manager**
Tony DeAnnuntis

The subscription price for *MASCA Research Papers in Science and Archaeology* is $20, payable in U.S. dollars. We also accept VISA/MASTERCARD. This price covers one main volume per year. In addition, we publish supplementary volumes which are offered to MASCA subscribers at a discounted price.

This is a refereed series. All material for publication should be sent to the Series Editor, *MASCA Research Papers in Science and Archaeology*. Subscription correspondence should be addressed to the Subscriptions Manager, MASCA, The University of Pennsylvania Museum, 33rd and Spruce Streets, Philadelphia, PA 19104-6324.